D1603326

UNITED NATIONS
PEACEMAKING

UNITED NATIONS PEACEMAKING

THE CONCILIATION COMMISSION FOR PALESTINE

DAVID P. FORSYTHE

PUBLISHED IN COOPERATION WITH

THE MIDDLE EAST INSTITUTE

THE JOHNS HOPKINS UNIVERSITY PRESS

BALTIMORE AND LONDON

Manufactured in the United States of America

The Johns Hopkins University Press, Baltimore, Maryland 21218
The Johns Hopkins University Press Ltd., London

Library of Congress Catalog Card Number 71-181557
ISBN 0-8018-1352-2

Library of Congress Cataloging in Publication data
will be found on the last printed page of this book.

TO MARY JUNE

"The dilemma confronting all hopes of
peaceful international change and settlement
is that there can be no change and no
settlement, not even peacefully, so long as
struggle is avoided. You may count on
the fingers of one hand the occasions
on which agreements have been made and changes
of sovereignty or transfers of territory have
occurred in the modern world without the
assistance of the possibility of a resort
to force, if not of force itself."

F. H. Hinsley, *Power and the Pursuit of Peace*

CONTENTS

FOREWORD

Two general questions were occasionally raised as I was interviewing diplomats and academicians regarding the Conciliation Commission for Palestine (CCP) and UN efforts at conflict resolution. The first was essentially, why study the CCP: was it not marginal in the Middle East, or was not the Arab-Israeli conflict always intractable irrespective of what the CCP did or did not do, or why study the CCP since it obviously failed? The second general question was this: even if the CCP was important during several eras, can one draw any generalizations from this one UN subsidiary organ in this one context? Is not every conflict and each attempt at peacemaking *sui generis*?

As I look back over almost five years of inquiry about the CCP as a focal point for the broader inquiry into the utility of UN peacemaking, I find a need to respond to these two questions. I am convinced that the CCP does indeed merit study and that some generalizations can be formulated about a variety of subjects when the case of the CCP is compared to other UN peacemaking efforts. It seems appropriate at the start of this book to indicate in brief fashion some of the reasons why I hold this view.

To the question, "why study the CCP," there is of course a glib answer. To find out whether or not the CCP deserves study, one has to study the CCP. The question is more difficult when rephrased: why write a book about the CCP after one has studied

xi

it? Those who would say a book is not deserved might focus their arguments on the criterion of success: the problem was insoluble, the CCP failed, and therefore extended treatment of the CCP is not in order. This approach is of course reinforced by the fact that at the time of writing the conflict had not been solved—by the CCP, Gunnar Jarring, the parties directly involved, the United States, or Allah and Jahweh working separately or together. This continuing stalemate *has* to affect the review of earlier efforts at peacemaking. Just as a solution would lead to examination of past events in terms of why the solution had not been reached earlier, so the continued animosity lends emphasis to the interpretation of permanent antagonism. As C. V. Wedgwood has said of interpreting history: "We know the end before we consider the beginning and we can never wholly recapture what it was to know the beginning only."[1] It is at least possible, however, that the general assumption of the permanence of the conflict is erroneous, thus spotlighting the role of the CCP. At the moment there is, of course, no definitive evidence that the CCP was in fact crucial in the heyday of its activity—that is, 1949. Nor is there definitive evidence that in 1962 the CCP was crucial in devising a way out of the refugee dilemma, when the Commission's Special Representative was the main channel for a renewed US effort to solve that problem. Arguments that the CCP *was* crucial depend on a series of what Inis Claude has termed "what if" questions that do not lead to definitive answers.[2] What if the CCP had pushed vigorously for direct negotiations? What if the CCP had dealt with the various Arab governments separately rather than *en bloc*? What if the Special Representative had devised the right formula but was ineffective in lobbying for support within US government circles? Thus the nondefinitive nature of historical interpretation is acknowledged. Be that as it may, I share the view of Nadav Safran.[3] On the basis of this study the conflict does appear more

[1] *William the Silent* (New York: W. W. Norton, 1968), p. 35, quoted in Dean Acheson, *Present at the Creation* (New York: W. W. Norton, 1969), Apologia.

[2] *Swords into Plowshares: The Problems and Progress of International Organization*, 3d ed. (New York: Random House, 1964), p. 209.

[3] *The United States and Israel* (Cambridge, Mass.: Harvard University Press, 1963),

malleable in 1949 than thereafter; this does add possible significance to the role of the CCP even if it does not guarantee
universal acceptance of that interpretation. Moreover, the Special
Representative mission of 1961–62 may yet prove significant
since it continues to be referred to indirectly by the highest
policymakers in the United States.

More important than all of the above is an awareness that
success is not the only criterion for measurement, perhaps not
even a valid criterion. Even if the conflict remains frozen, or
escalates to new dimensions of bitterness, an extended inquiry
into the 1948–68 record of the CCP seems merited. Numerous
new facts have been discovered in the process of this study which
add to the diplomatic record. For example, it is highly significant
that in the early 1960s a plan to solve the refugee problem was
thwarted primarily by Jordan, not Syria or the United Arab
Republic, for reasons entirely extraneous to the issues of Israel's
right to exist or the Palestinian refugees' legal right to repatriation
or compensation. To take another example, it is significant to
discover that France and the United States were not competing
with each other within the framework of the CCP in the 1949–51
period as has been argued in various sources previously; moreover,
it is of interest to note the difficulties for a UN commission
comprised of governments when that rivalry did occur in the
1960s. In addition to establishing these "whats," it has also been
possible to clarify some "whys": why the CCP in its negotiations
did not follow the pattern of negotiations employed by Ralph
Bunche in achieving the armistice agreements; why the Economic
Survey Mission was established when President Truman's previous
policy had been that a negotiated settlement had to precede any
economic approach to the problems of the area. Then too,
regardless of the ultimate success or failure of the CCP, a study of
that Commission is useful as a record of policy evolution and
intellectual trends. How did the Israelis come to place such great

---

pp. 124–26. See also the comments about the goals of pre-Nasser Egypt in J. C.
Hurewitz, *Middle East Politics: The Military Dimension* (New York: Frederick A.
Praeger, 1969), p. 460.

emphasis on the power of direct talks, and is such an attitude justified from diplomatic history? What was the basis for Arab requests for more UN involvement in the conflict in the early stages of CCP activity? On a smaller scale the CCP would seem as useful as the League of Nations in providing a framework within which one could analyze changing policies and attitudes of a particular period, some of which have continuing impact on the current political scene.

So much for "why study the CCP." What about drawing generalizations from this one case study on the basis of summary comparisons with other conflict situations and UN involvements? There is no denying that some facts, situations, attitudes, and UN processes are unique to each case study. If one can draw lessons from the much-written-about area of UN peacekeeping, then in the area of peacemaking one would expect to find both uniqueness and similarity in comparing cases. It should be evident at this juncture, for example, that what proved efficacious for the United Nations Emergency Force (UNEF) in the Middle East in 1957–67 did not prove to be exactly transferable to the Congo in 1960–64, because of different factors in the Congolese situation. But the UNEF record does provide a point of departure for analyzing the United Nations Operation in the Congo, and a number of similar processes can be discovered in the two operations. For instance, the general question can be raised regarding the difference between police actions and de facto enforcement actions by a UN peacekeeping force. Thus the analysis of both UNEF and the Organization des Nations Unies au Congo (ONUC) can be carried out within a common analytical framework, without denying the uniqueness of the two cases.

I have suggested elsewhere that one framework for analysis is possible as a background for studying UN peacemaking, peace-keeping, and peaceservicing in conflict situations.[4] In this book one will find an in-depth effort to verify that suggested framework with regard to peacemaking. For example, the question concerning

---

[4] "United Nations Intervention in Conflict Situations Revisited: A Framework for Analysis," *International Organization* 23, no. 1 (Winter 1969): 115–39.

the effect of a particular structure (UN subsidiary organs comprised of governments) on the effectiveness of the peacemaking function is raised; the trend toward UN use of individuals not instructed by national authorities as peacemakers rather than government commissions is noted; and the reasons for the trend are analyzed by comparing the CCP with the Conciliation Commission for the Congo, the United Nations Commission for Indonesia, the United Nations Truce Commissions for Korea, the Mediator and Acting Mediator on the Palestine Question, and the Mediators in Cyprus, *inter alia*. In addition to such general concerns with the interaction of structures and functions, there is also concern for specific processes such as whether a particular subsidiary organ did or did not lobby the parent body in support of particular policies and/or resolutions, a question of tactics which can be raised of any subsidiary organ.

To inquire into any of these subjects necessitates a comparative analysis if one is to evaluate the subject in terms of UN usefulness to the international political system. This book represents the point of view that that comparative analysis does indeed lead to general conclusions valid for a number of case studies, when certain conditions are present in the conflict situation. Moreover, is it not important that some questions raised do not seem to lend themselves to general conclusions? If one raises the question of the impact of an organ's terms of reference on its operations, and if one finds that neither specific nor general terms of reference seem to provide much guarantee of success for the organ, is not this in itself somewhat significant in that it directs the student toward other, more important, variables in UN peacemaking?

Perhaps in the last analysis, generalizations can be formed because, regardless of specific and apparently unique factors, common behavior can be identified in a number of conflict situations. Is Palestine ideologically and religiously significant for both Zionists and Arab nationalists? Then so is Kashmir of religious and ideological importance to India and Pakistan. Is Arab-Israeli bargaining impeded by fear of insecurity? Then so is flexible negotiation difficult to achieve between Greek and

Turkish Cypriots. It is suggested here that some of these generalizations can be formulated without reference to whether the conflict is international or intra-national, or to any other typology of types of conflict.

Finally, in writing about the CCP and UN peacemaking, I am aware that I am speaking to two, perhaps three, audiences. The mere title of the book, if not the substance, may attract specialists in international organization; the subtitle may attract Middle East specialists. Some weary methodologist in political science, desiring to be cured of insomnia, may leaf through the pages. None of the three may be satisfied with the effort, each desiring more that pertains to his interest. The Middle East specialist may want more about the dimensions of the refugee question and the work of the United Nations Relief and Works Agency (UNRWA); the specialist in international organization may want less case study and more comparative analysis; the methodologist may want a three-hundred-page introduction. Although aware of this problem of communication, I have elected to use this format because of a general need within political science as a discipline to merge case studies with framework- or theory-building. This is a modest effort to look at both the trees and the forest, something that has been decidedly lacking in political science.[5]

Acknowledgments are legion and must first go to Leon Gordenker and Oran Young of Princeton University who interested me in the subject and challenged me to think seriously about it. The Woodrow Wilson Foundation, the Leopold P. Schepp Foundation, and Princeton University provided generous grants that made interviewing in the United States, Europe, and the Middle East possible. The Princeton Center of International Studies, in cooperation with the Carnegie Endowment of International Peace, facilitated part of the rewriting stage. The Middle East Institute provided valuable criticism of the manuscript through readers still unknown to me. Colleagues at Georgia State University made helpful comments in the final stages. I am

[5] On this point see Stanley Hoffmann, *The State of War* (New York: Frederick A. Praeger, 1966), pp. 3–21.

particularly indebted to the many persons who granted candid interviews and who occasionally gave me access to classified information.

The final stages of preparation were most capably handled by Joanne Anderson and Amy Genins, with the much-appreciated cooperation of Charles Pyles, Acting Chairman of Political Science, Georgia State University.

One final acknowledgment must go to the late Quincy Wright. After his death in the fall of 1970, the Middle East Institute informed me that he had been among the reviewers of this work. It is with pleasure that I acknowledge his direct influence on this study through his incisive comments. A more indirect influence was no doubt already present from his wide-ranging writing on the subject of international relations in general. While not everyone agrees with all the arguments Quincy Wright has put forth with regard to the Arab-Israeli conflict, no one can fail to be impressed by his extensive knowledge of the subject, his persistent interest in the amelioration of the dangers from the confrontation, and his forthright judgments which were the hallmark of all his work.

INTRODUCTION

THE POLITICS OF PEACEMAKING

There is a plethora of terms purporting to describe UN involvement in conflicts: preventive diplomacy, peacekeeping, peace observation, UN presence, peace force, peaceful or pacific settlement. A number of observers tend to lump all types of involvements under the one term—"peacekeeping." Some prefer to call all conflict-oriented UN agencies "peace organs."[1] A caveat is in order, however, for such general terminology may reflect and help to cause misunderstanding and misapplied policy with regard to UN involvement in the maintenance of international peace and security.

The United Nations may become involved in three distinct but related ways in conflict situations.[2] (1) *UN Peacekeeping.* The goals of this UN function are to limit and, if possible, to curtail the violence of a conflict already initiated. A synonymous term is

[1] Yashpal Tandon, "Consensus and Authority behind United Nations Peacekeeping Operations," *International Organization* 21, no. 2 (Spring 1967): 254–83. Tandon lists almost seventy "peace organs" in the period of 1946–65, of which about one-third qualify as peacemaking organs as defined below.

[2] See also my article, "United Nations Intervention in Conflict Situations Revisited: A Framework for Analysis," *International Organization* 23, no. 1 (Winter 1969): 115–39. Conflicts may be compared to incidents and tensions. See further K. J. Holsti, *International Politics: A Framework for Analysis* (Englewood Cliffs, N.J.: Prentice-Hall, 1967), pp. 442–44. For a specific application of this breakdown among incidents, conflicts, and tensions, see Chapter 1 below.

1

"conflict-management." The most limited type of peacekeeping is the stationing of observers in the area of conflict—the action the United Nations took in Lebanon in 1958. The most extensive form to date is illustrated by the United Nations Operation in the Congo. (2) *UN Peacemaking*. Here the goal of the United Nations is to help resolve the basic, substantive issues of a conflict. Peacemaking is the same as "conflict-resolution" or "peaceful (pacific) settlement." The most limited type of such action is the creation of a UN presence, as was done in Yemen in the mid-1960s by dispatching a representative of the Secretary-General. The most extensive form is that of a full-fledged commission (for example, the Conciliation Commission for Palestine, the United Nations Commission for Indonesia) or a single individual supported by political and technical assistants (for example, Ralph Bunche, Frank Graham).[3] (3) *UN Peaceservicing*. Here the basic goal of the United Nations is to help avoid or ameliorate conflict through socioeconomic programs. Institutional forms of peaceservicing are exceedingly varied, ranging from technical assistance programs to administration of quasi-governmental programs (for example, the UN Civilian Operations in the Congo).[4]

These three functions are certainly related — at least because some types of investigation and fact-finding are usually involved in all. Moreover, peacekeeping may shade off into peacemaking. This was definitely true of the actions of the Secretary-General in the Congo crisis, as he found himself inadvertently resolving the

[3] For the purposes of this study, such single individuals, traditionally called mediators, are considered as field organs. They frequently operate with a battery of technical assistants, political advisers, and secretariat personnel; this gives their missions the characteristics of a field organ. The peacemaking role of the Secretary-General, as opposed to his representatives or appointees, is considered only marginally in this study. The reader is referred to the growing body of literature directly pertaining to the Secretary-General, especially to Leon Gordenker, *The UN Secretary-General and the Maintenance of Peace* (New York: Columbia University Press, 1967); and to Oran R. Young, *The Intermediaries: Third Parties in International Crises* (Princeton: Princeton University Press, 1967).

[4] There is a fourth function theoretically available to the United Nations, that of peacebreaking — viz., to use force to break a status quo deemed illegitimate, as perhaps to forcefully remove the Smith regime in Rhodesia.

2

substantive, constitutional issues at stake between the central government and Katanga province in the process of trying to accomplish what he thought was the essentially peacekeeping task of maintaining order. In addition, peacemaking may at some stage become peaceservicing. For example, in order to try to resolve some of the issues outstanding in the Arab-Israeli conflict the CCP proposed various plans for the regional economic development of the Middle East. Yet there remains a need to keep the three functions analytically distinct. For one reason, understanding is facilitated.[5] For another reason, policy is more likely to be accurately related to specific situations. What is efficacious for one type of operation (in terms of structures and functions) may not be appropriate for the others. In addition, various types of field organs may be working at cross purposes inter se because of a lack of a clear conception of the respective role of each organ.

By far, most writing on the role of the United Nations in the maintenance of international peace and security has dealt with peacekeeping: UN use of force and para-military ventures.[6] This study focuses on UN peacemaking as a distinctive area of operation for the United Nations, with tangential reference to peacekeeping and peaceservicing as needed.

For one to understand the UN peacemaking role *in its broadest sense*, it is necessary to be clear about the nature of international politics and the nature of international organization.

The terms "peacemaking" or "peaceful settlement" are often employed in an intuitive rather than an analytical manner. At first impression one might say that peacemaking — by any third party —is a role carried out without the exertion of any influence

[5] A case in point is Lincoln P. Bloomfield's "Peacekeeping and Peacemaking," *Foreign Affairs* 44, no. 4 (July 1966): 671–82. Here the differentiation between the two operations is presented in embryonic form initially, but the division of roles is not maintained conceptually throughout the article — thus marring some of its merits. The conclusions presented relate almost exclusively to peacekeeping, and the subject of peacemaking is left in limbo.

[6] See the detailed bibliography in Young, *Intermediaries*; and in Linda B. Miller, *World Order and Local Disorder: The United Nations and Internal Conflicts* (Princeton: Princeton University Press, 1967).

beyond verbal persuasion. Politics, however, is rarely ultimately peaceful in any absolute sense. Decisionmakers in international politics continually seek to influence other decisionmakers in order to resolve a conflict or avoid one (and sometimes to initiate one). It is normal for much of this influence to constitute what can be termed pressure on the target decisionmakers. And to say that no pressure is to be applied in the settlement of a conflict is to speak more of ideals than of the realities of international politics.

The differing forms of influence used in international politics can be represented by a spectrum, the right end of which represents the slightest form of influence, the left end the greatest.[7] The right end can be labeled "persuasion": the use of words alone—spoken or written—to exert influence either negatively or positively. The center sector of the spectrum can be labeled "pressure": the use of rewards and punishments to exert influence. Some normal forms of positive pressure are favorable tariff provisions, economic assistance, granting of diplomatic recognition, and establishment of cultural exchange programs. Some normal negative pressures are termination of foreign aid, restriction of private trade, unfavorable interest rates on loans, and recall or withdrawal of diplomatic personnel *inter alia*. As an intermediate sector between persuasion and pressure, one can conceive of a sector labeled "threats/promises of pressure." The left end of the spectrum can be labeled "force": the use of violence to exert influence. Force can be positive, through the varied means of military support, or it can be negative, through the varied means of military sanctions. As an intermediate sector between pressure

---

[7] For a sophisticated analysis of differing forms of influence see Raymond Aron, *Peace and War: A Theory of Intunational Relations,* trans. Richard Howard and Annette B. Fox (New York: Doubleday & Co., 1966), esp. pp. 6—70. For the purposes of this study, it has not proven necessary to construct a detailed spectrum listing the alternative means of influence available to actors in international politics. Particularly heuristic for the spectrum finally devised were Herman Kahn's *On Escalation: Metaphors and Scenarios* (New York: Frederick A. Praeger, 1965), and Thomas C. Schelling's *Arms and Influence* (New Haven: Yale University Press, 1966), esp. chap. 1.

and force, one can conceive of a sector labeled "threats/promises of force." The sum total of an actor's ability to use persuasion, pressure, and force is power.[8] That is the same as saying political power is the ability to influence another sector, as based on force and measures short of force.[9] This spectrum of influence represents a line of thought found consistently in the core literature of international law and politics.[10]

Spectrum of Forms of Influence

Force					
Force			*Measures Short of Force*		
Coercion		Pressure		Persuasion	
Negative	Positive	Negative	Positive	Negative	Positive
	Threats/promises of force		Threats/promises of pressure		

The rather continuous exertion of influence and counter-influence, frequently entailing the use of pressure and less

[8] The spectrum is thus one representing putative power rather than actualized power — i.e., the spectrum does not purport to represent the *effectiveness* of any form of influence; it seeks only to represent the forms available for exertion of potential influence. For a slightly different use of the terms "putative power" and "actualized power," see Klaus Knorr, "Military Power: Nature, Components, and Functions," mimeographed, Princeton Center of International Studies.

[9] The difference between force and measures short of force is exceedingly difficult to define in the abstract when one deals in terms of actualized power. What makes the distinction so problematical is that one series of actions in one context can have a different impact if the context is changed. Action X, undertaken by powerful state A against weak state B, may be exceedingly forceful — i.e., cause great destruction on B. The very same action (perhaps economic blockade) by A may have only slight impact on equally powerful state C. Cf. Kenneth Boulding, *Conflict and Defense* (New York: Harper & Bros., 1962), esp. p. 149.

[10] Clausewitz's oft-quoted dictum is applicable: "War is ... a continuation of political commerce, a carrying out of the same by other means," quoted in Aron, *Peace and War*, p. 23. Regarding the legal standpoint, see Fritz Grob, *The Relativity of War and Peace* (New Haven: Yale University Press, 1949), and Myres S. McDougal and Florentino P. Feliciano, *Law and Minimum World Public Order* (New Haven: Yale University Press, 1961).

5

frequently the use of force, is not basically altered when international politics is channeled through a UN framework. Force and threat of force are prohibited by the UN Charter, with exceptions for self-defense and use of force authorized by the Security Council, but the less violent forms of influence-exertion continue to be used as normal. In many situations the United Nations is indeed only an "institutional funnel"[11] through which traditional state behavior is channeled. It has been argued by some governments that force should be defined broadly and that force comprises most of the generally accepted forms of diplomacy, including most forms of pressure.[12] This propagandistic argument notwithstanding, state practice, the legal arguments of Western states, and political analysis all support the view that force can realistically, if minimally, be considered to encompass only those forms of influence that entail violence.[13]

Any UN peacemaking organ is very much a part of this influence-counterinfluence process, not only as an instrument or institutional funnel for state action but also at times as a relatively independent actor that may seek to mobilize influence for its own policy positions.

[11] Inis L. Claude, Jr., *The Changing United Nations* (New York: Random House, 1967), p. 53.

[12] See UN Doc. A/6230, *Report of the Special Committee on Principles of International Law Concerning Friendly Relations among States*, 27 June 1966. Such arguments were offered by communist and developing states. For a concise review of UN attempts to define such terms as force and nonintervention, see "Issues Before the General Assembly," in the September issues of *International Conciliation*.

[13] Much of the literature regarding international organization, however, does not deal adequately with the varying degrees of pressure found in international politics. A number of observers are still bitterly criticizing the United Nations because a certain mission "did not suspend internal or international politics." Ernest W. Lefever, "The Limits of U.N. Intervention in the Third World," *Review of Politics* 30, no. 1 (January 1968): 18. In general, there has been a rather pronounced tendency by many to consider UN activities as islands of pressure-free politics in a sea of pressure. The United Nations thus becomes a barrier against pressure behind which exists a world qualitatively different from state action. See, for example, UNESCO, "Techniques of Mediation and Conciliation," *International Social Science Bulletin* 10, no. 4 (1958); Y. Tandon, "The Peaceful Settlement of International Disputes," *International Relations* 2, no. 9 (April 1964): 555–87; and Elmore Jackson, *Meeting of Minds* (New York: McGraw-Hill Book Co., 1952).

This political fact of life is somewhat at variance with traditional legal concepts of UN peacemaking roles.[14] Both the Security Council and the General Assembly are authorized by the Charter under Chapter VI only to discuss and make recommendations on the subject of conflict-resolution. Theoretically there was, at least at the time of the UN's creation, the possibility that the Council would consider the lack of settlement of the substantive issues of a conflict a serious threat to the maintenance of international peace and hence invoke Chapter VII. Reference to Chapter VII would allow the Council to "decide" what measures were necessary to terminate the threat to peace, measures that entailed obligatory acceptance by member states (under article 25).

The US-USSR tension in the two decades after 1945 diminished to the point of extinction the likelihood that the Council would adopt this quasi-legislative procedure in conflict situations. At the moment, the Council's sanctions against Rhodesia are the exception to what seems to be the general rule. It has been argued that the decline of the probability of Council action under Chapter VII as a support for peacemaking efforts is compensated for in some degree by recommendations per se— that is, Council and Assembly resolutions.[15] The mere passing of resolutions, however, has severe limitations on influencing state behavior; the use of written words by the Assembly or Council— similar to the spoken words of debates—is of minor impact relative to the capability of nation-states for action.[16]

---

[14] The traditional conceptions of UN peacemaking possibilities are presented in Inis Claude, *Swords into Plowshares: The Problems and Progress of International Organization*, 3d ed. (New York: Random House, 1964), chap. 11, and Leland Goodrich and Anne Simons, *The United Nations and the Maintenance of International Peace and Security* (Washington D.C.: The Brookings Institution, 1957), esp. p. 250.

[15] See in particular Gabriella Rosner Lande, "The Effect of the Resolutions of the United Nations General Assembly," *World Politics* 19, no. 1 (October 1966): 83–105.

[16] In Claude, *Changing United Nations*, the passing of resolutions is termed "collective legitimization." In an otherwise perceptive analysis, Claude overestimates the important of this role by UN policy organs; he does not adequately stress that member states may have the power to oppose undertakings by other actors that have been legitimized but that they do not endorse themselves, and that states may have the power to carry out undertakings of their own without UN legitimization.

Yet it would be erroneous to assume that a UN peacemaking agency in the field was restricted to offering suggestions to the parties to a conflict because the agency's parent body had only the authority to discuss and make recommendations. While UN organs have neither a police force of their own nor an independently gained foreign aid program, they can have—in any given instance —both guns and butter. Take, for example, the case of General Assembly subsidiary organs of governmental membership. Composed legally of governments, these field organs are staffed by individuals appointed by national authorities. Such individuals may bring with them in serving the United Nations the participation of their national administrations. In actual operation, these subsidiary agencies may make national and international action coterminous. Such a meshing of international authority and national capability can in practice involve the exertion of pressure, and such pressure may reach maximum effectiveness because of the power of the nation-states involved coupled with the legitimizing framework of UN symbols.

In other cases, national and international action may not be coterminous, but they are closely intertwined. In these instances, too, pressure can be applied in the actual functioning of UN machinery. For example, a UN mediator is an international actor, operating under the jurisdiction of the Charter and under resolutions derived therefrom. Yet much of his success may depend upon his securing the backing of powerful national authorities who will give support to his efforts. A mediator responsible to the Assembly or Council whose recommendations have the support of one or more of the important member states is not viewed by the disputant parties *in vacuo* but as a part of the larger context. The parties are not likely to view the mediator's position independently of the ability of other states to implement his recommendations.

In many cases, the dividing line between national and international action may become blurred. The interaction of international and national actors may at times tend toward unity. Frequently the cooperation of national and international personnel follows this pattern: a national decisionmaker will initiate action; the United Nations will be asked to enter the process in order to provide an acceptable framework for action, personnel, expertise, channels of communication, an aura of impartiality; then the national actor will act in conjunction with the UN agency thus created to implement the chosen policy. Although a microanalysis can distinguish between national and international action in this field and a shifting pattern, the dividing line may indeed lose its practical importance to the parties to a dispute.[17]

Whether one says the United Nations acted or governments X and Y acted may become a matter of legal semantics. Such semantical differences may indeed have an important impact on the conflict, giving one course of action more legitimacy than another, thus leading to wider acceptance for that undertaking and a greater sense of obligation on the part of governments to cooperate with the mission.[18] Increasingly in international politics, collective decisionmaking and the symbols of international organizations are used as guidelines to judgments about legality and legitimacy. On the other hand, UN practice over the past twenty years indicates that law follows politics: what is politically feasible will usually be undertaken regardless of legal norms to the contrary, especially since there are frequently other legal norms that can be cited to justify the desired action.

Therefore UN peacemaking organs, operating under Chapter VI of the Charter, when commissioned either by the Council or Assembly, must be viewed in the larger context of the interaction between the subsidiary organ, the disputants, *and* member governments of the United Nations potentially or actually available as a supporting coalition for the peacemaking organ. While the active character of the UN system is limited by both legal authority and political capability, its institutional character may give rise to state action of an efficacious nature. States may, can, and do seek to persuade and pressure other states to do or not

[17] For an excellent example of this phenomenon, see Conor Cruise O'Brien, *To Katanga and Back* (New York: Grosset & Dunlap, 1962). US and UN action was indistinguishable at many junctures.

[18] See Oscar Schachter, "The Relation of Law, Politics and Action in the United Nations," Academy of International Law, *Recueil des Cours* 1 (1963): 203–4.

do something. Such third-party state efforts, when they are directed toward objectives established by the Council and Assembly, enhance the prospects for world order. The interaction of collective and unilateral decisionmaking, when directed toward consistent objectives, in fact constitutes a quasi-legislative process backed by effective implementation. Thus it is in the interaction of UN and national undertakings that the real impact of peacemaking missions is to be found.[19]

Recognition of the various forms of influence involved in peacemaking also requires recognition of the limitations of what influence can achieve. Success in attempts to promote a settlement is more likely when each party can accept the terms of settlement more or less voluntarily, out of a conviction that its interests are being promoted thereby. Thus, as the following pages will show, there may be a need for a very low level of third-party influence at the outset of a peacemaking effort in order to allow this largely voluntary meeting of minds to develop. Furthermore, no state is likely to be influenced into approving a settlement that in actual fact jeopardizes its security. And no state can be expected to endorse a radical alteration in the relative power positions of the parties to the conflict. There are very real limitations on third-party involvement, and they need to be recognized so that third parties do not overextend themselves and seek what cannot be gained. The third party that exceeds such limits subsequently loses the disputants' respect and its own future utility.

There is a further limitation to the use of influence in peacemaking, one that depends not so much on the attitudes of the parties directly concerned as on the availability of potential allies for the parties. UN peacemaking may be impeded not because the security of one of the parties is perceived to be threatened but simply because one of the disputant parties is able to mobilize effective support for its bargaining position. New states have frequently been able to mobilize support from other new states, thus helping to offset influence that might be directed

[19] "... the effectiveness of Council and Assembly resolutions (with regard to 'Colonial Wars') has depended on the susceptibility of incumbents and insurgents to bilateral pressures" (Miller, *World Order*, p. 63).

at them from the older, more developed states.[20] Where influence and counterinfluence are offsetting, UN peacemaking missions are restricted to means of persuasion—usually centered on verbal appeals to logic, justness, and self-interest. This was characteristic of the Arab-Israeli conflict in the late 1960s: each of the disputants had the backing of a superstate, and thus the maneuverability of UN intermediaries was limited. To expand the conflict in such a situation, to try to marshal enough support behind a UN policy to change the policy of one of the disputants, could be catastrophic for all involved.

Thus roles available to the United Nations may be exceedingly limited in any given conflict, and limitations inherent in the context of a conflict may prove decisive on third-party efforts. Yet one of the major dilemmas for third parties such as UN peacemaking organs is to avoid the problems of doing too little, even as the problem of trying to do too much is recognized. Especially in the wake of UN involvement in the Congo and the resulting controversies, there is a tendency on the part of some observers to see the United Nations as a last resort rather than a useful instrument.[21] While there is no denying that the UN system has weaknesses, there does seem to be some question about the wisdom of ideologically assigning the United Nations to a marginal status in international politics. Surely one of the factors leading to the demise of the League of Nations in the late 1930s was that it attempted to do too little, contenting itself with less controversial activities. Moreover, is it realistic to expect the United Nations to be simultaneously useful in international politics and yet free from controversy regarding the nature of its involvements? Is any institution that is centrally involved in a political system free from charges about the unwise exercise of power, whether it be the

[20] See *ibid.*, p. 170.

[21] See Lefever, "Limits of U.N. Intervention," pp. 3–18 for a case in point. See also Stephen Goodspeed, *The Nature and Function of International Organization* (New York: Oxford University Press, 1959), p. 217; Goodrich and Simons, *United Nations*, p. 316; and Miller, *World Order*, esp. pp. 169–72, although at times Miller seems to be arguing not against active UN peacemaking per se but against active peacemaking in support of *incorrect* solutions.

American Presidency, the UN Force in the Congo, or the UN mediator in Cyprus?

More to the point of this present study, is it not expected that some controversy will surround UN peacemaking and that charges of UN attempts to affect the conflict in a manner *ultra vires* will be made? And is it not true that where security interests are perceived to be involved in a conflict and where tensions are high, voluntary agreement is not probable—thus necessitating involvement beyond persuasion for the resolution of the conflict? And is not such involvement likely to be accompanied by charges of trying to do too much, whether or not well founded? F. S. Dunn stated the fundamental problem very well some thirty years ago:

> The things to be changed in disputes to be resolved ... are for the most part things which are highly valued and not willingly given up by existing holders. This fact cannot be disguised by any multiplication of specific institutions and techniques for dealing with demands for change. The widespread notion that by the mere calling of conferences, the establishment of international commissions of inquiry or the devising of new techniques of negotiation it will be possible to find acceptable solutions for all demands for change is largely the product of wishful thinking. It is useless to pile up additional institutions unless they take full account of existing values and attitudes which determine basic policies.[22]

In these disputes where the probability of agreement is slight, "There are ways of inducing a nation to yield to a particular demand in the interest of peace and friendly relations. There are ... ways of bringing pressure which are not incompatible with the notion of independence."[23] In short, at times there are legitimate ways of influencing a state to accept a settlement which a given disputant may view as detrimental to some of its interests — as long as its security is protected. The underlying objective of such a process is the achievement of a settlement that will prove itself beneficial to all concerned.

[22] *Peaceful Change*, United States Memorandum No. 3 (1937), p. 19.
[23] *Ibid.*, pp. 82–83.

In the de facto process of peacemaking, there are alternative roles available for the UN peacemaking organ. This typology of roles is used in the present study in part because neither international law nor political science has provided precise meanings for the traditional terms "good offices," "mediation," and "conciliation." The degree of involvement entailed under each term is unclear. The trend is to associate good offices with the least degree of involvement. The difference between mediation and conciliation is beginning to be based on the difference between involvement by an individual and by a multiplicity of actors. Perhaps only because of the alliteration involved in "conciliation commission," conciliation seems to mean group mediation, with mediation conceived as an effort at peacemaking that represents more involvement than the use of good offices. For purposes of continuity, roles 1–4 discussed below can be encompassed under the term good offices; and roles 5–9 can be termed types of mediation or conciliation, depending upon the size of the UN representative organ. The tenth role is the equivalent of legislation.[24]

The following ten-part typology of roles is based on increasing degrees of involvement in a conflict.[25] (1) *Serve as symbol of UN interest.* This slightest degree of involvement entails extremely little action. The subsidiary organ exists legally and may hold perfunctory meetings and make perfunctory reports to its parent body. It may not make contact with the disputants. Frequently this role will be undertaken when other roles have not been productive. Essentially, this role is a holding-technique, a

[24] See Elmore Jackson, "Mediation and Conciliation in International Law," *International Social Science Bulletin* 10, no. 4 (1958): 512–43; UNESCO, "Techniques of Mediation and Conciliation," in *ibid.*; and Goodrich and Simons, *United Nations,* pp. 291–92.

[25] Cf. Young, *Intermediaries,* esp. pp. 51–61, and the literature cited therein. Young discusses among other subjects a number of activities that can be undertaken by the third party outside formal negotiations by disputants. The typology presented here refers to involvement in the on-going process of negotiation, with the possible exception of (1). Many of the "independent" activities mentioned by Young are considered aspects of peacekeeping and peaceservicing in this study. This typology seeks to be more specific regarding what Young terms "participation" by the third party, and it presents a broader role for the intervenor in general than Young allows (see *ibid.,* pp. 43–45).

time-wasting device. The intent may be to maintain a legal entrée into the conflict in the hope that the disputants' attitudes will change over time and that the UN organ can undertake increased activity at a later date. Or the intent may be to maintain the validity of UN resolutions comprising the organ's terms of reference; to dissolve the organ entirely might be taken as a rejection of the original resolutions upon which basis the organ was constituted. (2) *Initiate procedural suggestions.* The UN organ may attempt to facilitate what remain essentially interstate negotiations without dealing with the substance of the conflict. The intervenor may seek to arrange meetings and convey communiqués. Such procedural suggestions may have a positive effect on the disputants. A disputant who hesitates to initiate negotiations for fear of giving the impression of weakness may find the third party's suggestions for talks a convenient excuse: "My government has agreed to honor the request of the United Nations in the interests of peace and justice." Procedural details are important to prestige-conscious disputants, and the third party concentrating on procedural details may be a catalyst for improvement of the state of the conflict. (3) *Clarify issues.* Here the task may be that of noting the major issues to be solved, thus helping to give some form to the negotiations by separating the trivia and propaganda from the major substantive issues. Conversely, the peacemaker may try to clarify some of the minor issues where agreement seems more probable, thereby contributing to initial agreement which might increase the confidence of the disputants inter se and give the negotiations a positive momentum. Or the third party might try to focus on facts under dispute rather than on more emotional tensions. (4) *Interpret issues.* This role is a hybrid one, partially administrative but also partially policy-creating. It is analogous to the role of a court in interpreting law — which is also a form of creating law. The third party may find it helpful to offer an interpretation of certain key issues to bring the policy positions of the disputants closer together. If the disputants feel that the interpretation does not entail unacceptable concessions, they may then accept the third party's statements as a basis for negotiations, preferring to negotiate the issues as interpreted rather than hold to original bargaining positions and risk the stalemating or collapse of the negotiations. (5) *Submit reports.* In many conflicts the third party can play an invaluable role in submitting factual reports to the disputants. The number and types of refugees may be in dispute. Census figures may be needed. Data for economic projections of various regions may aid a settlement. Such reports may facilitate compromise, particularly if the report appears as a reasonable midpoint between extreme allegations by the disputants. Or the report may make clear what a lack of settlement would mean for the future. In certain situations, reports can be essential to peacemaking when compensations, reparations, or technical assistance is part of the settlement. The presumably impartial status of a UN agency can be particularly helpful in providing an acceptable report. (6) *Submit policy recommendations.* The UN organ may try to circumvent disagreement by proposing new solutions to the conflict. More than likely these new recommendations would become the subject for intricate discussion and bargaining, although in both the Congo and Cyprus conflicts the UN peacemaker offered take-it-or-leave-it packaged proposals. Either way, the objective is to avoid adamant disagreement between the disputants. Frequently the third party runs the risk of being charged with acting *ultra vires* or outside its terms of reference by this action, but some risks may be undertaken in the hope of providing acceptable solutions to the issues outstanding. (7) *Mobilize persuasion.* A UN peacemaker, having submitted policy recommendations and having tried to get them accepted by the disputants, may seek to mobilize support for his position by asking interested actors to persuade the disputants to accept the recommendations. The third party may turn to governments for support, asking them to exert persuasion in support of the guidelines suggested.[26] Or the subsidiary organ may elect to use a more open process and seek a statement from

---

[26] A former high-ranking member of the Secretariat has indicated the Secretary-General's practice of asking governments to support his policy recommendations. See Andrew W. Cordier, "The Role of the Secretary General," in *Annual Review of United Nations Affairs 1960–1961,* ed. Richard N. Swift (New York: Dobbs Ferry-Oceana, 1961), p. 10.

its parent body indicating consensus of the members of that body in support of the organ's recommendations. In short, the subsidiary organ may lobby for its recommendations and ask other actors to reason with the disputants and perhaps to indicate by voting for appropriate resolutions their support for the subsidiary organ. (8) *Promise rewards—threaten deprivations.* The task here, pure and simple, is to develop quid pro quos, in either a positive or negative sense. The effort may be made to obtain a change in policy on behalf of one or more disputants through the promise of favors or the threat of deprivations. In making this attempt, the third party may represent other interested actors or may rely on its own status as an international agency. Rewards promised may be membership to a desired UN organ, technical assistance in the future, or facilitation of some bilateral transaction. A standard reward is that of offering to bear the financial burden, in part or *in toto,* of the costs of implementing a recommended settlement— whether it involves surveillance of boundary lines, aid for state-building, or underwriting the costs of population movement. Negative quid pro quos are well exemplified by the Thant Plan for economic sanctions against Tshombe in the Congo crisis, which was drawn up and informally discussed but never implemented. Another threatened deprivation was the denial of UN membership to Israel in 1949 until it agreed to certain policy positions, a proposal formally debated by the Assembly and seriously discussed by the CCP but never applied. The debate and discussion themselves, however, constituted informal threats. (9) *Mobilize pressure.* In the same way that a third party might seek to mobilize persuasion, it might seek to mobilize pressure on the disputants. Other actors could be asked to reduce or eliminate financial support to a particular disputant or a particular project important to one of the disputants. The third party might seek to have weapons or consumer goods denied to a disputant from a principal supplier. (10) *Mobilize force.* Again in the same process, the third party might seek to mobilize influence in the form of force against one or more disputants where the UN organ was supported by an overwhelming consensus against a weak disputant. Such action is highly unlikely in the foreseeable future and would require authorization by the Security Council under Chapter VII of the Charter. The *sine qua non* to the process would be great-power unity in the belief that the continuation of a conflict was a threat to international peace.

An understanding of the roles of UN peacemaking organs necessitates a further consideration of the problems of organizing peacemaking missions. There is a need to consider which structures facilitate the effective discharge of the roles discussed above.[27] As all students of the American Congress learn sooner or later, procedure does indeed affect substance.[28] Hence procedural or institutional questions regarding efficient forms of peacemaking missions are an important corollary to a typology of roles.

The basic question to be dealt with, one which unites role and structures, is this: what structures facilitate the efficient functioning of UN peacemaking missions as these missions act in conflict situations through a variety of roles. The typology of roles discussed above can be usefully evaluated through the use of five related questions concerning institutional forms. (1) What effect does the composition of the UN organ have on the functioning of that organ: is it more efficacious for the agency to be comprised of government members or of noninstructed individuals, and in either event how many members are desirable? (2) What effect do the terms of reference have on the agency's operations: is it desirable for the General Assembly or Security Council to give a specific mandate, or does the field organ fare better when it

---

[27] Thus this study may be considered as a somewhat bastardized form of structural-functional analysis that has been crossed with a modified case-study approach. The implicit central concern of this study is exactly "what structures fulfill what basic functions and under what conditions in any given system?" Oran R. Young, *Systems of Political Science* (Englewood Cliffs, N.J.: Prentice-Hall, 1968), p. 28.

[28] Procedural, institutional concerns have fallen into some disrepute in current political science, smacking of previous formal-legal analyses that tended to avoid the "real stuff" of politics. Institutions are, most fundamentally, formalized patterns of behavior; hence there is no attempt to replace the study of human action with formal-legal relationships. A concern with institutions for peacemaking represents awareness that effective role-playing requires procedures adequate to terminate conflict. See Boulding, *Conflict and Defense,* p. 324.

17

derives flexibility and maneuverability from an ambiguous mandate? (3) What are the tactics of the agency in the field: how formal are its procedures and what is the effect of formality; does it show adequate initiative; does it command the respect of the negotiating parties? (4) What is the relationship among the various field organs dealing with the same problem: is there an overlap of duties; does the action of one agency impede that of another; is there a detrimental tendency toward excessive egotism on the part of personnel in these agencies?[29]

In the pages that follow, the diplomatic history of the CCP, 1948–68, will be systematically described. The functioning of the CCP will be analyzed in terms of how its structures did or did not facilitate the roles it played. In the concluding chapter, UN peacemaking efforts in six conflicts (Palestine, Kashmir, Indonesia, Korea, Congo, and Cyprus) will be analyzed in summary form according to the same criteria.

[29] Under each of the four headings, subsequent questions are raised in the course of study. The list given here is instructive rather than comprehensive.

I

THE PALESTINE QUESTION AND

THE CREATION OF THE CCP

The origin of the Arab-Israeli conflict has been written about many times. Certainly to specialists in Middle East politics a historical review is unnecessary. Yet a brief look backward is included here for two reasons. One is to clarify this author's understanding of the events prior to the creation of the CCP in the fall of 1948. Second, pre-1948 events require a brief review in order to place the formation of the CCP in complete perspective.

The confrontation between Zionists and Arabs in the Middle East is, in its different dimensions, a multiplicity of incidents, a conflict, and a general tension.[1] The incidents, the minor provocations are legion: murders and assassinations, less violent harassments, public vituperations, violations of rules instituted by the British mandatory government, more recent border disputes, and so on ad infinitum.

The basic conflict is clear: at stake is control of the territory called Palestine.[2] Ruled by the United Kingdom under the aegis of

---

[1] The framework for this chapter is taken from K. J. Holsti, *International Politics: A Framework for Analysis* (Englewood Cliffs, N. J.: Prentice-Hall, 1967), chap. 15.

[2] The history of the Palestine conflict is well presented in J. C. Hurewitz, *The Struggle for Palestine* (New York: W. W. Norton, 1950). For a more general analysis of the political ramifications of the struggle for Palestine, see especially Charles D. Cremeans, *The Arabs and the World* (New York: Frederick A. Praeger, 1963); William R.

a League of Nations mandate after four hundred years of Turkish control, Palestine became the cause célèbre of both world Zionism and emergent Arab nationalism. Zionist claims to Palestine were initially based on a theory of ownership. The Hebrews had lived in what was now called Palestine thousands of years ago. The Jews of the twentieth century were the descendants of those Hebrews, and as such they were entitled to the land. The analogy of the owner-tenant was employed; the Jews were the owners of the land through a sense of ownership, even though they were not present on the land; the Arabs were the tenants, living on the land and caring for it while the owners were away.[3] Arab claims to Palestine were based on less theoretical grounds: the population was predominantly Arab and private property was overwhelmingly in the hands of Arabs, as evidenced by the records of the mandatory government. Other aspects of this basic conflict eventually developed: the location of official boundaries of the state or states created out of the mandated territory, the status of Jerusalem, the rights of—and current provision for—Palestinian refugees, navigation rights of the disputants, matters of diplomatic recognition, trading privileges, and the Middle East arms race. The core of the conflict has remained unchanged: is the territory to be controlled by Zionists or Arabs.

Yet to term the Arab-Zionist confrontation a conflict over territory is to oversimplify the problem grossly, for the territory is a symbol for a larger clash of destinies. As such, the magnitude of the confrontation can hardly be overstated. The very essence of Zionism is the belief that Judaism becomes meaningful to the fullest extent only when it has a territorial base. Thus Palestine is the *sine qua non* for world Zionism, other territorial substitutes having been long ago rejected. It is the geographical component of the ideology. But for the Arabs, too, the territory of Palestine has

---

Polk, *The United States and the Arab World* (Cambridge, Mass.: Harvard University Press, 1965); and Nadav Safran, *The United States and Israel* (Cambridge, Mass.: Harvard University Press, 1963).

[3] In addition to this theoretical foundation the Zionists subsequently made claims to Palestine on the basis of: the Balfour Declaration, the need to escape Nazi persecution and anti-Semitism in general, and the UN partition resolution, all discussed below.

meaning beyond the geographical sense. Arab nationalism, already prevalent for some time, took on renewed dynamism after World War II. Nationalism was proving its strength in Egypt, Lebanon, and Syria, and the same emergence was foreseen for Palestine. Successful nationalism—indigenous control of a nation-state—was one mark of modernity and status. Thus the control of Palestine was intertwined with the collective pride of the Palestinian Arabs. Moreover, Palestine was important to Arab peoples beyond Palestine, for the image of the Arab empire of history had not been forgotten; it was being resurrected in the form of pan-Arabism. What was also involved in the struggle for Palestine, therefore, was a clash of conceptions regarding the nature of the Middle East. Was it to be a more or less integrated Arab region, or was it to be poly-ethnic? Thus the Arab-Zionist confrontation is indeed a general, emotional tension in addition to being a specific conflict.[4]

In the struggle for Palestine, there were five modes of behavior theoretically available to the disputants:[5] voluntary withdrawal from the conflict, conquest-forced withdrawal, compromise, arbitration-adjudication, and passive settlement. At the time of the creation of the CCP in December 1948, it was clear from the history of the Palestine question that only two of the five modes of behavior were seen as realistic alternatives by the parties.

The conflict was perceived by the disputants to be too important either for voluntary withdrawal or for arbitration or adjudication by a third party. Neither of these alternatives appealed to the Zionists. They had interpreted the Balfour

---

[4] This distinction between conflicts and tensions is important particularly for policy prescription. From Holsti's general analysis, *International Politics*, it follows that the tension between Arabs and Israelis cannot be resolved except through historical processes which gradually may (or may not) reduce inter-society hostilities. It is possible (it may or may not be probable) to solve conflicts, usually by treating specific aspects of the conflict. Conflict-resolution may have the effect of making tensions less explosive and less dangerous. The difference between conflicts and tensions is especially important in the present study and should be kept in mind by the reader. See further Holsti, esp. pp. 442–44.

[5] This typology is a modified version of that presented in Holsti, *ibid.*, pp. 445–55.

Declaration of 1917 and its provision for a national home for Jews in Palestine as a British promise for a Jewish nation-state there. They had been confronted with the need to do something about the masses of European Jews fleeing the Third Reich. They had successfully worked for the passage of the General Assembly partition resolution in the fall of 1947, which resolved to partition Palestine into an Arab and a Jewish state, *inter alia*.[6] And particularly after British withdrawal from Palestine and the declaration of the state of Israel in May 1948 the Zionists had successfully defended their claims to Palestine with force and increased their control of territory beyond the boundaries allotted to the Jewish state in the partition resolution. Likewise the Arabs throughout the Middle East perceived the Palestine question to be of major importance, subject to neither third-party award nor voluntary withdrawal. For Palestinian Arabs, their political future was at stake. For other Arabs, their pride, dignity, sense of brotherhood, and ultimate political potential were seen to be jeopardized. They reminded the British of their World War I promises of aid to the Arabs pursuant to construction of an Arab empire in the Middle East, and they challenged the authority of the General Assembly to partition Palestine.[7]

Neither were conquest and forced withdrawal—two sides of the same coin—likely to occur. No doubt the Zionists had been relatively successful in competing for Palestine. Their actions had been effective in both the British and American political systems, and with the help of the Americans their actions had been influential in UN political processes. The Zionists had also been effective in organizing for more violent activity in Palestine, both before and after British withdrawal. In the winter of 1948, however, the Israelis were not in a position to make a conquest of all of Palestine and compel the Arabs to withdraw from the

---

[6] A/Res/181, 27 November 1947. The vote was 33–13–10, just above the necessary two-thirds majority required. In general, the partition resolution provided for two states of roughly equal size joined via an economic union, with Jerusalem an international city.

[7] See further George Kirk, *A Short History of the Middle East* (New York: Frederick A. Praeger, 1961), esp. p. 202 ff.

conflict. The Israelis had limited resources, both in terms of manpower and material, and a number of Israeli leaders considered the nation near exhaustion after the fighting of 1947—48. In short, the Israelis had won the Palestine war, but they were not in a position to dictate the terms of settlement; further fighting just after 1948 was highly unlikely. On the other hand, the Arab armies of Egypt, Lebanon, Jordan, Syria, and Iraq had been defeated in Palestine, but no territory was lost by any of these nations and no Arab state's existence was remotely threatened by Israel's army.[8] The only Arab loss in general, as opposed to the loss of a political future by the Palestinian Arabs, was a loss of pride and dignity. The Arab states remained in a relatively good bargaining position, surrounding Israel on three sides and outnumbering it overwhelmingly in terms of population. The Palestine war had been lost, but the Arabs could not be forced by the Israelis into accepting the presence of a Jewish state if the Arabs chose not to do so.

Therefore, of the five modes of behavior theoretically available, only attempts at compromise and hopes for a passive settlement existed as probable alternatives—and given the failure of these modes of behavior, perhaps a return to an attempt at conquest when historical change had altered the variables of the conflict. The past record of attempts at compromise and hopes for a settlement through the workings of history in the Arab-Zionist confrontation was not encouraging for the CCP. The British had tried for more or less thirty years to find modus vivendi to accommodate Zionist and Arab demands. In the end, the British managed to antagonize both parties. Zionists were infuriated that Palestine immigration limits were set on European Jews fleeing Hitler; Arabs were distressed that the immigration quotas were not

---

[8] Several of the Arab governments, while not directly threatened by Israel's army, were indirectly threatened by the very existence of Israel. The governments of Egypt, Jordan, and Syria were quite unstable at this time, and the obvious failure of the policies of these governments with regard to Palestine contributed to popular disaffection in these nations. Any tendency to accept the presence of Israel on the part of these governments could be very risky once the people had been stirred up to anti-Israel fervor through wartime propaganda.

enforced more strictly and not kept at low figures, thus upsetting the demographic status quo in Palestine. Each party considered the British ambivalent pattern of suppression of violence within Palestine to be favorable to the opponent.

After the British had given the Palestine question to the General Assembly in 1946, the UN record at facilitating compromise and hoping for passive settlement was not dissimilar from the British record.[9] The UN Special Committee on Palestine and the Ad Hoc Committee on Palestine could not strike a compromise solution to the conflict. Both opted for partition in 1946, but neither could find an acceptable plan for implementation in the face of adamant Arab opposition to any form of partition. The UN Palestine Commission, authorized under the partition resolution to oversee the implementation of partition, was totally insignificant in the rising tide of violence in the Middle East. The UN's attempts to enforce some limited compromises after the eruption of fighting in the spring of 1948 were for the most part ineffective. The UN Consular Truce Commission was a stopgap measure that was completely devoid of results.[10] Only in the summer of 1948 was the Security Council, using threat of sanctions for noncompliance, able to institute two truces directly supervised by a UN mediator, Count Folke Bernadotte of Sweden. Thus the United Nations, like the United Kingdom, had attempted to muddle through the conflict, hoping that somehow the conflict would disappear over time. Partition was voted without a compromise among the disputants but also without a plan for implementation; there was no preparation for the probability that the Arabs would resist partition with force; and there was a post-partition attempt to improvise on a day-to-day basis while

[9] The United Kingdom had concluded: "The fact has to be faced that there is no common ground between the Arabs and the Jews." British note to US government proposing Anglo-American commission of inquiry, quoted in Harry S. Truman, *Memoirs: 1946–1952,* 2 vols. (New York: New American Library, 1965), 2:168.

[10] An informative account of UN field operations in the winter of 1947–48 and the following spring is presented in Pablo de Azcárate, *Mission in Palestine 1948–1953* (Washington, D.C.: Middle East Institute, 1966), chaps. 1 and 7. UN personnel lacked means of transportation and protection and symbols of authority.

waiting for the conflict to somehow resolve itself. In all these activities, US attitudes were important. Throughout its involvement in the Palestine question, the United States was primarily concerned with checking Soviet influence in the Middle East.[11] Specific issues arising out of the Palestine question such as boundaries and refugees consistently took second place to the overriding concern with Soviet-American competition.[12]

By the fall of 1948, UN peacemaking and peacekeeping in Palestine were clearly characterized by naïveté and weakness, in part because the United States—the most powerful government in the world at that time—was content to let issues arising from the Arab-Israeli conflict go unresolved if the Soviet Union did not penetrate the Middle East. Events in Western and Central Europe seemed more important to American interests than a concerted effort to budge recalcitrant parties from their stated diplomatic positions. And because the British and French were both weak and because Britain was committed to withdrawing from the area, there was no other source of power in the West for the implementing of UN resolutions. Needless to say, the West in general was wary of permitting the USSR to act as an agent of the United Nations; and likewise the Soviet Union hesitated to see the West being authorized to involve itself in Middle East politics as spokesman for the United Nations. The Great Powers could only agree that a Zionist state was desirable (the Soviet view being then based on the assumption that a Zionist state would reduce British influence in the area and that the Arab League was little more than a front for British interests). In short there was no coalition of governments ready to implement UN resolutions vis-à-vis the protagonists. The two states with the greatest capacity for action in the area, the United States and the United Kingdom, both

[11] See Harry N. Howard, *The Development of United States Policy in the Near East, 1945–1951* (reprint from *Department of State Bulletin,* 19 and 26 November 1951; Washington, D.C.: Government Printing Office, 1952).

[12] See Truman, *Memoirs,* vol. 2, chaps. 10–11. As to the effect of US policies on the specific issues of the Palestine question and indeed even on the question of the future control of the territory, President Truman later wrote that this "was the kind of problem we had the UN for." *Ibid.,* pp. 166–67.

sought to avoid antagonizing Arab governments, whose oil and communication routes were deemed important. But neither did they want to antagonize powerful Zionist elements in their domestic political systems. Arabs and Israelis, therefore, could regard UN personnel as devoid of influence beyond persuasion.

Despite this unproductive record, a major effort at peace-making was initiated at the 1948 General Assembly. It was undertaken primarily at the request of the UN mediator. Count Bernadotte had had some success in the summer of 1948 in implementing the truces ordered by the Security Council, although not all the terms of both truces were scrupulously observed. This limited achievement in peacekeeping had not been matched in the field of peacemaking; Bernadotte's general recommendations for a settlement had met with little response from the parties concerned. Therefore the mediator, just prior to his assassination by a Zionist terrorist group, had drafted a report to the Assembly in which he asked that body to create a conciliation commission.[13]

Bernadotte believed that the United Nations had continuing responsibility in the Arab-Zionist conflict, but he was dissatisfied with the political stalemate that had persisted in spite of his peacemaking efforts. He thought a commission might succeed where he had not. Also contributing to his view that another form of peacemaking was needed was his feeling that personality conflicts had developed between himself and certain of those with whom he was dealing.[14] He felt that in such situations it was the mediator's job to be expendable. In calling for a conciliation

---

[13] GAOR: 3d Sess., Supplements, vol. 2 (A/638, *Progress Report of the United Nations Mediator on Palestine*). The final wording of the report was that of Ralph Bunche, then Bernadotte's assistant, who separated from Bernadotte in order to finish the report and thus missed the trip which resulted in ambush and the mediator's death.

[14] Statements of fact that are not common knowledge and that are not footnoted in this study are based on confidential interviews. At various points, statements of fact of particular importance that came from secret UN or government papers are footnoted with the phrase, "Unimpeachable source." A more complete documentation can be found in my 1968 Ph.D. dissertation, "The United Nations and the Peaceful Settlement of Disputes: The Case of the Conciliation Commission for Palestine," Firestone Library, Princeton University.

commission, Bernadotte restated his belief that a settlement was possible. He wrote in his report: "I do not conclude . . . that the problem is insoluble by peaceful means, or that a basis for agreement cannot ultimately be found. But the conclusion is inescapable that at some juncture vital decisions will have to be taken by the General Assembly if a peaceful settlement is to be achieved."[15]

The mediator's request for a conciliation commission met with an affirmative response at the third session, but there was divergence of opinion on virtually every detail of the commission's existence.[16] The mediator, and subsequently the acting mediator (Bunche), had recommended a commission that would reflect broad competence, have a specific mandate particularly on territorial matters, and be composed of individuals.[17] Although the mediator's report received strong support from the United Kingdom, it failed to gain a consensus on its specific proposals.

In general, there were two major points of contention reflected in Assembly debates:[18] what was to be the composition of the commission and what was to be its mandate. Several delegations, notably the US, argued for a commission composed legally of states on the ground that such a commission would have increased prestige and authority.[19] This position was finally

---

[15] A/648, *Progress Report of the United Nations Mediator on Palestine*, p. 3.

[16] The USSR first opposed the creation of a subsidiary agency, then changed its position. The Arabs maintained the official policy of opposing any field organ since, according to Arab public policy, no negotiation with a Jewish state would be considered. Hence a conciliation commission would be superfluous.

[17] Bernadotte and Bunche saw the commission as *the* UN field organ on the Palestine question, with competence to patrol the truce as well as to negotiate an overall settlement. They thought specific instructions were needed to strengthen the position of the commission vis-à-vis the recalcitrant disputants. Their views on the composition of the commission were not well known. Bunche was careful to maintain his independence from the US delegation, and this at times impeded the communication between himself and that influential delegation.

[18] See GAOR: 3d Sess., 1st Comm., 1: 771–867; and GAOR: 3d Sess., 1st Comm., Annexes, Agenda Item 67.

[19] This attitude was consistent both with League of Nations experience and with early UN action. See UN Doc. A/AC.18/68, *Measures and Procedures of Pacific*

accepted, over the opposition of Guatemala and Colombia, *inter alia*, who urged a commission of individuals without government directives in order to protect the impartial status of the field organ. It was finally agreed that the states should be three in number rather than five, in the interests of speed in making decisions and of efficiency.

With regard to the commission's terms of reference, or mandate, the mediator's report provided one obvious possibility. The United Kingdom pushed this alternative and argued publicly that Assembly endorsement of this document was needed to prod Arabs and Israelis into negotiations. More importantly to the British, they realized they would gain by incorporation of the report into the commission's mandate. Jordanian territory would be increased, thus desirable locations for British bases would become available, and ultimately the British bargaining position would be enhanced with the Egyptians regarding treaty negotiations in the immediate future.[20] But other governments sought to return to the partition resolution as a basis for a mandate, in some cases for the sake of consistency with past resolutions and in some cases to block advantages accruing to the United Kingdom from the mediator's report.[21] Consistency and the partition resolution were to prevail only on the subject of Jerusalem, as the original plan to create an international city again received endorsement. In most other respects, Assembly resolution 194(III), destined to be quoted and misquoted for years to come, followed neither the mediator's report nor the partition resolution in the terms of reference it provided for the CCP created thereby.[22] The subject of territory and boundaries was omitted in

---

Settlement Employed by the League of Nations, 29 June 1948; Elmore Jackson, "Mediation and Conciliation in International Law," *International Social Science Bulletin* 10, no. 4 (1958): 535–36.

[20] See Hurewitz, *Struggle for Palestine,* pp. 487–88; and Safran, *United States and Israel,* p. 223. The mediator, and Great Britain, wanted Jordan to control the southern Negev, giving that kingdom a land link to Egypt.

[21] Communist delegations took this latter point of view.

[22] GAOR: 3d Sess., Supplements, 2: 21–25, contained in its entirety in Appendix A below.

the resolution, apart from the Jerusalem issue. As for refugees who had left areas of fighting, the resolution established only a general principle: the right of repatriation or compensation for those desiring to live in peace. Only on the question of Jerusalem was the CCP tied to specific instructions; on that issue the Commission was not to facilitate negotiation but to implement the Assembly's judgment. On the other issues, the actual membership of the CCP was seen as the key factor as to whether Arab and Israeli positions could be bridged. After much controversy, the permanent members of the Council were designated as a committee of the Assembly to name the Commission's members, subject to final approval by the Assembly.

The five permanent members of the Council met in closed session immediately after the adoption of A/Res/194. Both the United States and the Soviet Union entered the meeting with plans for a CCP without Great Powers. The United Kingdom, however, wanted the United States on the CCP. The British policy was that the United States should be directly responsible for decisions taken on the Palestine question since US power would have to be involved in any permanent settlement. The French agreed to this policy, and the United Kingdom and France persuaded China to vote with them. Thus the United States became the first member despite its own initial opposition. Subsequently it was deemed advisable not to have another Anglo-Saxon state on the CCP, nor an obvious small power that would appear to be completely dominated by the United States. For these reasons, and because the head of the French permanent delegation to the United Nations, as a career diplomat, was keenly interested in the complexities of the Palestine question, France became the second member. Turkey was chosen as the third member since it was a Moslem state that had extended de facto recognition to the state of Israel. It was hoped in some quarters that Turkey, without being adamantly pro-Arab, could serve as a bridge between the CCP and the Arab states.[23]

---

[23] In the subsequent plenary session, the USSR and others objected to the inclusion of Great Powers on the CCP, and other delegations objected to the inclusion of Turkey. Nevertheless, A/Res/194 was finally adopted by a vote of 40−7−4.

After the creation of the CCP, events continued to transpire rapidly in the Middle East. Egypt notified the United Nations that it was ready to enter into armistice negotiations with Israel under the provisions of the Security Council resolution of 16 November. That resolution had called for armistice talks under the supervision of the acting mediator for Palestine (Bunche). The acting mediator, however, had previously indicated that he thought the new Commission should conduct all further negotiations and handle all UN tasks relating to the Arab-Israeli dispute.[24] But the individual members of the CCP had not been named yet. Only the French delegate, Claude de Boisanger, was ready to serve in his new capacity.

Recognizing that the Egyptians were serious in their request for armistice negotiations[25] and not wanting to miss this opportunity to end the fighting, the Security Council urged the CCP to take action as quickly as possible.[26] In the meantime, the acting mediator did what he could so that the opportunity for peace was not lost.

The request for action by the Security Council had its effect on the member governments of the CCP, as the Turkish and US members were appointed within a week. Turkey nominated Huseyin Cahit Yalchin, and the United States named Joseph Keenan. The Commission was not yet ready to function, however, because of the first in a series of personnel problems that was to plague the US delegation throughout the coming year. After having been sworn in on 4 January at a White House public ceremony attended by the highest ranking State Department personnel, Keenan resigned on 15 January for "personal reasons."[27] To add to the problems of the CCP in this most

---

[24] GAOR: 3d Sess., 1st Comm., pt. 1, p. 770.

[25] The Egyptians had been defeated twice in succession by the Israelis; subsequently the United Kingdom had threatened to intervene in Egyptian affairs to protect British interests in the Suez. Egypt disliked the prospect of dealing with Israel, but it disliked even more the prospect of UK intervention.

[26] UN Doc. S/1169, 28 December 1948.

[27] *Palestine Post*, 5 and 16 January 1949, p. 1. Keenan's name has been removed from all UN records.

inauspicious debut, the acting mediator continued to adhere to his position that the Commission should be the agency to supervise the armistice talks.[28] The CCP finally assembled in full strength in Jerusalem approximately two months after its legal creation as Mark Ethridge, the new appointee from the United States, arrived on 2 February.[29] The acting mediator had meanwhile gone to Rhodes where he was met by Egyptian and Israeli officials.

The CCP started its peacemaking efforts with high hopes for success, especially since the disputants had indicated a willingness to parley. But to Israel and the Arab states, the CCP was viewed with some reservation. They had not been consulted concerning its composition: the Arabs were unhappy with the inclusion of two Western states; Israel was aware, *inter alia*, that both France and the United States had voted for an international status for Jerusalem. The CCP's mandate was objected to by various parties for various reasons. The Commission's personnel problems and slowness in organizing did not add to its initial prestige. The disputants also had reservations about the CCP because of the UN's tradition of inconsistent and indecisive action on the Palestine question.

At this point perhaps it is well to provide some overview of the 1949–69 conflict, during which the detailed activities of the CCP can be set. As a three-government organ, the CCP was to be most involved during 1949; for two years thereafter it sought to bring about Arab-Israeli rapport with decreasing vigor. After 1951 and the issuance of the Tripartite Declaration by Britain, France, and the United States, which constituted a Western endorsement of the status quo, the Commission became largely a symbol of UN concern that the outstanding issues be resolved. This dormant posture was altered in the early 1960s when the Kennedy Administration activated the CCP by creating a Special Representative of the Commission to solve the refugee problem, still perhaps the most central and most pressing specific issue in the

[28] UN Doc. S/1215, 17 January 1949.

[29] On these early problems of the CCP, and for a review of meetings prior to the arrival of Ethridge, see Azcárate, *Mission in Palestine*, p. 139 and *passim*.

overall Arab-Israeli dilemma.[30] This peacemaking undertaking in 1961–62 proved as devoid of results as earlier efforts, at least in the 1960s. In the late 1950s and 1960s, CCP staff personnel carried out technical work on the identification and evaluation of Arab refugee property in Israel, but the Commission's efforts in all dimensions seemed consistently to face the problem of being dated by events.

As negotiations on the refugee question bogged down, the Assembly created the United Nations Relief and Works Agency (UNRWA) in 1949 as a peaceservicing agency designed to coordinate socioeconomic assistance to the refugees. Because of the natural increase of refugees and because of the unfortunate conditions in the refugee camps, UNRWA itself became a channel for efforts to solve the refugee problem as well as a channel for technical assistance such as educational and vocational training. As the refugees doubled in population, their condition as the most directly and severely affected group of those Arabs affected by the Palestine question led to the presence of a large pool of manpower potentially, and to some extent actually, available for radical movements. While the exact relationship is difficult to define between Palestinian refugees and membership in Arab terrorist-commando organizations in the late 1960s, there is no doubt that the Arab organizations such as *Fatah* do some of their recruiting from the refugee areas. The increasing popularity of such groups throughout the Arab world makes it difficult for UNRWA and the Arab governments in whose territory UNRWA operates to curtail such activities, even when the actions of the terrorists-commandos endanger the stability of the Arab government, as on occasion in Lebanon and Jordan. That same popularity also impeded prospects for negotiations on the refugee question, for the militant posture of the nongovernmental groups made it difficult for any government to offer to negotiate differences with Israel without giving the appearances of "being soft on the enemy."

---

[30] This phrase—"Arab-Israel dilemma"—is borrowed from Fred J. Khouri, *The Arab-Israeli Dilemma* (Syracuse: Syracuse University Press, 1968). This important work, published after the completion of the research and writing of this present effort, presents an excellent overview of the conflict and role of the UN through the mid-1960s.

It had, of course, always been difficult to keep all the phases of the Arab-Israeli conflict within tolerable limits of animosity after the stalemate in negotiations in 1949, even prior to the appearance of the guerrilla movements. The Armistice Agreements of 1949 and the related United Nations Truce Supervision Organization—Mixed Armistice Commission (UNTSO-MAC) apparatus had become a sort of tally sheet for violations of the agreements claimed by one party or the other. Thus UN peacekeeping through these agents had never been completely successful. Although the government in Cairo had long maintained the dubious argument that the agreements did not end the state of war with Israel (hence Egypt could claim to bar shipping by or to or from Israel through Suez), the UNTSO-MAC phase of peacekeeping largely collapsed with the Anglo-French-Israeli invasion of Egypt in 1956, at which time the Israelis denounced the Egyptian-Israeli Agreement as null and void. While UNTSO-MAC remained operative on the other boundaries, the introduction of the United Nations Emergency Force (UNEF) into Sinai restored tranquility to the Egyptian-Israeli boundary for the decade following the Suez crisis. But this successful peacekeeping did not lay the foundation for an increase in mutual respect and Israeli-Egyptian negotiations. Economic pressure on Israeli shipping through the Gulf of Aqaba combined with military maneuvers and the ordering of the withdrawal of UNEF brought the United Arab Republic into yet another war with Israel in 1967, after which it has thus far proved impossible to reinstitute the peacekeeping that had existed prior to the war.

Thus the UN record of peacemaking, peaceservicing, and peacekeeping in the Arab-Israeli confrontation is one of frustration. General territorial questions have been "solved" by occupation, and specific issues such as Jerusalem have been "treated" in the same fashion. UN service to the refugees continues, but in a context of ever-growing need and frustration.[31] And UN observers in the Suez canal area serve as little

[31] See further David P. Forsythe, "UNRWA, the Palestine Refugees, and World Politics, 1949—1969," *International Organization* 25, no. 1 (Winter 1971): 26—45.

more than commentators on the relatively extensive on-going process of coercion between Egypt and Israel, interrupted only by violence across one of the other three Arab-Israeli boundaries.

It is time to look into the record of the CCP, to analyze its performance, and to discover if there is something valuable in that record for current students of UN and Middle East politics.

II

THE CCP AND CONFERENCE DIPLOMACY IN
THE CRUCIAL YEAR 1949

M uch was to transpire in the year 1949, and in retrospect it can be argued—without definitive conclusion to be sure—that an Arab-Israeli peace was more within reach in that year than at any time since. There was more direct contact among the Arab and Israeli delegations on the island of Rhodes, in the area of Lausanne, Switzerland, and secretly in the Middle East; and there was more serious attention given to the issues that would make a peace. The CCP was a hub around which much of this diplomatic activity occurred, a status it was never to know again.

While armistice negotiations continued under Ralph Bunche, the CCP engaged in an early probing of the parties to discern both how to proceed and what issues to treat first. In so doing, it accomplished a major objective—getting the Arab governments to drop their insistence on Israel's repatriation of Palestinian refugees as a precondition for talks and to agree to meet for talks in Lausanne where, just by chance, the Israelis could also be found. There followed in the summer of 1949 the Lausanne conference; in the first phase of this conference the Lausanne protocol was signed which linked the refugee and territorial issues into one package as a presumably negotiable matter to the parties, but it was a package that remained unnegotiated despite threat of pressure on Israel by the United States. The second phase of the conference led to limited offers of repatriation by Israel and to limited offers of resettlement by several Arab delegations, but the gap between the offers was not bridged, and the thrust of discussion turned to blocked bank accounts and provision for the needs of the refugees who remained in political limbo.

The year started with the CCP optimistic: Arab governments were negotiating at Rhodes and being flexible vis-à-vis the Commission, despite a good bit of inflammatory, bellicose propaganda designed in no small degree for Arab domestic consumption. This double-deckered diplomatic style emerged early and continued late into the active life of the CCP. But the flexibility and pragmatism were there in the Arabs' diplomacy, as indicated by negotiations under Bunche and under the CCP at Beirut prior to Lausanne. The flexibility existed at least until the armistice agreements were signed, reducing the threat of Israeli coercion, and until the weakness of Western prodding on the Arabs indicated the reduction of an outside stimulus to peace-making. The year ended with the CCP barely existing: Israel believed the CCP had become an obstacle to peacemaking by its failure to obtain formal, tête-à-tête negotiations, a view that deemphasized the secret direct talks that occurred around Lausanne behind the back of the Commission and that were also going on in the Middle East between the Israelis and Jordanians, not to mention the formal, direct talks of a limited nature that did occur under CCP auspices. By comparing Bunche and the CCP, Israel strengthened its belief in the efficacy of direct talks per se: if men would just talk together, agreement would eventually be reached. But several Arab governments reached the conclusion that there were few positive incentives to make peace, given the Israeli terms of settlement indicated in these private talks, once a halt to the fighting had been agreed upon.

As the Arabs began to hold out for a return to the terms of the partition resolution that they had once rejected, and as the Israelis began to hold out for consolidation of the status quo established through force of arms, the CCP began to fade in importance—a drift currently culminated in what one Secretariat member terms its "somnolent stance." But the opportunity was there in 1949, had the CCP been able to mobilize the firm and consistent support of the United States. Or was it?

The three heads of delegations to the CCP that assembled in Government House, Jerusalem, in early 1949 were quite different in background. Yalchin was an elderly journalist, well known in Turkey, prominent for his anti-Soviet views. De Boisanger was a career diplomat, respected for his ability and prestige, a lover of the arts and of the French way of life. Ethridge was a southern journalist who had been special envoy to Rumania and Bulgaria at the close of World War II and then chief US delegate to the UN Commission of Inquiry concerning Greek Frontier Incidents.

As to the influence exerted by Yalchin, there is no indication that he ever said or did anything of positive significance.[1] De Boisanger was well thought of in diplomatic circles, and his presence gave the Commission an early degree of prestige. He made numerous contributions to the work of the CCP and was respected by many Arab delegations dealing with the Commission. From the outset, however, he deferred to the leadership of the US member on the CCP since he regarded his own efforts as insignificant in relation to the power of the United States. Moreover, he was generally characterized as not very forceful. His status on the Commission was at times impaired because of his being "typically French"—that is, because he enjoyed Paris, night life in general, cars, and a number of other things that led to his being termed lazy and indifferent by some. His appearance to the contrary, he was without doubt conscientious in his CCP duties. He was not unimportant, but neither was he the driving force of the CCP in its early activities.

The most influential member of the Commission was the US member, and this was true throughout the 1948–51 period regardless of who that person actually was. All parties involved in the negotiations looked to the United States for leadership on the Palestine question because of US political power. The personal ability of the US member was an important factor in the functioning of the CCP since a great number of decisions on this question were initiated in the field and not in Washington. Ethridge was well

---

[1] For analyses of CCP individuals, cf. Pablo de Azcárate, *Mission in Palestine 1948–1953* (Washington, D.C.: Middle East Institute, 1966), pp. 136–37; Walter Eytan, *The First Ten Years* (New York: Simon & Schuster, 1958), p. 56; James G. McDonald, *My Mission in Israel: 1948–1951* (London: Victor Gollancz, Ltd., 1951), pp. 161–62.

suited by temperament to occupy this position of leadership, even if he was not particularly suited for the rigors of Middle Eastern diplomacy. He worked hard and was anxious to make progress on the problems. His was a likeable personality, and he got along well with his colleagues on the CCP and with the delegates of the parties directly involved. But he had no experience in Arab-Israeli affairs, and he became impatient with the lack of progress along what he thought were rational guidelines.[2] What contributed to his impatience, in addition to personality factors, was the fact that he had accepted membership on the CCP on a short-term basis and from the outset was looking for a rapid solution both to the variety of problems that had not been solved in the last thirty years and to the many problems that had been generated by the Palestine war.

The government delegations under these three chief representatives were quite capable. In the case of Turkey, the number two and three men were far more vigorous than Yalchin. In the case of France, the lower-rank personnel were more dynamic than de Boisanger—particularly with regard to the question of the status of Jerusalem. On the US delegation, too, there were capable lower officials; and James Barco, who arrived on the scene later in the spring of 1949, was an excellent diplomat who was to become the idea-man and stimulating force in the CCP's post-1949 activities.

The government members of the CCP were supported by a capable secretariat, headed by Dr. Pablo de Azcárate y Flores as principal secretary.[3] Azcárate had been a senior official with the League of Nations and also Spanish Ambassador to the Court of Saint James's in the late 1930s. He had had a good deal of experience in Palestinian affairs with the United Nations and was thus a valuable counselor to the government members. He was an activist in the sense of advocating action by the CCP, but there are no data to suggest that he took action on his own or in any way exceeded

[2] McDonald thought that Ethridge relied too much on rationality and not enough on expert advice (*Mission to Israel*, p. 162).

[3] The word "secretariat" when not capitalized refers to the international civil servants of the field organ, as compared to the Secretariat in New York.

the normal duties of an international civil servant. The other members of the CCP secretariat were, for the most part, capable and dedicated in their respective tasks. As time went on they developed good esprit de corps[4] and a high respect for Azcárate. The secretariat aided the work of the CCP by advising the government members, by offering suggestions and revisions to all manner of documents, and by other "extra-curricular duties" such as trying to arrange for the Arabs to meet the Israelis "accidentally" as the parties went to and from meetings with the CCP.

The CCP secretariat did feel itself "cut off" and "detached" from the New York Secretariat. Early in 1949 it was not able to receive from New York what it thought was adequate support necessary for efficient functioning. As a result, the CCP had poor means of transportation and lack of protection from the sporadic violence that still occurred.[5] In February the CCP was unable to obtain a plane from the Secretariat so that a trip to the various Arab capitals could be undertaken, despite the fact that one of the planes assigned to Bunche at nearby Rhodes was not in use. If the Turkish government had not come to the aid of the Commission, the trip could not have been made.[6] In addition to hampering the actual work of the CCP, this lack of provision by the Secretariat cost the Commission a certain amount of its prestige. In comparison with the resources made available to both the mediator and acting mediator, the CCP had access to few external symbols of power. It is probable that this lack of support from New York stemmed both from a general lack of resources within the United Nations at this time and from certain conflicts between the CCP secretariat and the New York Secretariat which were to last through the first three years of CCP activity. On occasion, officials at the very highest level in the New York Secretariat took a policy position contrary to the policies pursued by the CCP.[7] In

---

[4] Azcárate, *Mission in Palestine*, p. 138.

[5] *Ibid.*, pp. 140–42.

[6] *Ibid.*, p. 146.

[7] See n. 97 below.

addition, there were personal differences between the Secretary-General and the CCP's principal secretary.[8]

With its prestige diminished somewhat from lack of physical provisions and from events concerning the abortive appointment of the first US delegate, the CCP made its first major decision in early February—a course that was to cost the CCP further loss of status with Israel. It was decided that the CCP would stay out of the armistice negotiations; Bunche would carry on independently. Ethridge had stopped at Rhodes on his way to Jerusalem, and in talking with Bunche he found that the negotiations there had reached a delicate stage. UN personnel knowledgeable on the state of the armistice talks feared that any alteration in the form of UN involvement might disrupt the talks and impede gains then in sight. Assistants to the acting mediator conferred with the CCP in Jerusalem during the first week in February,[9] and it was the consensus that the CCP should do nothing to jeopardize the Rhodes negotiations. After the Egyptian-Israeli Armistice was signed on 24 February, the CCP elected to stay out of further armistice negotiations.[10] Numerous Israeli officials were to say in retrospect, although the attitude probably had little currency in early 1949, that it seemed the CCP did not want to "dirty its hands" with the problems involved in achieving the armistice agreements.

While the peacekeeping talks continued at Rhodes, the CCP

[8] For references to this conflict and to some of the issues involved, see Azcárate, *Mission in Palestine,* pp. 31, 36. Some members of the CCP secretariat thought that Azcárate's former standing with the League and his extensive experience led to resentment on the part of some of the younger members of the New York Secretariat. The CCP in general was aware of the conflict. Azcárate was removed from office by the Secretary-General in 1952, despite requests that he be retained by the US permanent mission to the United Nations.

[9] *Palestine Post,* 2, 8, and 9 February 1949, p. 1. Paul Mohn, advisor to Bunche, came to Jerusalem on 1 February. Another adviser, Constantine Stavropoulos, spoke with the CCP on 7 February.

[10] See the first progress report of the CCP, GAOR: 4th Sess., Annexes, vol. 2 (A/819, 15 March 1949). The CCP was not acting *ultra vires* in taking this course since the General Assembly had instructed it "to assume, *in so far as it considers necessary* in existing circumstances, the functions given to the United Nations Mediator on Palestine . . . " (A/Res/194(III), 11 December 1948). Emphasis added.

concentrated its peacemaking efforts on initiating negotiations on nonmilitary subjects. Invitations were sent to interested Arab governments asking them to come to Government House and state their policies on any matters they wished. The Arab governments declined to come and gave a single reason: the only road to Government House went through Israeli territory, and the Arab governments would not allow their delegations to use such a road. Moreover, the Arab governments showed no inclination to correspond with the CCP and put their policies in writing. The CCP then decided to make a tour of Arab capitals in order to get the Arabs to state their views. Meanwhile, the CCP had created a subcommittee on Jerusalem.[11]

Having finally secured means of transport from the Turkish government and having established contact with the Israeli government, the CCP started its tour at a time when movements for Arab unity were gaining ground. The activity of the CCP contributed to these movements. Secretary-General Azzam Pasha of the Arab League was hard at work trying to overcome the fragmentation that had torn the Arab world during the winter of 1948. He was receiving able assistance from the tireless Palestinian, Ahmad Shuqayri. Inter-Arab conflicts were prevalent, as usual, and the acting mediator was not treating the Arab states *en bloc* for the armistice negotiations. But the Arabs minus Transjordan —were meeting together in Cairo and were preparing to deal with the CCP *en bloc*.[12]

The CCP arrived in Amman in early February and promptly received notification that Transjordan was prepared to negotiate a

[11] The CCP had debated whether or not to build a road to Government House from the Transjordanian side of the neutral zone in which the house was located. The view was expressed within the CCP that such a road would emphasize UN responsibility for the city of Jerusalem. Initial contacts were made with Transjordan (*Palestine Post,* 8 February 1949, p. 1), but the United States and the Secretariat did not think the expenses involved were justified. The work of the Jerusalem subcommittee that started at this juncture is covered below, pp. 65–67.

[12] On the history of movements for unity and conflicts impeding unity, see Polk, *United States and the Arab World,* pp. 189–91; Jon Kimche, *Seven Fallen Pillars* (London: Secker & Warburg, 1953), pp. 303–8; and Nadav Safran, *From War to War* (New York: Pegasus, 1969), pp. 36–42, 65–68, and *passim.*

separate peace treaty with Israel. The Foreign Minister, Tawfiq Pasha, "hinted at the possibility of bilateral negotiations" to the CCP *in toto;*[13] he made his position more explicit to government members during less formal conversations. The CCP declined to pursue this course of action, since it felt that it had a mandate to conclude a peace treaty between Israel and all the Arab belligerents and it was optimistic at this point that such a peace treaty could be achieved.[14] Moreover, strange as it may seem, the CCP was ignorant of the procedure of separate negotiations employed at that very time by Bunche at Rhodes, communication between the two UN field organs being most imperfect. In the other Arab capitals, the Commission found an emphasis on the refugee question. Arab governments cooperating with the Arab League pursued the policy that the Arab refugees who had left Israel-controlled Palestine had to be repatriated as a prior condition to any peace talks. Otherwise, the Arab governments were inarticulate on the subject of territorial boundaries, the future of Jerusalem, and regional economic plans for the future.[15]

The CCP did not accept the argument that the Arab refugees should be settled prior to any peace talks, but it believed the refugee question would have to be dealt with in some fashion in order to get the negotiations off the ground since this was the primary focus of most of the Arab governments.[16] The Commission consulted with experts on refugee affairs, then called a conference at Beirut of all Arab governments visited so that discussion on the refugee question could be continued in one place.[17] The CCP did not think it could make repeated trips to Arab capitals; and since the Arabs would not come to Government House or state their views in writing, there seemed no alternative to bringing the Arabs together in Beirut. But in doing so, the CCP

[13] Azcárate, *Mission in Palestine,* pp. 142–43.

[14] Azcárate defends this decision, pp. 143–44.

[15] See UN Doc. A/1367, 2 September 1950, p. 5; and Azcárate, *Mission in Palestine,* p. 145.

[16] UN Doc. A/1367, p. 6.

[17] *Ibid.*

was acting against the advice of the US Ambassador to Israel, certain British officials, and the Israeli government.[18] These parties feared that if the Arab representatives were brought together in one location, each would be so wary of the intentions of the others and so concerned with not leaving his country open to propaganda attack by any of the others that meaningful discussion would be impossible. It was thought that the Arab delegations, because of mutual fears, would try to surpass each other in making propaganda attacks against Israel. The CCP, in order to counteract this possible tendency, sent separate invitations to the Arab governments and decided to deal with each Arab delegation separately in Beirut.[19]

After the Beirut conference was announced on 2 March, there was a lull in the Commission's official activities until the meeting started on 21 March. Optimism had increased regarding the outcome of the peace talks following the conclusion of the Egyptian—Israeli Armistice Agreement on 24 February. Much of the optimism was based on the wording of the agreement where it was stated that the parties had signed the armistice "to facilitate the transition from the present truce to permanent peace in Palestine. . . ."[20] And the CCP said the agreement would "facilitate its own task considerably."[21] In addition, the government of Transjordan remained predisposed to a separate peace treaty with Israel and was at that time meeting the Israelis secretly at Shuneh pursuant to that goal. The CCP stated in its first progress report that on its initial round of contacts it had found the parties in a state of mind conducive to peace, and it had hopes of instituting direct talks.[22]

---

[18] McDonald, *Mission to Israel,* p. 162. The advice was not expressed very forcefully. A number of CCP secretariat people, as well as some government members, were not aware that such advice had been given at all.

[19] Azcárate, *Mission in Palestine,* pp. 148–49.

[20] Quoted in J. C. Hurewitz, ed., *Diplomacy in the Near and Middle East, A Documentary Record: 1914–1956* (New York: D. Van Nostrand Co., 1956), p. 300.

[21] UN Doc. A/819, 15 March 1949, p. 1.

[22] *Ibid.,* pp. 1–2. For a concise account of the secret Israeli-Jordanian talks, see Safran, *From War to War,* p. 37.

Also during the lull, Ethridge dispatched one of his assistants, Fraser Wilkins, to Rhodes to find out what was going on there. After the decision in early February to separate the peace talks from the armistice negotiations, communication between Bunche and the CCP had broken down. There was little concern with how the armistice talks were to mesh with the peace talks. There seemed to be an assumption, both in the field and in New York, that the two operations would mesh of their own accord. For his part, Bunche appeared to be too busy to keep the CCP informed on how matters were progressing. For the Commission's part, it made little effort to stay in touch with Rhodes.[23] Hence either because of intentional bypassing or because of an assumption that contact was not needed, there was little rapport between Rhodes and Jerusalem. One of Bunche's assistants was assigned to Government House; this would have facilitated contact considerably had rapport been desired. But the relations between General W. Riley and CCP personnel were casual for the most part and became strained in later years. Contrary to much speculation, Bunche had only a slight interest in the 1949 work of the CCP. At the close of the Beirut conference, he made a courtesy call on the CCP at the latter's invitation, but it was more of a social call than one for the purpose of giving advice. The later armistice negotiations involving Israel with Transjordan, Lebanon, and Syria had almost no relation to the peace talks, although both types of negotiations were pursued at the same time.

While Wilkins was at Rhodes, Ethridge sought to get from Israel a policy statement on the refugee issue that would be conducive to a settlement of the question in keeping with the CCP's terms of reference. In an earlier meeting with Israeli officials at the end of the trip to Arab capitals, the CCP had been told that Israel would not agree to repatriation except in the context of an

---

[23] McDonald was of the opinion that the CCP *in toto* wanted no liaison with Bunche (*Mission to Israel*, p. 162). The French in particular were skeptical of Bunche's ability; they were still thinking in colonial terms, and they had little regard for "that colored man." The dispute over the plane had not improved relations between the peacekeeping and peacemaking operations.

overall settlement.[24] Ethridge sought to get some alteration in this policy so that the Arabs could be asked at Beirut to change their policy. In seeking a "softer" refugee policy from Israel so that the Arabs might be induced to moderate their stand, Ethridge used the channels of the US government, and asked Ambassador McDonald to make the appropriate inquiries. McDonald contacted Foreign Minister Moshe Sharett, But the Israeli policy remained unchanged.[25]

The Beirut conference opened on 21 March, as Yalchin and de Boisanger returned from consultations in their respective capitals. The Arab governments sent delegations headed by men at the foreign minister and prime minister rank; also in attendance was George McGhee, soon to be Assistant Secretary for Near Eastern Affairs in the US State Department. The CCP also heard spokesmen from various refugee groups such as the "Gaza Government," the "Committee of Arab Refugees from Nazareth and Haifa," and the "Jerusalem Arab Conference." Designed as a "probing operation," the Beirut meeting quickly uncovered two Arab interests: unqualified and immediate repatriation, and release of refugee accounts frozen in Israeli banks.[26] The CCP accepted the validity, in principle, of the Arab legal argument regarding the absolute right of repatriation but realized the implementation of the principle would not be acceptable to Israel.[27] The Commission agreed with Israel that the government could not be expected to undertake a large-scale repatriation project in the face of continuing threats to Israeli security and statements advocating a "second round" in the Palestine war by various Arab leaders. Hence the CCP sought to persuade the Arab governments at Beirut

---

[24] Azcárate, *Mission in Palestine*, p. 145.

[25] McDonald, *Mission to Israel*, p. 163. The Ambassador, however, could not be termed overly cooperative toward the CCP, and this irritated members of the Commission. To McDonald, the CCP was "a three-headed monster which proved to be as self-defeating as Bunche was effective . . . " (*ibid.*, p. 159).

[26] On the first issue, see A/1367, p. 6. On the second, see Don Peretz, *Israel and the Palestine Arabs* (Washington, D.C.: The Middle East Institute, 1956), p. 223.

[27] A/1367, p. 30. To the CCP, the "practical application" of the right necessitated some "observations" by the Commission.

not to adhere to their policy of demanding repatriation as a precondition for settlement negotiations. During the separate meetings with the different delegations, the CCP used "hours and hours" of reasoning in an effort to convince the Arabs that their policy on the refugee question was detrimental to their own interests. Stressing that no gains could be made on the basis of present Arab policy and that the onus for the failure of the talks would fall squarely on their shoulders, the CCP was successful in getting all the delegations except Iraq to drop the policy of repatriation as a precondition for peaceful settlement negotiations.[28] The matter of blocked accounts was put on the agenda for the upcoming talks with Israel, which the Arabs agreed to attend in a neutral place.

The pattern of the Beirut conference had unfolded on two levels. On one level there was the Arabs' "mass of declarations overflowing with acrimony and . . . violence, and worthy to go on record as models of irrelevance and futility. . . . "[29] On the other level there was rationality, flexibility, and cooperation with the CCP. Action on the first level was seen to be necessary because of a need to accommodate bellicose Arab public opinion, which the Arab governments had themselves partly created. Action on the second level was based on reasoned judgment. This two-level pattern was to appear again and again in the CCP's work.

Upon returning from Beirut, the Commission met immediately with Prime Minister David Ben Gurion in Tel Aviv. The CCP sought from the Prime Minister a statement that he accepted the principle of repatriation.[30] In the few weeks prior to that meeting, the CCP had been seeking Arab acceptance of the principle of resettlement.[31] It was the Commission's hope that

[28] *Ibid.*, p. 6.

[29] Azcárate, *Mission in Palestine*, p. 149.

[30] A/1367, p. 31.

[31] In its second progress report, written just after the Beirut Conference, the CCP indicated quite clearly that its policy was that the refugees should know what repatriation to Israel would entail in terms of social adjustment and, concomitantly, that resettlement was an important part of any settlement. GAOR: 4th Sess., Annexes, vol. 2 (A/838, 19 April 1949), p. 3.

46

once the two principles had been agreed to in a general manner, negotiations could begin in a "favorable atmosphere" on the actual implementation of the two principles—or, as the CCP thought more likely, on partial implementation of the principles.[32] Ben Gurion, however, would not endorse the principle of repatriation. Instead, he sought to avoid giving a direct answer to the CCP's request by stressing that part of A/Res/194 that required refugees who returned to "live at peace with their neighbors."[33] It seemed clear to the CCP that Israel would not agree even to the abstract principle of repatriation as long as threats were being made against Israeli security by Arab leaders. Yet the CCP had also found that a number of Arab leaders had taken the stand, officially, that the threats against Israel would not stop until it had agreed to repatriate the Arab refugees.

The lack of a "favorable atmosphere" notwithstanding, the CCP announced in early April that the Commission would go to Lausanne on 27 April and be available to the parties for an exchange of views on all matters outstanding in the dispute. In order not to cause any Arab government trouble with its own domestic public opinion and hence jeopardize the outcome of the talks in Lausanne, the nature of the meetings was played down. There was no reference to any peace talks or treaties. In a press release, the CCP said explicitly that the conversations scheduled for Lausanne did not constitute a round-table conference and that no effort would be made to get the parties in the same room at the same time. The intention of the Commission, according to this public statement, was to assemble the various delegates in this one locality in order to facilitate an exchange of views.[34]

As the details of the Lausanne meetings were being arranged by the secretariat, the CCP used its multiple membership to make a variety of contacts in the Middle East. This appears to be one of the few times that a multiple membership facilitated the work of the Commission. CCP envoys were trying to persuade the parties

[32] A/1367, p. 31.

[33] Ibid.

[34] Palestine Post, 8 April 1949, p. 1.

to change their policies on the refugee question, which was seen to be the key issue in the upcoming talks.[35]

At the Lausanne conference, the parties marked time for the first few days because Israel had applied for admission to the United Nations, and the General Assembly was at that very time debating the question.[36] None of the parties directly involved at Lausanne wanted to undertake settlement negotiations until it was seen what arguments were accepted as valid by the Assembly and until it was clear what influence might be brought to bear in support of previous Assembly resolutions.[37]

The CCP met with the Israeli delegation during those opening days and sought some concessions on the refugee question in order to initiate compromises on the subject. Israel responded with an

[35] At this time Yalchin wrote two articles that undermined whatever usefulness he had to the Commission. In *Ulus,* the voice of the Turkish goverment, he wrote two pro-Arab articles. These were publicized almost immediately in the Middle East and of course did nothing to inspire Israel's confidence in the impartiality of the CCP. Yalchin advocated a Turkish-Arab rapprochement. He wrote, in part: "The Arab today is unhappy. A dire defeat he did not deserve has stirred his soul to deep indignation . . . I have personally assured them that we (Turks) are deeply concerned with the destiny and future of Arabia. . . . " (*Palestine Post,* 25 April 1949, p. 3). Cf. Rony E. Gabbay, *A Political Study of the Arab-Jewish Conflict: The Arab Refugee Problem (A Case Study)* (Geneva: Droz, 1959). And McDonald, *Mission to Israel,* pp. 161–62.

[36] Israel sent an eleven-man delegation to Lausanne headed by Walter Eytan, Director-General of the Foreign Ministry, who had represented his goverment at Rhodes. Lebanon's delegation was chaired by its Director-General of the Foreign Ministry, Fuad Bey Ammoun. Syria sent its Minister to France, Achan Atasi. Transjordan, somewhat belatedly, sent its Defense Minister, Fawzi al-Mulki Pasha. Egypt sent the well-known Abdal-Munim Mustafa Bey. Saudi Arabia and Iraq faded out of the picture as both sent messages saying their views would be represented by other Arab states. Israel, following the procedure that had worked so well at Rhodes, moved into the same hotel that the CCP was using for its headquarters, with the hope that the Arabs would do likewise and hence that informal conversations could be initiated. The Arab delegations, however, took up residence in another part of town. Helping to hold the Arabs together in a common front was Shuqayri, then a "Palestinian adviser" to the Syrian delegation at Lausanne.

[37] At the start of the conference Ethridge told the press the CCP was confident of achieving a settlement, although it might take some time. He was candid in giving the reason for the initial delay, but he indicated the CCP believed any cooling-off periods would do no harm. The refugee question was said to be the key to the negotiations (*New York Times,* 28 April 1949, p. 16; *Palestine Post,* 28 April 1949, p. 1).

offer to repatriate members of Arab families whose chief "bread-winner" was already in Israel. The plan was termed the family reunification scheme.[38] The CCP then met with the Arab delegations, *en bloc,* but the Arabs still had hopes of keeping Israel out of the United Nations—at least until Israel had agreed to repatriate large numbers of Arab refugees and internationalize Jerusalem (Transjordan excepted to the latter). Hence they did not want at that time to abandon any bargaining positions at Lausanne useful to them at the General Assembly. Therefore the Arabs refused to be drawn into a quid pro quo on the refugee question.[39]

At the General Assembly session, the Arabs were arguing that Israel's entry into the United Nations without preconditions would negate the work of the CCP as it tried to achieve a settlement on the basis of A/Res/194.[40] Hoping to mobilize support for their position, the Arabs stressed the precondition of internationalizing Jerusalem since the Assembly had displayed in the past a consensus in support of internationalization.[41] A second important precondition asked was Israel's agreement to the principle of repatriation. The Arab argument received substantial support from member governments of the Assembly; of the CCP members, Turkey supported the Arab draft resolution and France was ambivalent. Israel, perceiving clearly that the Assembly was already threatening deprivations against its bargaining position and would be applying deprivations if it adopted the Arab draft, argued that flexibility and not fixed guidelines were needed for a settlement at Lausanne.[42] This argument won the support of

[38] UN Doc. A/AC.25/W.82/Rev. 1, *The Question of Compensation,* 2 October 1961, p. 6. For the reasons why this concession also furthered Israel's interests, see Peretz, *Israel and the Palestine Arabs,* p. 51.

[39] The Arabs belatedly accepted Israel's offer on 27 July (*Palestine Post,* 28 July 1949, p. 1). The first families were reunited in December 1949 through the machinery of the UN Mixed Armistice Commissions.

[40] See GAOR: 3d Sess., Ad Hoc Political Committee, 2: 226, 316.

[41] *Ibid.,* p. 222. This emphasis was, of course, contrary to what the Arabs had emphasized to the CCP; the CCP had been told explicitly that the refugee issue was of foremost importance for "humanitarian and political" reasons (A/1367, p. 29).

[42] GAOR: 3d Sess., Ad Hoc Political Committee, 2: 234–35, 301, 342.

enough delegations—including that of the United States—to defeat the Arab draft by six votes. Israel was admitted to membership without preconditions.[43]

In Lausanne, the CCP was still trying to get the negotiations going. In order to have a starting point and in order to try to structure the negotiations, the CCP asked the parties to sign a protocol which, in effect, linked the territorial question and the refugee issue. Not only was it true that Israel emphasized the need to achieve a permanent settlement on boundaries while the Arabs stressed repatriation (Arab comments in the General Assembly notwithstanding), it was also true that the two issues were interrelated inherently. Until the border issue was settled, there would be some question as to who was entitled to return to Israel as a refugee. And the return of certain Arabs to their former homes would be considerably facilitated if land then held by Israel were to wind up under the control of Arab authorities. Therefore the Commission asked the parties to sign the following protocol:

> The United Nations Conciliation Commission for Palestine, anxious to achieve as quickly as possible the objectives of the General Assembly resolution of 11 December 1948, regarding refugees, the respect for their rights and the preservation of their property, as well as territorial and other questions, has proposed to the delegations of the Arab states and to the delegation of Israel that the working document attached hereto [a map of the boundary lines of the Arab and Jewish states according to the partition resolution] be taken as a basis for discussion with the Commission.
>
> The interested delegations have accepted this proposal with the understanding that the exchanges of views which will be carried on by the Commission with the two parties will bear upon the territorial adjustments necessary to the above-indicated objectives.[44]

Israel hesitated to sign the protocol, since it feared that in the future the protocol might be used as propaganda against it by

---

[43] To personnel on the CCP in general, including Ethridge, and to several others in the State Department, it seemed that a coherent UN policy on the Palestine question required a concerted effort to get Israel to agree to repatriation, at least in principle; and Israel's application to the United Nations seemed an obvious occasion to several US diplomats for the United States to exert some influence pursuant to that goal.

[44] UN Doc. A/927, 21 June 1949, Annex A.

Arabs arguing that Israel had thereby accepted the boundaries given to the Jewish state under the partition resolution, which would reduce Israeli territory—as then controlled, especially in the Galilee and Negev areas. The CCP worked hard to persuade Israel to sign, and as Israel regarded the protocol as a "procedural trick" to get the Arabs into negotiations, it finally agreed to sign. In accepting the protocol, Israel on 9 May appended a letter to the CCP as an integral part of that document in which Israel made clear its interpretation of the protocol. In that letter Israel stressed that the map was accepted as just one basis for discussion and that Israel reserved its right to resort to other bases as the need arose.[45]

The Arab governments were willing to sign the protocol, especially since the protocol recognized the Arab delegations as one party, even though it also indicated the Arabs were recognizing the validity of the partition resolution for the first time and were apparently accepting a negotiated solution to the conflict.[46] It could be argued that at this point the Arabs seemed ready to accept the existence of a smaller Israel, although it is to be kept in mind that a smaller Israel carrying out repatriation would be more susceptible to Arab attack from without and within. But it also could be argued that the Arabs at this time seemed more concerned with regaining prestige and dignity and with winning some propaganda victory rather than with creating conditions conducive to any physical victory over Israel. Moreover, some apparent victory would have to be displayed back home if Arab governments were to come to terms with Israel. Some sense of achievement, if only a legal prize, was needed to ward off domestic and inter-Arab charges of "selling out" to the Israelis.

The Lausanne protocol was signed on 12 May in separate rooms on separate copies. The Arabs then made a proposal centering around the right of refugees from the area designated as an Arab state under the terms of partition to return immediately, a proposal rejected by Israel and countered with an Israeli

[45] UN Doc. A/1367/Rev. 1, p. 3.

[46] Gabbay, *Arab-Jewish Conflict*, pp. 241–42, draws this same conclusion.

proposal that would largely consolidate the post-1948 status quo.[47] This the Arabs rejected without making a further counteroffer, at which point the limited offers to bargain broke down.[48] In these exchanges the CCP acted only as an intermediary among the parties and did not pass judgment on the proposals.

The US government in Washington had been following the events of the Lausanne conference closely but had limited most of its involvement in Middle East affairs to its regular diplomatic channels.[49] The government had given Ethridge no precise instructions and indeed had taken a "hands-off" approach to the CCP's efforts, while, of course, it continued to give communiqués to the American ambassadors in the Middle East on a whole range of related issues. But as the stalemate at Lausanne crystallized with the failure of the protocol to lead to progress in reaching agreement, the United States made an attempt to involve itself directly with those negotiations. On 29 May the United States delivered a diplomatic note to Israel through its embassy in Tel Aviv.[50] In that note the United States asked Israel to reconsider its policies on the refugees, boundaries, and Jerusalem. General Assembly resolutions on those subjects were asked to be taken as guidelines for action. The note contained the implication that the United States might reconsider its relation to Israel in the event that Israel adhered to its former policies. At this same time, Ethridge and McDonald were speaking with Israeli officials and talking in terms of a repatriation project involving some 200,000 refugees—a figure representing less than one-third of the number of refugees at that time.[51] Ethridge, speaking for the CCP,

---

[47] A/1367/Rev. 1, 2 October 1950, p. 19. In summation, Israel proposed that its permanent boundaries be based on the armistice lines except in central Galilee, where Transjordanian control was not challenged, and in the Gaza area, where Israel claimed territory up to the old mandate boundary despite Egyptian control.

[48] A/1367/Rev. 1.

[49] Dean Acheson gives the core of US policy in his *Present at the Creation* (New York: W. W. Norton, 1969), p. 259.

[50] McDonald, *Mission to Israel*, pp. 165–66.

[51] Peretz, *Israel and the Palestine Arabs*, p. 41. The Commission's subcommittee on refugees reported in August 1949 that the total number of refugees was 711,000.

emphasized that the Commission's stand was still that the refugee question could be solved only on a broad scale,[52] which meant that the rest of the refugees would have to be resettled in Arab lands with international financial assistance. The day after the note from the United States, the Arab delegations at Lausanne presented the CCP with their formal rejection of Israel's previous boundary adjustment offer.[53]

On 6 June, Israel, in its reply to the United States, rejected the guidelines contained in the note and maintained its previously indicated policies.[54] Later it issued a press release criticizing influence-exertion by foreign parties.[55] The United States subsequently backed away from its effort to get concessions from Israel through this type of formal threat of pressure. The next US note to Israel "abandoned completely the stern tone of its predecessor":[56] thereafter the United States did not suggest specific solutions to the parties directly concerned.[57] Far from achieving its intended objective, this abruptly applied and hastily withdrawn attempt at exerting influence had antagonized Israel, impaired future US power, and had had the indirect effect of weakening the CCP since it discredited the Commission's most powerful member.[58]

GAOR: 4th Sess., Annexes (A/AC.25/3, 7 September 1949), p. 2. Later work by UN officials indicates that this figure was essentially correct although a bit low by several thousand. Cf. Don Peretz, "Arab Palestine," *Foreign Affairs* 48, no. 2 (Winter 1970): 322–34; and Fred J. Khouri, *The Arab-Israeli Dilemma* (Syracuse: Syracuse University Press, 1968), p. 390 n.

[52] A/1367, p. 32.

[53] A/1367/Rev. 1.

[54] McDonald, *Mission to Israel*, p. 167.

[55] *Palestine Post*, 12 June 1949, p. 1.

[56] McDonald, *Mission to Israel*, p. 167.

[57] *Ibid.*, p. 168.

[58] Nevertheless, Berger is incorrect in his conclusion that this episode constituted a US "plan" to impose a settlement on the basis of "Arab demands" (*The Covenant and the Sword* [London: Routledge & Kegan Paul, Ltd, 1965], p. 44). The United States had no plan or overall blueprint for a settlement at this time, and were that not true, it would still require more than one incomplete act to constitute a plan. That the United States did not act consistently at this time is evidence that its operation on this question

After Israel had replied to the United States, it made a joint refugee-territorial offer to the CCP—at the suggestion of Ethridge and others.[59] Israel offered to take control of the Gaza area and all the refugees therein if international funds were made available.[60] The CCP transmitted the proposal to the Arab delegations without comment, and the Arabs rejected it.[61] Once more an impasse had been reached.

Israel made numerous suggestions designed to break the impasse and designed in particular to bring about direct contact under CCP aegis. The Israelis had been meeting with members of Arab delegations, Syrians excepted, in the small towns around Lausanne such as Vevy, but nothing of importance had resulted from these private contacts.[62] Israel obviously hoped that more formal contact might lead to something and also that the Armistice Agreements should be substituted for the Lausanne protocol as a basis for negotiation. But the Arabs did not respond

---

was ad hoc rather than strategically planned. Moreover, the United States was not supporting "Arab demands." Its note did not coincide with the Arab scheme for repatriation and de facto acceptance of partition boundaries. The note asked for Israeli policy to be in keeping with Assembly resolutions, which, in the context of the situation, meant some territorial concessions and limited repatriation.

[59] That Ethridge and refugee experts did suggest that Israel should make the offer is found in a statement by Eban in the Fourth General Assembly. GAOR: 4th Sess., Ad Hoc Political Committee, p. 323. See also Gabbay, *Arab-Jewish Conflict,* p. 244. His sources are debates in the Knesset.

[60] A/1367, p. 33. Gabbay listed 300,000 refugees for the Gaza area (*Arab-Jewish Conflict,* p. 245). According to State Department figures, the total was 230,000 (*United States Participation in the United Nations: Report by the President to the Congress for the Year 1949,* Department of State Publication 3765 [Washington, D.C.: Government Printing Office, 1950], p. 40).

[61] It was reported that part of the reason for the Arab rejection was a conflict between Transjordan and Egypt. Egypt controlled Gaza, but Transjordan wanted it in order to have an access to the Mediterranean in the event that a strip of land across the Negev could be gained from the Israelis. According to newspaper reports, Egypt and Transjordan agreed in a procès-verbal in April not to act on the subject of Gaza without prior consultation. Hence Egypt, even though it was in control of Gaza, could not give it up because Transjordan had interests there (*Palestine Post,* 14 June 1949, p. 1; *ibid.,* 12 July 1949, p. 4).

[62] On the Arab-Israeli private contacts in Switzerland, see Eytan, *First Ten Years,* p. 54. For a discussion of the proposals made by Israel at this point, see Gabbay, *Arab-Jewish Conflict,* pp. 246–47.

favorably. Therefore the CCP, having no fresh approaches to solutions, established a technical committee to study the refugee situation and declared a recess in the conference. For its part, the United States sought not only new ideas but a new chief delegate to the Commission.

Three days before the scheduled resumption of the conference, the United States still did not have a permanent replacement for Ethridge, and thus began one of the most bizarre episodes in the history of the CCP.

The choice of Ethridge and President Truman was Paul A. Porter, a Washington lawyer. Porter had no expertise on the Palestine question, had not followed events in the Middle East up to this time, and did not want the post. He had declined CCP membership with the excuse that he could not leave his law practice because his partners were away. Two days prior to the second opening of the conference, Truman arranged with Porter's partners for him to go to Lausanne. Faced with this *fait accompli*, Porter accepted the appointment—after he had been assured by Ethridge that progress was being made in the negotiations, that the disputants had changed their policies during the recesses, and that a peace settlement was imminent. Porter conferred with Truman, was briefed by the State Department for about a week, then left for Lausanne under the assumption that he was going to put the final touches on a peace treaty.[63]

When Porter discovered the deadlocked nature of the negotiations and the impact—or lack of it—that his suggestions for breaking that deadlock made, he became disillusioned and pessimistic quite quickly. Moreover, Kentuckian Porter was by nature brusque, impatient, and "folksy."[64] Hence he contrasted

---

[63] Cf. Azcárate, *Mission in Palestine*, p. 137.

[64] In one conversation with an Arab delegate, Porter was presented with a request for US arms so that preparation could be made for the up-coming "second round" against Israel. Porter replied to this effect: if a second round comes, my government will be on the side of the Israelis because there's not one damn Arab vote in most of the American constituencies.

On another occasion, when faced with an Arab request for a strip of land in the Negev connecting Transjordan and Egypt so that Arab leaders would not have to travel

boldly with the traditional diplomatic style of de Boisanger and Azcárate and with the dignified posture of the Arab delegations. This is not to say that Porter was an incompetent member of the CCP, for he brought an independence of action and a zestful drive to the Commission that it had not known before. He had, moreover, the same excellent access to high political leaders in the United States that Ethridge had possessed. But it is to say that Porter was not a diplomat in any sense of the word and that his limited interest in the Palestine question faded rapidly in the context of the complex difficulties the CCP faced.

As the second phase of the Lausanne conference started the last week in July, discussion again focused on the issue of repatriation and what an Israeli policy on that question might be that would be acceptable to both the Israelis and the Arabs. This focus eventually led to Israel's limited and qualified offer to repatriate 100,000 refugees, which finally became an unqualified offer to repatriate the same number, which nevertheless did not break the deadlock as the Arab militants thought this too far short of the absolute right of repatriation that they asserted. Whereupon the CCP turned its attention to the subject of blocked bank accounts by Arab and Israeli citizens, a subject in which there was enough mutual interest to lead to direct and formal discussion. But eventually the CCP and the parties gave up on the effort to negotiate the refugee question with its territorial dimensions, as the United States relied on the advice of Porter and sought to provide for the needs of the refugees on a longer-term basis without waiting for a diplomatic breakthrough. This change of policy signaled the beginning of the demise of the CCP as anything but a symbol, with the exception of a brief renaissance in the early 1960s.

As the conference resumed, the CCP stressed that it had a mandate to achieve the repatriation of the refugees and that some progress was necessary on this issue if the Arab governments were

---

across Israeli territory, Porter was supposed to have replied to this effect: I don't know how fast your camels can go, but we've got some that can go 900 miles an hour and can cross that strip of land before you can pronounce it; now let's talk some sense.

ever going to be drawn into serious negotiations leading toward a peace treaty. Israel responded with a proposal to discuss the refugee question first (to consider it the foremost issue in the talks rather than territory) and to make a definite offer if that offer were considered as a first step toward an overall peaceful settlement.[65] This policy was put forward on 28 July, and on 2 August the Arabs replied that this was acceptable to them. The following day Israel made what was to be its only offer for relatively large-scale repatriation. It offered to repatriate 100,000 refugees, who would be relocated in parts of Israel according to the economic and security needs of the state, irrespective of the former location of the refugees' residence. The CCP transmitted this proposal without comment to the Arabs.[66] The Arab governments, however, because of a lack of pressure brought to bear upon them to accept this offer, were aware that the Israeli proposal did not have the CCP's support. The Arab rejection was not expressed formally until 15 August, but it was clear prior to that time that the offer would not be accepted.

In making the formal reply, however, the Arabs did offer a counterproposal, which was in essence a more extreme variation of their previous position on the territorial issue. They accepted the Israeli offer of 100,000 if that number were taken to apply to those refugees who were to return to their homes in territory allotted to the Arab state according to the partition resolution. Relatedly, those refugees who had lived in territory allotted to the Jewish state under the partition resolution were to be compensated in kind for not returning—that is, they were to receive territory, not money, out of that same Jewish state according to partition. Israel's signature on the Lausanne protocol was cited as

---

[65] Sharett told the Knesset that the United States was trying to influence Israel on this subject (*Palestine Post,* 3 August 1949, p. 1). Cf. Peretz, *Israel and the Palestine Arabs*, p. 43, and Gabby, *Arab-Jewish Conflict,* p. 254.

[66] A/1367, pp. 34–35. Peretz argues that Israel's offer was made not because of international pressure but because of Israeli domestic politics (*Israel and the Palestine Arabs*, p. 32), and the unyielding nature of Arab demands (p. 49). Only later, at the time when the progress report was written, did the CCP express the conclusion that the Israeli offer was "unsatisfactory" (see A/1367, pp. 35–36).

evidence that it had agreed to accept the partition boundaries.[67] Hence the Arab governments were trying to reduce Israel-controlled territory in two ways, not only by creating the Arab state foreseen in the partition resolution, but also by shrinking the Jewish state outlined therein through territorial compensation to those Arab refugees who did not choose to return to what was then Israel. Needless to say, this proposal appeared ludicrous in the eyes of the Israelis.

Prior to the Arabs' formal reply and counteroffer, the Commission's technical subcommittee on refugees had reported back to its parent body after almost two months of interviewing refugees and government officials, visiting the refugee camps, and maintaining contact with other international organizations involved with the refugee problem.[68] The subcommittee's report made little immediate impact—partially because Israel had already decided what offer it could make on the refugee question —although the CCP used the report as a basis for numerous suggestions to the parties.[69]

One of these suggestions led to Arab-Israeli agreement—at a general level—on the subject of blocked accounts, and a mixed committee was created. Not only was this agreement the first of any importance since the Arabs had belatedly accepted the family reunification scheme; it was also the first time since the armistice negotiations that a delegate of Israel and one from the Arab side

[67] A/AC.25/W.82/Rev. 1, p. 11.

[68] A/AC.25/3. The technical committee on refugees reported, *inter alia*, that there was a "strong sentiment for return" among the refugees. The committee made a number of detailed recommendations, based on these fundamental conclusions: the refugee problem was "intricate" and could not "be resolved in a matter of months"; the committee had taken "into consideration" the resettlement in Arab lands of "a large number" of refugees; and UN efforts to aid the refugees should be coordinated more closely.

[69] On the basis of the report the CCP attempted to set up a mixed committee on orange groves and conservation of Arab property in Israel, but Israel objected (A/922, 22 September 1949, p. 2; A/1367, p. 40). The CCP also wanted a mixed committee to look into identification and evaluation of Arab property in Israel, but again Israeli opposition curtailed the plan (A/AC.25/W.82/Rev. 1, p. 8). The CCP recommended that refugees be allowed access to their fields in Israel, but Israel countered by arguing that such matters were under the jurisdiction of the Mixed Armistice Commissions (A/992, p. 9).

had met tête-à-tête under UN supervision. Both the Israelis and the Arabs took this opportunity to send to the direct talks not a financial expert but a negotiator versed in more general goals and tactics. The Israeli and the Egyptian met in the presence of Azcárate, and a series of meetings followed that were characterized by a reasonable tone and an amicable relationship between the two negotiators.[70] But whereas there was general agreement that Arab accounts in Israeli banks and Jewish accounts in Arab banks should be mutually unfrozen, problems developed because only Iraqi banks had frozen Jewish assets. Hence the sum of frozen Jewish property was too small, from the Israeli viewpoint, to provide a basis for reciprocal action. [71] The talks on blocked accounts were to continue for some time, and new approaches were to be tried at various stages, but it was to be four years before any tangible results were derived. There was no progress on noneconomic matters.

After the parties had failed to come to an agreement on the refugee and territorial issues, and after the CCP's suggestions drawn from the subcommittee's report had failed to produce positive results, the Commission asked the parties to clarify their policies. In requesting these policy statements on 15 August, which was the same day that the Arabs presented their formal rejections of Israel's refugee offer and their extreme counterproposal, the CCP also asked the parties to sign a declaration on the refugee question. It was the CCP's hope that the proposed declaration might enable the parties to clarify their policies according to a common guideline so that some agreement could be achieved.

The questionnaire dealt with a number of items, perhaps the most important being a request for views on the CCP's judgment that the 100,000 to be repatriated under Israel's offer should not be restricted in any way and on the CCP's judgment that the Arab governments should indicate how many refugees they could resettle. Other items dealt with cooperation with an economic

[70] See Azcárate, *Mission in Palestine*, pp. 152–53; and A/1367, p. 41.

[71] A/1367/Rev. 1, p. 16.

survey mission if one would be created to study the economic factors related to the CCP's mandate, *inter alia.*[72]

There were no replies from the Arabs and Israelis for two weeks, during which time the CCP for the most part simply waited, having exhausted most of its ideas on how to make some progress on the various questions outstanding. Porter was already in Washington, D.C., indicating his pessimism and looking for a way to return to his law practice. On 29 August the Arabs gave a common reply that was phrased in very general and noncommittal terms.[73] Arab territorial policy remained based on adherence to the terms of the partition resolution. Both Jordan and Syria, however, indicated they were prepared to accept some of the refugees. Egypt reported that it would have to study this issue further since it had very little fertile land available, but Egypt said that prospects for its accepting refugees might be improved if its eastern borders were readjusted. Only Lebanon stated that it definitely would not accept any refugees, and this stand was taken because of the overpopulation that Lebanon was already experiencing. Israel replied to the CCP two days later and agreed to drop the restrictions on the 100,000 to be repatriated.[74] Israel reserved its position with regard to an economic survey mission until created. Its territorial policy continued to be founded on the status quo, legitimized already to some degree by the armistice agreements. It understood the role of UN assistance in repatriation and resettlement programs. On the question of the total number of refugees it would be willing to accept, Israel reported its policy was that the solution to the refugee problem should be sought "primarily" in the Arab states. Israel's policy on the refugees, then as earlier, was stated most clearly in a letter sent by Ambassador Abba Eban to the CCP during early September. In the letter, Eban said that the security needs of the state of Israel would have to take precedence over the individual needs of the refugees, that Israel thought it had made this policy clear at the 1948 General

---

[72] A/AC.25/W.82/Rev. 1, pp. 11–15; cf. A/1367, pp. 37–38.

[73] *Ibid.*

[74] *Ibid.*

Assembly, and that recent events in the Middle East had only "aggravated our fear" that repatriation would jeopardize Israel's security.[75] In sum, as long as the Arabs spoke of a "second round," Israel would not accept the principle of repatriation or undertake large-scale repatriation.

The Commission deliberated over what to do with the replies to its proposed declaration for almost two weeks. Most of that time was taken up by consultations with Washington and Paris by the members of the CCP.[76] In the end the CCP decided to adjourn the conference. The major reason why little follow-up was made with regard to the explicit commitment of two Arab states to resettle part of the refugees, and the explicit commitment of Israel to drop the restrictions on the 100,000, was that the decision had been made already—without waiting for the replies of the parties —to create an economic survey mission and hence to look for some solution to the refugee problem through economic channels.

Whereas the replies of the parties were not received until 29 and 31 August, the CCP had established its Economic Survey Mission on 23 August. Porter had been in Washington for some two weeks prior to this date, and it was his opinion that there was no hope for a negotiated settlement. Porter advocated an economic approach, and his recommendations resulted in the creation of what was commonly known as the Clapp Mission after the chairman of the Mission, Gordon Clapp, former chairman of the Tennessee Valley Authority.

Economic planning was not a new aspect of the Palestine question, for at least since the spring of 1949 it had been assumed by most of those seeking a solution to the Arab-Israeli conflict that some form of regional economic development project would be needed. It was generally recognized that any state undertaking either repatriation or resettlement would require international financial assistance, and these "carrots" had been put before the parties on several occasions by members of the CCP, and US

[75] A/AC.25/W.82/Rev. 1, p. 15.

[76] This occasion was the first time that the French delegation to the CCP sought explicit instructions from the Quai d'Orsay.

officials as well. The chief exponent of the economic approach had been the State Department's George McGhee throughout late spring and summer of 1949, but it was largely Porter who persuaded Truman and Acheson to rely on this approach.[77] Prior to that time Truman, while considering economic assistance as one part of the total picture in any settlement, had believed that a negotiated solution was a prerequisite for effective economic assistance. Porter persuaded the President to change that policy, primarily because Porter was so pessimistic about the prospects for a negotiated settlement.

Thus the Clapp Mission was launched not because of any belief in an economic approach per se but because there seemed no other alternative, aside from giving up in the effort to find a solution to the conflict. Moreover, the longer the settlement talks dragged on, the greater became the need for an efficient relief program to provide for the immediate needs of the refugees, who, being primarily farmers, had absolutely no means of income since they did not have access to their fields. Hence the mission was given a three-fold task: to report on how to overcome the economic dislocation caused by the Palestine war; to report on how to facilitate the repatriation, resettlement, and rehabilitation of the refugees, and the payment of compensation to them; and to report on how to promote economic conditions conducive to the maintenance of peace and stability in the area.

Despite the fact that the emphasis had been shifted to the economic sphere, and that in the context of the creation of a research and study mission it was clear to the parties that no breakthroughs were foreseen in the immediate future on the negotiating front, the CCP made two last efforts to salvage the Lausanne conference. On 5 September the Commission sent a letter to the parties involved stressing that the armistice agreements were not a final solution to the problems discussed at Lausanne since those agreements pertained strictly to military

[77] See further Benjamin Shwadran, "Assistance to Arab Refugees," *Middle Eastern Affairs* 1, no. 1 (January 1950), p. 3; and *Palestine Post,* 10 October 1949, p. 4.

matters.[78] The letter did not attempt to coordinate the replies received from the parties on 29 and 31 August. The CCP dispatched another letter on 12 September asking for a reexamination of policy. But now not only did the parties have no new reason to deviate from their past policies; in addition, they were waiting for the upcoming General Assembly and how that Assembly would review the events of 1949. Thus the parties' motivation for further negotiation at this point was nonexistent. The CCP finally adjourned the conference with the statement that the parties' policy statements on the territorial question, initiated by the signing of the Lausanne protocol, had exceeded what the Commission could call adjustments of the map attached to that protocol.[79]

After a month had elapsed, the CCP resumed contact with the parties in New York in an effort to make some progress prior to the start of the General Assembly debate on the Palestine question. Concomitantly, the United States was trying to persuade Israel to accept a token number of refugees while trading part of Galilee and the southern Negev regions for the Gaza strip.[80] Israel resisted this persuasion.

Moreover, Israel launched a new policy, directed toward lessening the role of the CCP. It was the opinion of a number of Israeli officials that third-party roles by the United Nations had been an impediment to peace talks because the formal conference attended by all the Arab states had "frozen the gap" between Israel and the Arabs. The opinion had arisen in Israel that, had there been no UN involvement, Arabs and Israelis would have met face-to-face long ago. To this school of thought, it was the very presence of the United Nations in the conflict that had given the Arabs the opportunity to carry out their policy of nonrecognition of Israel. It was an attitude that had originated as early as February 1949, even while Bunche was guiding meaningful

[78] A/1367/Rev. 1, p. 19.

[79] A/1367, p. 46.

[80] Peretz, *Israel and the Palestine Arabs*, p. 64.

negotiations at Rhodes.[81] Those who held this view argued that progress had been made at Rhodes largely because of the negotiations that went on in private rather than because of the efforts of Bunche. Therefore in the fall of 1949 Israel stated that CCP activity in the future might be "harmful."[82] Confidence in the CCP's ability was not formally questioned, but Israel indicated that it thought CCP efforts would be "fruitless" as long as the Arabs refused to meet Israeli representatives around a conference table.

The Arabs, on the other hand, presented the CCP with a request for more activity.[83] The Arabs were critical of the CCP's role as a go-between and asked the Commission to play a more active role in implementing General Assembly resolutions. Undecided about how to handle these diametrically opposed requests, the CCP en masse conferred with State Department officials in Washington.[84] Both McGhee and Acheson met with the CCP, as did lesser-rank personnel—one of whom, Stuart Rockwell, was then the acting US member on the Commission; Porter had resigned by this time. The CCP finally decided to protect its status as a third party. In a letter to the parties concerned on 10 November, the CCP stated officially for the first time that it preferred direct negotiations among the parties. But since the Arabs had stated a desire for contact through the Commission, and since the CCP had a mandate from the General Assembly, the CCP indicated that it would continue its operations as a third party.[85]

Israel, however, replied that it would prefer not to undertake any new settlement talks until after the General Assembly debate.[86] In making this request, Israel was aware of the fact that during the early fall, discussion had been under way in the UN

[81] *Palestine Post,* 11 and 16 February 1949, p. 1.

[82] A/1367, p. 12.

[83] *Ibid.*

[84] Azcárate, *Mission in Palestine,* pp. 137–58. Such action contravened the "impartial" status of the Commission.

[85] A/1367/Rev. 1, p. 5.

[86] *Ibid.*

Secretariat and in the State Department about the future of the CCP. There was some movement at that time to replace the Commission with a single mediator.[87] The CCP's image fell far short of that of Bunche and of Bernadotte. And with a lack of tangible results to show for ten months in the field, there was some question about what the General Assembly might do with the CCP. By November the United States had decided, however, to back the continued operation of the CCP, even though the thinking of US officials on the Palestine question remained something less than clear.[88]

As the General Assembly opened debate on the Palestine question, it became evident that the early focus of debate again was to be the status of Jerusalem. The CCP had separated rather completely its work on Jerusalem from the general negotiations. The Commission had a precise mandate from the Assembly on Jerusalem but not on other aspects of the conflict. Yet the CCP's subcommittee on Jerusalem, at work since the early months of 1949, was very much aware that that precise mandate calling for "a permanent international regime" for the city was at variance with the de facto situation. The subcommittee was also aware that the Israelis and Transjordanians were firmly committed to maintaining their sectors of the city.[89] The subcommittee, therefore, sought a broad interpretation of its mandate. Its goal from the start was to find a compromise between the parties in de

[87] Azcárate, *Mission in Palestine,* pp. 157–58.

[88] See McDonald, *Mission to Israel,* pp. 180–82.

[89] Israel's Prime Minister Ben Gurion had said: "But with all respect to the Conciliation Commission of the United Nations, the decision with regard to Jerusalem was made 3,000 years ago when Ben Yishai (King David) made Jerusalem the Jewish centre" (*Palestine Post,* 14 February 1949, p. 1).

Transjordan wanted the status that came from being protector of the holy places, the population and commerce from the city, and to avoid being in an inferior military position. See Sir John Bagot Glubb, *A Soldier with the Arabs* (London: Hodder & Stoughton, 1959), pp. 291–92.

Nevertheless, the CCP subcommittee, led by the French Catholic Philippe Benoist, was particularly interested in at least some international responsibility for the holy places in Jerusalem.

65

facto control of the city, then phrase that compromise in language permitting some international responsibility.[90]

The CCP approved and defended the work of its subcommittee. The Commission presented a draft statute for an international regime to the Assembly[91] and emphasized its practicality.[92] Israel opposed the draft in no uncertain terms: " . . . the instrument still adheres to conceptions which experience and reality have proved to be impracticable . . . it also contains a number of specific proposals which the Government of Israel and the Jews of Jerusalem cannot possibly accept."[93] Transjordan continued to oppose any form of international responsibility in the city,[94] but the rest of the Arab governments held out for a complete *corpus separatum* rather than accept the CCP plan which left Israel and Transjordan with some authority in the city.

The CCP sought to counteract the disputants' criticisms of its draft statute by formal and informal lobbying. It issued a public

[90] At one point the subcommittee distributed a questionnaire in an attempt to discover acceptable compromises. Israel later argued at the Assembly that this action was proof that internationalization was a dead letter. The Arab delegations cited the action as proof that the CCP had exceeded its terms of reference.

[91] See UN Doc. A/973, 12 September 1949. In general, the Israeli and Transjordanian sectors of the city were not abolished, and any competence not exercised by UN authorities was reserved to the local officials in each sector. No state officials could have competence in the city, and no immigration into the city was permitted that upset the then-current demographic pattern. The city was to be demilitarized; and there was to be a UN Commissioner, General Council, and judicial system. The Commissioner was to have exclusive control of the holy places.

During the summer of 1949 the CCP had appointed an interim commissioner for Jerusalem, as it had been instructed to do by the Assembly, when Israel began transferring some of its government offices from Tel Aviv. Dr. Alberto Gonzalez-Fernandez was appointed, but he never assumed his duties. The CCP never made another appointment, for it believed that no commissioner could take action in the face of de facto partition. The CCP decision was accepted by the Secretariat.

[92] See GAOR: 4th Sess., Annexes (A/AC.25/1, 1 September 1949); GAOR: 4th Sess., Ad Hoc Political Committee, Annex to the Summary Records, 1 (1949): 10. The CCP also sought acceptance by the parties of a declaration guaranteeing the protection of holy places outside Jerusalem. This was rejected by the disputants since it provided for an extension of the Jerusalem draft statute.

[93] *Palestine Post,* 14 September 1949, p. 1.

[94] *Ibid.,* 9 October 1949, p. 1. This was an Associated Press report.

letter dealing in detail with points made in opposition to the draft,[95] and M. Benoist made a number of contacts in behalf of what had become his "pet project." This was one of the very few times that the CCP lobbied for a policy recommendation. As a general rule CCP individuals informed their governments about factors regarding the Palestine question, but it was unusual for these individuals to lobby qua commission or qua individuals in their international status. CCP lobbying in this case was impeded, however, by the fact that the French delegation to the Assembly did not support the draft statute that the French delegation to the CCP had been instrumental in producing.[96] Moreover, both the Vatican and the Secretariat opposed the draft—the former quite vigorously.[97] The United States gave only "unenthusiastic" support to the draft, as did the United Kingdom.[98] Of the delegations directly involved, only Turkey endorsed the draft unequivocally.

In the end the CCP efforts were to no avail; the Assembly voted to endorse the concept of a *corpus separatum* for Jerusalem and removed the matter from the Commission's purview. The Trusteeship Council was asked to revise its earlier drafts on the subject.[99]

[95] A/973/Add. 1, 12 November 1949. The CCP arguments were well reasoned. See further my 1968 dissertation, "The United Nations and the Peaceful Settlement of Disputes: The Case of the Conciliation Commission for Palestine," Firestone Library, Princeton University.

[96] The delegation to the CCP had sought the advice of the Quai d'Orsay with regard to the Jerusalem statute prior to the Assembly session. A negative reply was received whereupon the French members of the CCP went ahead with their plans to submit the draft as originally written.

[97] On the influential opposition of the Vatican, see Edward B. Glick, "The Vatican, Latin America and Jerusalem," *International Organization* 1, no. 2 (Spring 1957): 213–19. The Vatican thought the CCP draft did not go far enough toward internationalization. High-ranking Secretariat personnel opposed the draft for embodying too much internationalization, given the de facto situation. See further Azcárate, *Mission in Palestine*, p. 157.

[98] Paul Mohn, "Jerusalem and the United Nations," *International Conciliation*, no. 464 (October 1950), p. 468.

[99] Arab arguments against accepting *faits accomplis* were supported by many Latin American and European Catholic governments. Thus the Assembly opted for a more pure form of internationalization, even though Israel's attitude had been "totally

Midway through the debates the interim report of the Clapp Mission had brought the refugee question to the forefront of the Assembly session.[100] The mission had tabulated that there were not more than 726,000 Arab Palestinian refugees outside Israel and that there were 31,000 Arab Palestinian refugees inside Israel. According to the survey, there were 17,000 Jewish refugees from the Palestine war in Israel. Of the total of 774,00 refugees from the war, the mission concluded that 652,00 of them needed international assistance. The mission's most important conclusion was that the political stalemate precluded an early solution to the refugee question by large-scale repatriation or resettlement; therefore, efforts would have to be undertaken in the meantime to try and provide meaningful lives for these people.[101] The mission warned that if the Palestinian refugees were "left forgotten and desolate in their misery," peace would "recede yet further from these distracted lands."

The work of the Clapp Mission was well received by the Assembly, and the US and the Arab delegations agreed upon a compromise draft resolution encompassing many of the mission's

---

negative" (A/AC.31L.35, 15 November 1949) toward the CCP's limited internationalization. Of the CCP members, France voted with the Assembly majority.

The status of Jerusalem doubtless became a dead letter for the CCP a short time later. The Trusteeship Council referred the matter back to the Assembly the following June, and the Assembly declined to take any action. M. Benoist had continued his personal interest in the question, and he had sought unsuccessfully to have parts of the CCP draft introduced into the Council's work through the role of his colleague, M. Carreau, then President of the Council.

[100] UN Doc. A/1106, 17 November 1949. The Clapp Mission submitted its final report in December (UN Doc. A/AC.25/6, vols. 1, 2). The Mission was composed of the CCP members plus the United Kingdom and the chairman. From September to December it operated independently of the CCP.

[101] Detailed recommendations were: continuation of international emergency assistance, but on a reduced scale; initiation of work projects for the refugees; and creation of an administrative UN agency.

The final report recommended: payment of compensation to refugees prior to negotiation of a final settlement and without nexus to repatriation claims (thus stimulating de facto resettlement). In general, the Clapp Mission followed the principle of recommending initiation of programs, even if incompletely planned and administered, to get some action under way. It adhered to the principle that political problems blocked economic progress.

suggestions.[102] This draft resolution was easily adopted, thus creating the United Nations Relief and Works Agency for Palestine Refugees (UNRWA), responsible for administration of UN welfare programs.

Most of the Assembly session had been occupied with the question of Jerusalem and charges and countercharges by the disputants. But some attention had been given to the general performance of the CCP, although it cannot be said that the problem of negotiating a general settlement had been reviewed in a systematic and comprehensive perspective. At one point the Australian delegation sought to enlarge the CCP to seven members and to extend its life for specifically one year.[103] At another point the Soviet Union sought to dissolve the Commission.[104] But neither alternative was pressed with vigor, and in the end the CCP was instructed to continue its efforts with the same composition and the same mandate—minus the question of Jerusalem. The Assembly had not supported the CCP's draft statute for Jerusalem, and it had not given the CCP new instructions on how to deal with territorial and refugee questions. There was no indication that the stalemate would be broken through an overwhelming international consensus for a particular policy or through the introduction of new ideas.

The year in which the CCP as a three-government commission proved to be most active was 1949. It continued to function as an operating field organ in that form for the following two years, on

---

[102] The Arab delegations were willing to accept the Clapp Mission's report even though it clearly leaned toward de facto resettlement as the long-range solution to the refugee question. The Arabs were content to insert references to the validity of paragraph 11 of A/Res/194, thus protecting legal rights to repatriation.

[103] GAOR: 4th sess., Ad Hoc Political Committee, p. 225. To the Australian spokesman, the CCP "was not sufficiently representative. . . . Furthermore, the Commission had sometimes given the impression of Governments engaged in diplomatic negotiations rather than that of an organ of conciliation designed by the United Nations."

[104] *Ibid.*, pp. 281, 363. According to the Soviets, the CCP was an agent of imperialism and an obstacle to peace. The USSR attempt to eradicate the CCP was defeated in plenary session: 45—5—8.

a reduced scale of importance; and it is after a review of the years 1950–51 that an analysis of the early CCP will be attempted in some depth, when 1949 can be put into larger perspective. It suffices at this juncture to indicate some of the points that will be taken up in extended analysis at the end of the following chapter.

As far as the roles undertaken by the Commission were concerned, it is obvious that once the CCP arrived in the Middle East and tried to establish contact with the parties it quickly discarded the idea that it could make a positive contribution through the relatively passive role of making procedural suggestions—that is, through serving as a good offices agent—although the CCP did revert to this role at times during the Lausanne conference. Early in 1949 the Commission not only sought to interject its interpretations and clarifications of the Assembly resolutions that comprised its terms of reference, it also sought to institute policy recommendations and substantive reports— starting with its successful efforts at Beirut to persuade the Arabs to change their stated policy with regard to repatriation as a precondition for talks. Beyond that point, the general drift of the CCP's recommendations was to persuade Israel first to accept the validity of the abstract principle of repatriation and later to make tangible offers of limited repatriation. Combined CCP-US persuasion toward the latter objective, plus domestic politics in Israel, did eventually lead to such an Israeli offer. But there is little if any evidence that there followed a concerted effort to persuade the Arab governments to accept Israel's offer to make a counteroffer that would bridge the gap between total repatriation and the limited offer of 100,000.

Probably the composition of the CCP led it into several tactical errors as it sought to execute these roles, and other freely chosen tactics clearly impeded the objectives sought by the Commission. Diplomacy by conference is a necessity when the third party consists of a multiplicity of governments, but it can be questioned whether conference diplomacy pursuant to a formal, public treaty was an appropriate format for dealing with Arab governments caught between an aroused, anti-Israel public opinion and a governmental desire to regain prestige in the real or imagined eyes of the world. Conference diplomacy and formal treaties were no doubt part of the conventional wisdom of the era, namely, the accepted approach to peace. Neither past Assembly debates nor events at Rhodes, however, confirmed the efficacy of this approach in the Arab-Israeli confrontation. Moreover, the decision to treat the Arab states *en bloc* at Lausanne and the related failure to maintain communication with Bunche and profit from his successful experience in the peacekeeping negotiations were clearly tactical errors that undermined the impact of the CCP's substantive recommendations.

In 1949 the CCP ultimately failed to persuade the Arabs and Israelis to reach a compromise on the central issue of the refugees —and failed to persuade the United States to commit itself firmly and consistently to any particular compromise on the same issue. Thus the parties were free to disagree inter se without fear of pressure to conform to UN resolutions purporting to be guidelines to a settlement. With regard to CCP-US relations, it is of interest to note that the initial flow of decisionmaking was frequently from CCP personnel to Washington personnel, as in the case of Porter's recommendation to establish an economic survey mission or in the case of Ethridge's lack of instructions. Thus the Commission can be described as a slightly or relatively independent organ somewhat apart from the US government, a description most clearly validated by the CCP's proposals for the internationalization of Jerusalem which the US government failed to support in Assembly debates.

71

III

THE CCP AND ATTEMPTS TO

ALTER THE POST-1949 STATUS QUO

After 1949 the CCP became less important to all concerned with the Arab-Israeli conflict. None of the parties directly involved preferred negotiations involving compromises to maintaining previous policy positions. Israel adopted no changes in basic policy, because it believed that de facto resettlement would erase the refugee question and that the Jerusalem and territorial questions had already been solved in a de facto manner. The Arab states, having successfully avoided dealing with Israel officially in 1949, saw no reason to start compromising thereafter. Events within Jordan lessened the likelihood for a separate Israel-Jordanian settlement. No less importantly, interested third parties —particularly the United States, the United Kingdom, and France —endorsed the status quo in the Middle East. Given this milieu, the CCP was unable to alter the configuration of the Arab-Israeli conflict. It made only procedural suggestions to the disputants throughout most of 1950. Its substantive policy suggestions to the Assembly in 1950 and to the disputants in 1951 failed to break the stalemate. For the rest of the decade the CCP served primarily as a symbol for UN interest in a negotiated settlement. In the wake of the 1956 Suez crisis, the CCP remained dormant and the Secretary-General represented the United Nations in Middle East negotiations.

For the CCP, 1950 was a lost year. During the first part of the year it sought unsuccessfully to bring Israel and the Arab states into discussion on the issues outstanding. Further time was consumed in competition with UNRWA over the question of which of these two subsidiary organs was primarily responsible for action on the question of repatriation and/or resettlement of the refugees. Finally, CCP contact with the protagonists convinced the Commission that nothing could be done to alter the configuration of the conflict without a change in mandate, and thus, with no progress to record from the field, the CCP reported back to the General Assembly (this, as a matter of fact, was one of the more constructive things the Commission did).

The CCP had assembled in early 1950 with the intention of resuming a conference or round of meetings with high-ranking officials.[1] But Israel and the Arab governments sent lower ranking and smaller delegations.[2] The CCP almost immediately sought to bypass these delegations and make an impact on the more important officials in the respective capitals. It was clear to the CCP from the nature of the delegations named that the probability of reaching settlement had receded further into the background, as had the importance of the Commission itself. The CCP tried to keep the hope for a settlement alive and issued a press release which stated that the lower-ranking delegations indicated the Middle Eastern governments "have cooled off. . . . The atmosphere is calmer now, and it may be easier to think in terms of a permanent settlement."[3] The CCP indicated clearly, in a later press statement free from diplomatic euphemisms, two changes in its policies. The Commission officially endorsed "the establishment of *direct contact* between the parties and this course

[1] Pablo de Azcárate, *Mission in Palestine 1948–1953* (Washington, D.C.: Middle East Institute, 1966), p. 158. The US chief delegate was now Ely Palmer, former ambassador to Afghanistan. James Barco was to become the most forceful man behind the scenes.

[2] Israel, for example, in place of the eleven-man delegation headed by the Director-General of the Foreign Ministry, sent at first the head of its permanent delegation to the Geneva office of the United Nations, then a lower official from the Ministry. Likewise, Lebanon did not send its Director-General again, and so forth for the other governments.

[3] *Palestine Post*, 22 January 1950, p. 1.

appears . . . all the more indispensable if [the CCP] is to mediate effectively. . . . "[4] In addition, the Commission indicated its readiness "to assist the parties in reaching agreements whether collectively or separately, both on the larger issues and on questions of a more local character."[5]

In general the governments of Egypt, Syria, and Lebanon showed little interest in direct contact during 1950, and Jordan seemed content to continue its private conversations with Israel. At one point Egypt did make a claim vis-à-vis the CCP regarding an issue of "local character," whereupon the CCP tried to use the question as a format for instituting more general talks through a committee of mixed membership: partly Egyptian, partly Israeli, and partly CCP.[6] The claim concerned the right of refugees in Egyptian-controlled Gaza to work their fields in Israel, but Israel preferred to bypass the issue by replying to the CCP that the Mixed Armistice Commissions set up to handle questions arising out of the Armistice Agreements had jurisdiction over the matter. For its part, Egypt, when the CCP suggested the format of a mixed committee for general discussions on all issues, demanded that Israel agree to the principle of repatriation as a precondition for talks. Thus Egypt was returning to the Arab policy position of one year earlier, which the CCP had successfully circumvented at Beirut. Although the Commission believed the mixed committee format to be suitable, given Israel's desire of direct contact and the Arabs' desire to have an intermediary, the hope for a mixed committee was reluctantly abandoned in the face of Israel's unwillingness to deal with the specific issue raised and Egypt's unwillingness to enter broader negotiations.

Being persistent if not creative, in March the CCP tried to institute a series of mixed committees. Israel responded quickly and affirmatively but was not optimistic regarding the outcome of

[4] *Ibid.*, 31 January 1950, p. 1. Emphasis added.

[5] *Ibid.*

[6] See UN Doc. A/1367, 2 September 1950, p. 15; and Don Peretz, *Israel and the Palestine Arabs* (Washington, D.C.: The Middle East Institute, 1956), p. 67. The CCP was relying on its relatively successful experience in 1949 in getting an Egyptian and an Israeli to discuss blocked bank accounts and other subjects at a meeting chaired by Azcárate.

any talks.[7] To secure Arab acceptance of its suggestion, the CCP dispatched de Boisanger on a tour of Arab capitals and thus sought to bypass the Arab delegations to the CCP.[8] The Egyptians continued to insist that Israel accept the principle of repatriation prior to talks, however, and the CCP was unable to persuade the Egyptians to alter this policy or the Israelis to endorse the principle.

Then an event occurred which, to a great extent, froze the status quo that the CCP was trying to break apart. On 25 May the United States, the United Kingdom, and France issued the Tripartite Declaration. The immediate effect of article 3 of the declaration was to guarantee the existing frontiers in the Middle East from external attack.[9] The larger implication of the declaration was that it solidified the Arab-Israeli conflict as a whole in its then-current form, for the thought underlying the declaration was that a negotiated settlement was not likely.[10] This impact was perceived by the members of the CCP.[11]

The Tripartite Declaration was a clear indication that the CCP's mandate was being dated by events in the Middle East, but it was not the only such indication. At the end of 1949 both Jordan and Israel had strengthened their hold on their respective sectors of Jerusalem—which affected part of the territorial and refugee questions with which the Commission was concerned. Moreover, in April Jordan had officially incorporated the west bank of the Jordan River into the Hashimite Kingdom of Jordan, thus further settling aspects of the territorial and refugee questions in a de facto process despite the censure of Jordan by the Arab League.

---

[7] Cf. UN Doc. A/AC.25/W.82/Rev.1, *The Question of Compensation*, p. 18, and *Palestine Post*, 14 April 1950, p. 1. Israel was critical of a number of Arab policies, rejected compensation payment in general, and threatened to withdraw its offer to repatriate 100,000, *inter alia*.

[8] Unimpeachable source. The CCP also sought to avoid publicity about its efforts.

[9] J. C. Hurewitz, ed., *Diplomacy in the Near and Middle East, A Documentary Record: 1914–1956* (New York: D. Van Nostrand Co., 1956), p. 310.

[10] See Nadav Safran, *The United States and Israel* (Cambridge, Mass.: Harvard University Press, 1963), p. 225.

[11] Unimpeachable source.

75

Throughout the early months of 1950, the Arab League's resolutions had reflected an increasing reluctance to reach an agreement with Israel. While it is best not to use these public documents as the only index of Arab attitudes, it can be noted that, in the spring of 1950, resolutions were passed stating opposition to any Arab state's concluding a separate peace with Israel, providing sanctions for the state that did so, and reiterating the Arab public policy of liberating Palestine and returning it to its Arab owners. The CCP tried to brush off such proclamations, with de Boisanger telling the press that such resolutions were "deceiving" since the Arabs usually took an extreme position prior to negotations in order not to yield anything they did not have to in the talks—a somewhat plausible answer that, of course, did not affect the Arab reluctance to negotiate.[12]

The Tripartite Declaration was likewise an indication that the CCP would not be supported by the declaration's sponsors if the Commission sought changes in the territorial status quo, and the declaration constituted a reasonably clear sign that their influence would not be forthcoming on other questions still outstanding since there was little hope of achieving a settlement. Once again the Tripartite Declaration was only one of several indicators pointing in this direction. The Commission had already discovered earlier in 1950 that the potential exertion of US influence vis-à-vis Syria was not a very reliable support for the CCP because of the United States' being considered, a priori, pro-Israel by the Syrian decisionmakers.[13] And the CCP had already learned that possible exertion of US influence on Egypt was unlikely, given the small degree to which the Commission was actively supported during its April efforts to persuade the Egyptians to accept the procedure of mixed committees.[14]

[12] For a review of the League's statements, see Muhammad Khalil, ed., 2 vols. *The Arab States and the Arab League* (Beirut: Khayats, 1962), 2: 165–67. Cf. Robert W. MacDonald, *The League of Arab States* (Princeton: Princeton University Press, 1965), pp. 348–77; and the Carnegie Endowment, *Egypt and the United Nations* (New York: Manhattan Publishing Co., 1957), pp. 165–80. See *New York Times,* 18 April 1950, p. 20, for the de Boisanger statement.

[13] Azcárate, *Mission in Palestine,* p. 162.

[14] *Ibid.,* p. 163.

Despite the obvious impact of the Tripartite Declaration on the work of the CCP, the Commission continued to doggedly seek negotiations through a series of mixed committees. Policy statements by the Arab League and the Israeli government proclaimed that the post-1949 situation was not seen as the final answer to Arab-Israeli relations. Ben Gurion told his Knesset: "There is also a need to support and accelerate the negotiations for an enduring peace . . . and for this purpose it is essential to employ the full authority and resources of the United Nations."[15] According to the League: "The Arab states take note of the assurance that they have received to the effect that the three powers did not intend by their declaration . . . to affect the final settlement of the Palestine problem. . . ."[16] Thus the CCP professed to see reasons for continuation of its efforts.

In late May the CCP outlined the terms of reference for the mixed committees it wanted to create, but the Arab states continued to ask the same precondition for negotiation—Israel's acceptance of the repatriation principle. Jordan, after a month's delay, did inform the Commission that it might be willing to enter negotiations if the Israelis altered some of their policies; but nothing resulted from this apparent attempt to bargain, as neither the Israelis nor the CCP pressed the issue.

At this point the CCP, figuring that the end of the road had been reached in the search for negotiations, formally recessed its efforts for the summer. Quite clearly out of the Commission's proposals for one, general mixed committee and then for a series of mixed committees dealing with specific topics there emerged an Arab intransigence against negotiation that was more firm than in the previous year—Jordan excepted. Israel's policy on the central refugee question began to solidify into a nonnegotiable stance too, as it began to reevaluate its offer to repatriate 100,000 and as it maintained tough bargaining terms with Jordan.

Upon resumption of its meetings in August, the CCP decided to make a tour of the capitals of the parties concerned in order to determine what action could be taken prior to the fifth General

[15] Quoted in Hurewitz, *Diplomacy*, p. 310.
[16] *Ibid.*

Assembly. The Commission stressed the subject of compensation in these talks,[17] while the parties showed primary interest in blocked accounts as a subject on which negotiations could take place at any time.[18] The Arab governments seemed more receptive to the idea of de facto resettlement than the CCP had expected.[19] The CCP finally then concluded that there was hope for negotiations through the procedure of mixed committees.[20] Moreover, the Commission concluded that there was virtually no hope for achieving either boundary adjustments or repatriation.[21] The CCP, recalling the report of the Clapp Mission, thus decided to try to get Israel to agree to pay compensation to the Arab refugees without a comprehensive settlement and without tying payment of individual compensation to reparations claims made against a given Arab state. It was the CCP's view that such payment would be an inducement to resettlement, which would tend to accelerate the de facto resettlement that the Arab governments seemed ready to accept, and UNRWA concurred in the CCP's decision.[22] But CCP agreement with UNRWA was a rare commodity during most of 1950.

Until late summer there had been only one official meeting— in April—between the CCP and UNRWA. This was the case despite the inherent relationship between their functions. The progress that the CCP made on the issue of repatriation related to UNRWA plans for providing for the refugees not repatriated. CCP efforts to get the Arab governments to facilitate de facto resettlement as a solution to the refugee question overlapped with UNRWA efforts to resettle the refugees in order to reduce unnecessary UNRWA expenditures and to provide the refugees with a higher standard of living. The plan of the CCP to secure

[17] A/AC.25/W.81/Rev. 2, *The Question of Reintegration by Repatriation or Resettlement*, 1961, p. 30. By this time Yalchin had been replaced by Rustuv Aras for the Turkish government in the first non-US change of top personnel.

[18] Unimpeachable source.

[19] A/AC.25/W.81/Rev. 2.

[20] A/1367, pp. 22–23.

[21] Unimpeachable source.

[22] *Ibid.*

compensation payments from Israel obviously related to UNRWA's resettlement talks then in progress, for compensation would be paid first to those resettled. Israeli policies, expressed to the Commission, affected the undertakings of UNRWA, which dealt primarily with the Arab governments.

Yet there was little rapport between the two UN subsidiary organs. Like the relationship between the CCP and the acting mediator, there seemed to be an assumption on the part of all concerned that the efforts of the CCP and UNRWA would mesh of their own accord. And during the first half of 1950, neither organ sought to coordinate its activities with the other.

Increased CCP emphasis on resettlement and compensation caused UNRWA to ask the CCP for a joint meeting in August. UNRWA wanted to know about the resettlement work of the CCP, and it also wanted to protect its position vis-à-vis the Commission. There followed a series of CCP-UNRWA meetings during 1950 characterized by friction between the two agencies. The origin of the conflict was basically a matter of institutional jealousy.[23]

The most important point of friction was the question of resettlement per se and which agency should handle discussions on this matter.[24] UNRWA asked the CCP to limit Commission activities on the refugee question to repatriation in order to leave itself as the organ responsible for resettlement talks. It appears clear from the records that personnel were concerned primarily with protecting the status of their organ. There was a secondary concern with the possibility that the Arab governments would become confused with two organs working simultaneously on the same question of resettlement. But the primary and motivating concern was that the CCP would consider itself an executive organ superior to UNRWA on the matter of resettlement. CCP members

[23] During 1950 there is nothing in the CCP's progress reports about this friction. Azcárate writes of the conflict in an ambiguous fashion (*Mission in Palestine,* chap. 11 and *passim*). The present study is based on unimpeachable sources.

[24] There was also initial friction regarding tactics employed. UNRWA wanted the CCP to develop more formal ties with the Arab League, in order to facilitate Arab acceptance of resettlement. The CCP maintained that de Boisanger had adequate rapport with officials of the League and that informal ties were sufficient.

resisted UNRWA efforts to preempt the field on the subject of resettlement; they warned of trying to draw too fine a line between the activities of the two agencies. In the exchange between personnel of the two organs, which became heated at times, Frenchman argued against Frenchman, and the US representative on one organ against his counterpart on the other organ. It was clear, therefore, that neither the Quai d'Orsay nor the State Department was trying to coordinate the activities of the two organs—nor was the New York Secretariat. It is also interesting to note that initial decisionmaking was clearly being made in the field rather than in a particular capital, as was noted to be the case with the CCP during parts of 1949.

UNRWA's position on the matter of jurisdiction over the issue of resettlement provoked the Commission into an isolationist reaction. Although both organs dealt with the subject of resettlement, neither would tell the other what it intended to report to the fifth session of the General Assembly.[25] The ramification of this mutual isolation was that action was taken at the fifth Assembly, on the basis of the separate reports; that action led to further conflict between the two organs during 1951, as will be seen below.

The CCP and UNRWA did concur on a number of subjects—for example, resettlement was the most likely solution to the refugee question and Israel's payment of compensation would facilitate that process. With this goal in mind and with little hope of carrying out the rest of the terms of reference, the CCP drew up its progress report for the fifth General Assembly. Because it felt that it had exhausted its role under its general mandate, the CCP compiled an extensive review of its activities during 1949–50, revised the published report in order to add material, then

[25] During the course of debate on the Palestine question, Aras was to make the revealing statement that he was glad to see that UNRWA's recommendations coincided with those of the CCP, it being obvious from this that there had been no prior consultation. GAOR: 5th Sess., Ad Hoc Political Committee, p. 203.

There was CCP-UNRWA consultation prior to the following, sixth session of the Assembly. The process was this: compile report, consult with other UN organs, clear with government members, and complete final form.

submitted an additional report containing analytic comments and recommendations. Although these reports omitted several important points, as most public documents do, they constituted a more improved guide to the actions of the CCP than the Commission's bland reports of the previous year. And in making judgments and recommendations, the CCP helped to direct the attention of the Assembly to its problems and needs. It is true that in 1950 the CCP had a better idea than in 1949 of the possible role of the Commission and of the nature of a feasible settlement. To a large degree, the apparent lack of solutions to problems and the set nature of the parties' policies made reporting in 1950 a great deal easier for the CCP because of the lack of alternatives it perceived for the settlement of the conflict. Nevertheless, the CCP, in making an analytic report, did a great deal to obtain improved oversight and review by the General Assembly.

The core of the Commission's report was that the status quo should not be accepted by the General Assembly and that further efforts should be made to obtain a settlement. The CCP wanted a "positive peace" in place of the "negative peace" then present.[26] According to the Commission,

> it is obvious that, though a situation based exclusively on negative undertakings of non-aggression may last a long time and result in a consolidation of existing circumstances, it will never succeed in providing the guarantees of stability which are the characteristics of a peace based on the final settlement of all questions outstanding between the parties, accompanied by the establishment of normal relations between them.

The CCP believed that the armistice agreements had not provided the security intended. The existing anxiety of the parties had hindered the peace negotiations, in the CCP's view, for insecurity had prevented both direct negotiations among the parties and effective negotiations through the CCP.[27] The Commission also believed that the signing of the armistice

---

[26] GAOR: 5th Sess., Supplement No. 18 (A/1367/Add.1, 24 October 1950), p. 3. All direct quotations in the following two paragraphs are also taken from this document.

[27] Ibid., p. 4.

agreements was detrimental to its efforts because these agreements "had the effect of eliminating military considerations and of greatly reducing, in the minds of the parties, the immediate necessity of taking further steps towards a final settlement." The Commission advised that a continued state of armistice would have "adverse effects" on all parties involved, because regional security would be undermined, economic growth impeded, and world peace threatened.

According to the CCP, "the continued assistance of the United Nations and the constant presence of its agencies in the area will be the most effective guarantee for the early re-establishment of stability and harmony in the Middle East." But the Commission added that compromise by the parties was necessary, even though in the past there had been no desire to compromise by any party. Israel had to "counteract the dislocations caused by its own establishment"; the Arabs had to "endeavor to adapt their policy to the new state of affairs." The Commission saw no early return to stability since "readjustments among the peoples and the States concerned" were necessary. It was the CCP's judgment that "no immediate 'solution' of all outstanding issues could have been expected in this case. . . . " The CCP asked the General Assembly, however, to urge the parties concerned to undertake settlement negotiations directed toward the refugee question so that a start could be made on returning stability to the region.

Although the CCP in its progress report continued to mention steps leading toward a general settlement, emphasis was clearly on the refugee question. The CCP continued this theme in personal contacts at the fifth session and concentrated on improving its ties with the Assembly. In addition to making the customary introductory statement to the Assembly on the nature of the Commission's work, the CCP participated in the debate on several occasions. At one point, questions were raised that only CCP personnel were able to answer, and subsequently Palmer took part in an unplanned exchange with government spokesmen which represented a debate on issues in the truest sense—rare for the General Assembly and rarer still for the Assembly on the Palestine question. Palmer said candidly at one point that the CCP desired new terms of reference so that the refugee problem could be considered apart from the other issues still outstanding.[28]

The Arab position at the fifth session was essentially that what was needed was implementation of past resolutions—such as repatriation and internationalization of Jerusalem—rather than bargaining, and a new office was demanded under the CCP to secure the property rights of the refugees.[29] The CCP was attacked both for sharing Zionist views[30] and for being lax in seeking repatriation.[31] The acrimonious nature of Arab speeches gave a preview of the sterility of UN debates on the subject for years to come. At the fifth session, Israel continued to call for direct negotiations even while it offered to make payments in UNRWA's "reintegration" fund—at the suggestion of the United States along with the CCP.[32] But Israel had told Palmer earlier in the fall that the offer to repatriate 100,000 no longer stood.[33] Thus the central stalemate continued: the Arab official policy was to demand full repatriation; the Israeli policy emerged as an offer of limited repatriation—less than 100,000.

In this situation the one apparent avenue of action by consensus was to study the subject of compensation and to support the creation of a CCP suboffice designed primarily for work on compensation factors. The original Western-sponsored proposal asked for direct negotiations. The General Assembly, however, adopted this draft with the reference to direct negotiations omitted.[34] The Soviet Union made its usual and unaccepted request for the dissolution of the CCP.[35] And there was some

[28] GAOR: 5th Sess., Ad Hoc Political Committee, p. 452.

[29] *Ibid.*, pp. 391–410.

[30] *Ibid.*, p. 403.

[31] *Ibid.*, p. 409.

[32] Peretz, *Israel and the Palestine Arabs*, p. 196.

[33] A/AC.25/W.82/Rev.1, p. 18.

[34] A/Res/394(V). All operative paragraphs pertained to the refugee question.

[35] The Soviets used the same arguments in supporting their position—to wit, the CCP had acted *ultra vires* and as an imperialistic arm of the United States. They also added a new one: the CCP had proven incapable of carrying out its terms of reference. These arguments got no more support at the fifth session than they had previously, since only the Soviet satellites voted for the draft.

concern, for the first time, about the number of UN subsidiary organs in the field in the Middle East, but delegations speaking on this subject were content to have the new office under the CCP rather than separate. Otherwise the Western draft was adopted without undue friction. For the first time in the last three years, some parties directly concerned were relatively satisfied with results of the fifth session, even though once again the General Assembly had not debated the requisites of a general settlement per se.

The CCP worked on creating its Refugee Office until late July 1951; the amount of time used for planning and organization was due either to necessity or to the conviction that time spent in quest of negotiations was wasted. The lethargy of the CCP on the diplomatic front was finally shaken by an activist in the US delegation whose prodding brought about the Paris conference in the early fall of 1951, which was to be the last conference in the Arab-Israeli confrontation to the time of this writing, the final act of diplomacy of the CCP as an active three-government organ, and an excellent format for the clarification of the policies of the protagonists.

In early 1951 the Commission took the view that the fifth Assembly had brought about a "new phase" in the life of the CCP. In the light of A/Res/394, the CCP argued that its task was to concentrate exclusively on the refugee problem from a practical point of view rather than on the principled basis used up to that time.[36]

But in the "practical" creation of the Refugee Office, the Conciliation Commission once more had conflict with UNRWA.[37] In meetings during January, February, and March, UNRWA again asked the CCP to consider UNRWA as the organ responsible for resettlement matters. Again the CCP took the position that UNRWA was trying to make a distinction in theory that would not hold up in practice. In particular, UNRWA was concerned

[36] A/AC.25/W.82/Rev.1, p. 21.

[37] This paragraph is based on unimpeachable sources.

about the creation of the Refugee Office, since the lack of UNRWA-CCP consultation in 1950 had resulted in UNRWA's being uninformed about the role and function of the new office. UNRWA wanted the Refugee Office to be closely supervised by the Commission so that the new office would not usurp the duties of UNRWA. At one point UNRWA asked explicitly that the Refugee Office not be headed by a well-known personality.[38]

With the views of UNRWA thus expressed, the Commission continued its building of its Refugee Office at an extremely leisurely pace. Some informal CCP-Israeli talks took place on the subject of Israel's payment of compensation directly to individual refugees, but the issue was not pressed. The only communication of any importance in the life of the Commission during the spring of 1951 related to the issue of blocked accounts, and on this subject there was no appreciable progress at that time.[39]

By mid-May the CCP's Refugee Office began some of its substantive work. At the outset of its technical work of indentification and evaluation, the office and the CCP were buoyed by information from UNRWA indicating that the Arab governments were preparing for resettlement.[40] Thus stimulated, the Refugee Office undertook a rapid survey on the basis of records readily available regarding Arab refugee property in Israel.[41] The goal of

[38] In addition, the CCP was to have conflict with UNTSO during 1951. During the Israeli-Syrian border clash near Lake Huleh, the CCP wanted to use the incident to reestablish contact between the parties and to try to build some larger settlement out of the efforts to stop the fighting. UNTSO excluded the CCP from UN activities. See Azcárate, *Mission in Palestine,* pp. 172—73.

[39] In early 1951 the Iraqi government impounded the accounts and property of Iraqi Jews who registered for immigration to Israel. Israel called the matter to the attention of the CCP and stated that if the policy continued Israel might reconsider its offer to make a contribution to UNRWA's reintegration fund. Moreover, Israel stated that the sum of Iraqi Jews' property so impounded would be deducted from any compensation payments Israel might be willing to pay. The CCP transmitted this policy statement to Iraq without comment and received no reply. The CCP was not involved in further discussions on this subject during the rest of the year. See further A/AC.25/ W.81/Rev. 2, pp. 38—39.

[40] Unimpeachable source.

[41] Holger Anderson headed the Refugee Office. Much of the work was done under John Berncastle who was experienced on the refugee subject. See further Don Peretz, "Problems of Arab Refugee Compensation," *Middle East Journal* 8, no. 4 (Autumn

the CCP was to obtain property estimates so that compensation payments could be used to induce resettlement. After research during the summer of 1951, the Refugee Office arrived at the estimate of $240 million for Arab refugee property in Israel of a permanent or immovable nature.[42]

With this information, the CCP began planning still another conference. Throughout much of 1951 James Barco of the US delegation to the Commission had been dissatisfied with the lethargy of the CCP and had been advocating some activity so that the Commission could justify its existence. He had been unhappy with Palmer's reluctance to pursue the subject of compensation payment vis-à-vis the Israelis, even after he had made preliminary soundings and had arranged a meeting of Palmer and Israeli officials to discuss that subject. Therefore Barco had begun advocating the need for a new diplomatic effort, for making "one last try" under the CCP's terms of reference. Palmer hesitated to endorse this initiative, despite approval from the other CCP members, for the same reason that he had not taken action on the compensation question. He feared that the CCP would not be supported by the US government and that as a result the Commission would find itself "out on a limb." At this point Barco offered his resignation at a stormy session of the CCP, and at this prodding from his colleague Palmer agreed to the calling of a conference—if Barco took the responsibility for initiating and planning the conference as far as US participation was concerned. Subsequently, Barco returned to Washington in early summer, drew up a number of draft proposals with the aid of State Department personnel, and obtained a letter from the Secretary of State instructing Palmer to undertake a more active and structured diplomatic effort on the Palestine question.[43]

1954): 406. Berncastle had reservations that an adequate job could be done in the time span asked by the CCP. Later CCP efforts were to validate his reservations.

[42] GAOR: 6th Sess., Supplement No. 18 (A/1985), p. 6. The official figures were given as 100,000,000 Palestinian pounds for Arab refugee immovable property and P£ 19,100,000 for movable property. The P£ was worth $2.40 in 1947.

[43] Azcárate misunderstands the actual origins of what was to be the Paris conference (*Mission in Palestine,* pp. 174—76). Because of his limited information, he

Upon Barco's return to the Middle East and the CCP's resumption of meetings, elements within the Commission expressed some hesitation about holding the conference, although the CCP had given approval to the idea before Barco had gone to Washington. De Boisanger had been replaced by M. Marchal during the recess, and Marchal was reluctant to follow through on what de Boisanger had approved. The French delegation to the CCP under Marchal was no longer as independent of the Quai d'Orsay as previously. French foreign policy in the Middle East was undergoing a reorientation at that time in favor of Israel. Since the CCP's draft proposals contained several aspects which could be presumed to be disliked by Israel—in particular, the reopening of the repatriation issue—the French were not enthusiastic about the conference. Nevertheless, the invitations to the conference were sent on 10 August, with the conference scheduled for Paris a month later.

The timing of the conference hardly could have been worse; every contextual factor pointed to the failure of the conference prior to its start. Nothing at this time pointed to a change of policy by the Arabs. Jordan was in its most unstable period since the end of the mandate. King Abdallah had been assassinated on 20 July, and the heir to the throne, Amir Talal, had been out of the country prior to late summer of 1959 because of his mental instability. He was named king just four days before the

---

ascribes to Acheson's letter the start of the decisionmaking process that led to the conference. Thus in his presentation, the CCP appears to be dominated by US officials in Washington. In fact, the initial decisionmaking was made in the field and by CCP personnel. Of course, in either analysis the role of the US government is important, but it does make a difference whether US members on the CCP had freedom to initiate policies, and whether US personnel on the CCP had access to the top decisionmakers in Washington.

Azcárate also misunderstands the role of the CCP secretariat in the preparation of the proposals that were presented to the parties at the Paris conference. Whereas Azcárate states that the secretariat, and in particular Hamilton Fisher, drew up the proposals, interview findings indicate conclusively that US officials alone drew up the proposals under Barco's supervision. CCP secretariat personnel—and the government members of the Commission—entered the decisionmaking process at the later stage of revising the draft proposals. While valuable service was rendered by both secretariat and government personnel, and in particular by the secretariat's Alexis Ladas, Azcárate's presentation remains formal-legal and factually incorrect.

87

conference, had uncertain political support in the country, and his ability to stay on the throne was questionable. In the context of Abdallah's assassination (which probably resulted from his private negotiations with Israel), and in the face of unsure support from Jordanian public opinion (a large segment of Jordanians were Palestinian refugees), a public agreement with Israel was not probable. Moreover, Egypt was involved in a conflict with the United Kingdom over revision of treaty rights concerning Suez. Because of this conflict, agreement with Israel was again improbable, for Egyptian attention was riveted on the treaty question and Egypt's anti-Israel policy was helpful to it in the conflict. As long as a de facto war with Israel was asserted to be present, Egypt could use this asserted state of affairs to justify its tight control over Suez and concomitantly its barring of British influence. Thus an Egyptian-Israeli rapprochement was unlikely. And a Security Council condemnation of Egypt for blocking Israeli shipping in the Suez Canal just prior to the conference only inflamed Egyptian public opinion against Israel, Great Britain and the United Nations.[44] In addition, Egypt was being requested to participate in the Western-sponsored, anti-communist Middle East Command structure. Hence the exertion of influence on the Arabs to modify their policies on the Palestine question was unlikely not only from the United Kingdom but also from the United States. The latter state had additional reasons to hesitate in applying pressure on the Arabs because of the Korean War and the need to keep material for that war passing through Suez.

Israel, too, had little reason to change its policies. On the all-important refugee question, international thinking was clearly tending toward resettlement. At the time of the conference, UNRWA was trying to implement the "Blandford plan" through use of the reintegration fund established by the General Assembly. The aim of the Blandford plan was to liquidate UN responsibility for the Palestinian refugees with a UN grant of 250 million dollars to Arab governments. The Arab governments were being asked to

[44] See Rony E. Gabbay, *A Political Study of the Arab-Jewish Conflict: The Arab Refugee Problem (A Case Study)* (Geneva: Droz, 1959), pp. 328–29.

provide land and services for the refugees, and UN aid was to be changed from direct relief provisions to rehabilitation projects.[45]

Hence the two UN organs working on the refugee question were undercutting each other's efforts. While the CCP was trying to obtain agreement to limited repatriation from Israel, UNRWA was trying to implement de facto resettlement. Israel was quite aware of the intended results of UNRWA's program; thus there was even less reason than previously to yield on the issue of repatriation.[46] Nor was influence likely to be exerted on Israel to obtain policy changes. The French, as noted above, had been reluctant even to call the conference because of not wanting to undermine budding French-Israeli ties. The British had very few, if any, points of influence with the Israelis. The United States had tried sporadic persuasion and threats of pressure in 1949 with unfavorable results. And issuance of the Tripartite Declaration had pledged support for the status quo.

Neither did the replies of the parties to the CCP's invitation give any cause for optimism. In accepting, Israel stated some "preliminary observations" which, in fact, constituted extensive reservations.[47] Israel asked for an Arab guarantee that discussions would be entered into pursuant to a settlement and stated it would not discuss specifics until the CCP had obtained that guarantee. Moreover, Israel expressed reservations about the CCP's assuming the role of suggesting proposals to the disputants and argued that these would only become new points of contention in the conflict. The Arabs, too, expressed reservations and asserted that there should be no direct contact, no deviation from past UN resolutions, and no proposals presented at the conference not presented to the Arab governments ahead of time.[48] Despite the

[45] Peretz, *Israel and the Palestine Arabs,* pp. 14–15.

[46] On the other hand, the Arabs hesitated to cooperate with UNRWA on resettlement as long as there was any hope of obtaining repatriation through the CCP.

[47] UN Doc. A/1985, 19 November 1951, p. 2. A more informative account of Israel's policy statement was published in the *Jerusalem Post,* 11 September 1951, pp. 1, 6.

[48] A/1985, p. 2; *Al-Ahram,* 7 September 1951; *Al-Ahram,* 1 September 1951. This last policy represents one of the clearest examples of what has been described as the Arab conception of an "almost super-humanly clever and able" Zionist, an image which

tone of the replies and, in particular, the Israeli stand regarding an active role for the Commission, the CCP assumed that the replies constituted reason to hold the conference as planned.[49]

The Paris conference was thus initiated in mid-September by a CCP statement, read by Palmer. It contained three main points: the solutions to the outstanding problems had to be "sought in a fair and realistic spirit of give-and-take"; the Palestine question had to be considered in its entirety because the specific problems were interrelated, and thus the parties should not emphasize particular paragraphs, or sections thereof, in A/Res/194 or A/Res/181; and each party had to respect the security of the other since this was the basic starting point for securing compromises and concessions from any party.[50]

The Commission then proceeded to present to the parties a draft of a nonaggression declaration for adoption.[51] It was the hope of the CCP that the signing of this "Preamble" would improve the atmosphere of the talks. Its presentation, however, had the reverse effect. The Preamble was rejected by the Arabs, which increased Israeli fears of subversion through return of refugees, and thereby doomed the CCP's specific proposals for a general settlement before they were presented. The heart of the issue was that the Preamble was based on the armistice agreements among Israel, Lebanon, Jordan, and Syria—the wording of which forbade all kinds of force. The armistice agreement between Israel and Egypt prohibited use of military force only, and Egypt was unwilling to extend its commitments under the CCP's Preamble.[52] An Arab draft preamble only worsened the situation, for the Arab draft was based on the Egyptian-Israeli Armistice Agreement and would have had the effect of undermining the commitments of Syria, Jordan, and Lebanon under their armistice agreements.[53]

"helps to explain the Arabs' reluctance to negotiate . . . " (Charles D. Cremeans, *The Arabs and the World* [New York: F. A. Praeger, 1963], pp. 182–83).

[49] A/1985, p. 2.

[50] *Ibid.*, p. 3.

[51] *Ibid.*

[52] See Azcárate, *Mission in Palestine*, pp. 174–76.

[53] A/1985, Annex B, Appendix II, p. 16.

By mid-October the CCP sought to bypass the entire subject and to institute discussion of the proposals for a general settlement it had drawn up. Israel objected, saying such an effort was pointless since the Arabs had shown that a basis for negotiations was clearly absent.[54] Nevertheless, the CCP presented its blueprint for a general settlement.

The substance of the Commission's proposals stand in bold contrast to the nature of the conference in which they were presented. But they were presented at a conference that was poorly timed to begin with, then engulfed in pessimism by the time the proposals were presented. It was not surprising that the replies to the proposals "were a veritable exercise in the critical spirit."[55]

The CCP first suggested the mutual cancellation of claims for war damages. In the opinion of the Commission, "any attempt to go back to the origin of the conflict in order to determine the responsiblitity for the outbreak of the hostilities would have been . . . a step backwards."[56] With regard to the refugee question, the CCP asked for limited repatriation for those refugees who wanted to live at peace with Israel and who could be integrated into Israel's economy, and for resettlement of others with compensation. According to the CCP, two fundamental principles were involved in a realistic approach to repatriation: Israel must be given a definite number, and the refugees must be told what repatriation to a Jewish state would entail.[57] The Commission stated frankly that its mandate on the subject of repatriation, under the terms of A/Res/194, could not be implemented: a realistic solution to that problem required a

---

[54] Israel, which had accepted the CCP's "Preamble," challenged the CCP's statement that the replies of the parties on the question of nonagression "constituted a basis for the consideration of its comprehensive pattern of proposals . . . " (A/1985, pp. 7–8). See the pessimistic statement by Foreign Minister Sharett in *Jerusalem Post*, 28 October 1951, p. 1.

[55] Azcárate, *Mission in Palestine*, p. 178.

[56] A/1985, p. 4.

[57] A/AC.25/W.82/Rev. 1, pp. 24–25.

91

departure from wording of paragraph 11 of that resolution.[58] Israel was asked to pay compensation on the basis of the estimates compiled by the Refugee Office of the Commission. The CCP called for further negotiations on blocked accounts. And finally, it asked for a revision of the boundaries outlined in the armistice agreements with a view toward the creation of international river authorities; the discussion of the future of the Gaza area; and the establishment of a free port at Haifa, free access to the Holy Places, health controls, and arrangements for mutual economic growth.[59]

In brief, the Arab comments on the proposals reflected previous policy and the continuing efforts of Arab League Secretary-General Azzam Pasha and Shuqayri, now Assistant Secretary-General of the Arab League.[60] The Arabs did not agree to mutual cancellation of reparations claims, to any limitation on the right of repatriation, or to limiting Israel's payment of compensation to its ability to pay—with the United Nations' meeting the balance (as the CCP had suggested). The Arabs did agree to the mutual release of blocked accounts once more, and they accepted, in principle, the general idea of revisions in the armistice boundaries.[61] The Arabs also questioned the authority of the CCP to induce general negotiations rather than implement General Assembly resolutions, and they raised some question about the desirability of having a UN organ composed of government representatives.[62]

For its part, Israel did not agree to drop its reparations claims, nor did it agree to accept repatriation. Israel did accept the responsibility to pay some compensation, but it did not endorse

---

[58] A/1985, p. 5.

[59] For the entire list of proposals, see *ibid.*, pp. 3–5.

[60] Azzam Pasha and Shuqayri were denouncing the CCP's efforts from Cairo throughout the Paris conference. On occasion they denounced Commission proposals as Israeli ones, even before the CCP had presented them to the parties. See *Al-Ahram*, 1, 19, and 20 September 1951, and 6 October 1951; *Al-Misri*, 1 and 6 October 1951; and *Al-Zaman*, 19 September 1951.

[61] A/1985, p. 9.

[62] *Ibid.*, p. 6.

the estimates presented by the CCP's Refugee Office. Israel would not accept individual compensation claims, and its agreement to pay global compensation was qualified by previous deduction of reparations.[63] Israel also agreed to work toward the release of the blocked accounts and to negotiate territorial revisions in the armistice agreements.[64]

Confronted with these attitudes, the Commission adjourned the conference on 19 November. The US members of the CCP had requested that influence from the State Department be exerted on the parties during the conference. While the Department supported the calling of the conference through regular diplomatic contact, there was no extra effort to persuade any of the parties to deviate from past policies.[65] The CCP concluded that it was not able to secure discussion of the proposals "in a fair and realistic spirit of give-and-take."[66] The Commission criticized both the Israeli policy of not accepting the principle of repatriation and the Arab lack of "readiness to arrive at . . . a peace settlement with the government of Israel."[67]

In addressing its progress report to the sixth General Assembly, the CCP stated:

> The Commission is of the opinion . . . that the present unwillingness of the parties fully to implement the General Assembly resolutions under which the Commission is operating, as well as the changes which have occurred in Palestine during the past three years, have made it impossible for the Commission to carry out its mandate, and this fact should be taken into consideration in any further approach to the Palestine problem.
> Finally, in view of its firm conviction that the aspects of the Palestine problem are inter-related, the Commission is of the opinion

[63] A/AC.25/W.81/Rev. 2, p. 49.

[64] *Ibid.*, p. 8.

[65] The US and UK ambassadors to Egypt did have one meeting with Azzam Pasha in which a number of issues were discussed, including the work of the CCP. See *Al-Ahram* and *Al-Misri* of 2 October 1951.

[66] A/1985, p. 10.

[67] *Ibid.*

that in any further approach to the problem it is desirable that consideration be given to the need for co-ordinating all United Nations efforts aimed at the promotion of stability, security and peace in Palestine.[68]

One of the ironies of the situation at this time was that while the CCP was terminating its efforts and stating that there was no solution to the Palestine problem under its terms of reference, the Arab governments through the Arab League were approving UNRWA's "Blandford plan." This program for turning the refugee problem over to the Arab governments for de facto resettlement programs had been before the Arab governments at the same time as the CCP's series of proposals. UNRWA had encountered increased resistance to its plan at the start of the Paris conference,[69] but it had finally been discussed realistically by the Arab League.[70] And the Secretary-General of the United Nations found the Arab governments preparing for resettlement at this time.[71]

In any event, at the sixth General Assembly the Palestine question was debated to a large extent in terms of the future of the CCP. The progress report of the Commission seemed to many

[68] *Ibid.* The CCP considered adding a paragraph stating that repatriation was impossible, given a realistic assessment of the situation in the Middle East. UNRWA advised for inclusion, but the US and UK governments were opposed to such a declaration. French personnel supported the inclusion of such a statement (unimpeachable source). The report of the CCP's Refugee Office is found in Annex A of A/1985.

[69] Unimpeachable source.

[70] *Al-Ahram* and *Al-Misri,* 5 October 1951.

[71] Trygve Lie, *In the Cause of Peace* (New York: Macmillan Co., 1954), p. 196. Peretz argues that the Arab governments were not serious concerning resettlement (see *Israel and the Palestine Arabs,* pp. 13–15).

It could be argued that the work of the CCP and UNRWA, rather than being mutually detrimental as argued earlier, was mutually beneficial: because the CCP's Paris conference gave the Arabs a chance to maintain the "hard line" on the subject of repatriation, they could then accept the Blandford plan in a less publicized process. While this hypothesis is logically sound, the difficulty that UNRWA experienced during the conference indicates that the efforts of the two organs, as perceived by the Arabs, were mutually undercutting. Resettlement would not be accepted as long as there was hope for repatriation. There is no doubt that the two organs were working at cross-purposes with regard to Israel's policy on repatriation, as noted earlier. Israel saw no point in making concessions on the repatriation issue while UNRWA was working for resettlement.

to contain a de facto resignation. But Marchal indicated to the Assembly's Ad Hoc Political Committee that it was the Commission's idea to remain in operation and be available to the parties, although a negotiated solution would not be sought immediately.[72] The CCP secretariat, too, was of the opinion that the CCP should continue to be available to the parties and "chip away" at the problems.[73] In the succeeding days, however, there was debate regarding the future of the CCP. No direct attention was given to the substantive proposals presented at the Paris conference.

In the Ad Hoc Political Committee in the fall of 1951 there was significant opposition to maintaining the same membership of the CCP. A move to enlarge the CCP to seven members was successful as far as committee voting was concerned, but the United States was able to reverse this vote in plenary session after intensive private diplomacy. The member governments of the CCP —led by the United States—were unwilling to bear the responsibility for the failure of the peacemaking effort, a responsibility which they thought a change of membership would signify.[74] Nevertheless, the committee vote indicated widespread dissatisfaction with the composition of the CCP. This in turn was an indirect reflection of dissatisfaction with the role played by the Commission. The issue of where the CCP's headquarters were to be was symbolic of the question of the role of the CCP in the future. Presumably, an active Commission would be based in Jerusalem (and would symbolize UN interest in that city), while a less active Commission would be based in New York. In the end, the Assembly reached no decision on this question.

Israel had finally moved for indirect termination of the CCP and argued that negotiations could continue through the Mixed

[72] GAOR: 6th Sess., Ad Hoc Political Committee, p. 175.

[73] Azcárate, *Mission in Palestine,* p. 169.

[74] In particular the US delegation to the United Nations did not want to contradict its government's position that it was the attitudes of the disputants that had blocked a settlement. Thus the United States saw in the move to enlarge the CCP an attempt to use the CCP as a scapegoat for failure—especially by the Arab states. At this point Israel supported the continuation of the CCP as originally created.

Armistice Commissions or through a good offices committee.[75] This recommendation for less UN involvement in the future picked up support from significant neutrals such as Canada, but a number of delegations—including Arab ones—had been working for more UN involvement directed toward implementation of past resolutions. The Assembly elected not to change the CCP's mandate, despite the CCP's earlier statement in its progress report that it was not able to carry out its terms of reference.

Three years of CCP peacemaking efforts had produced, if anything, even more differences of opinion in the General Assembly than ever before. After all the criticism of the Commission, the disputants, and anyone else, member governments of the Assembly still could not reach a consensus on what changes to make in the UN peacemaking effort. Thus the CCP seemed little different after the sixth session than before. It still had a general mandate to facilitate the settlement of all questions outstanding, with the same composition, with its headquarters where it chose. The Arab states seemed to agree that the CCP would continue as previously, as did the Commission's principal secretary.[76] But the United States saw no prospect for breaking the status quo,[77] and therefore the Secretary-General recommended a budget in which the CCP was presumed to be based in New York with no major expenditures.[78]

Thus the CCP entered a new phase, one of decreased activity on the diplomatic front while "marking time" with technical work

[75] Israel believed that the CCP had blocked direct negotiations. Israel also wanted the General Assembly to change the UN form of involvement as a way of not endorsing past Assembly resolutions. Thus Israel argued that the United Nations should create a good offices committee with membership the same as the CCP's but with a different mandate. The USSR also made its annual move for the explicit termination of the CCP, but its draft resolution failed 5–48–1.

[76] For a survey of Arab opinion see *Mideast Mirror: A Review of Middle East News* (Beirut, yearly), 1952, p. 12. See also Azcárate, *Mission in Palestine*, p. 178.

[77] This decision appears to have been made without the intense Zionist lobbying presumed by Azcárate in *ibid.*, although State Department officials were aware that the Zionists would not oppose such a decision.

[78] GAOR: 6th Sess., Annexes, Agenda Item 24 (A/2072, 24 January 1952), p. 6. The CCP had cost circa $10 million in 1949–51 (see Peretz, *Israel and the Palestine Arabs,* p. 302).

on identification and evaluation of Arab property in Israel. For the next eight years the CCP was to be primarily a symbol of UN concern for the unresolved aspects of the Arab-Israeli conflict.

Since the CCP was, in the words of one of its more recent principal secretaries, "a different animal at different times," it is appropriate at this point to review the first three years of the CCP's work. The period 1949-51 was the only time in the life of the Commission when it operated as a three-government organ pursuant to a general settlement of the Arab-Israeli conflict.

In 1949 and thereafter, the Arab states dealing with the CCP did not prefer a negotiated settlement to the maintenance of the early 1949 status quo. Such a status quo did not require the recognition of the state of Israel, nor admission of past failures, nor renunciation of claims to Palestine. Therefore Egypt and Syria "used" the CCP to avoid explicitly affirming the de facto situation in the Middle East; they sought to give the appearance of cooperation with the CCP when realistic negotiation based on bargaining was not desired. Jordan and Lebanon supported this policy for fear of propaganda attack from other Arab states—and because Jordan did not get what it considered favorable settlement terms from Israel.

There were four main factors in the configuration of the Arab-Israeli conflict that led the Arabs to this general disposition. First, the signing of the armistice agreements gave the Arab governments limited security vis-à-vis Israel without requiring the Arab states to recognize Israel or deal with it as a permanent fixture in the Middle East. As the CCP concluded in its tenth progress report, the agreements had reduced the disputants' sense of urgency in pursuing a general settlement and had removed military matters—and a number of territorial considerations—from the purview of the CCP. Thus the Arabs had less desire to bargain with Israel under Commission aegis and did not have to reach a general settlement with Israel in return for immediate relief from Israeli military force.[79]

[79] On the other hand, the very presence of the CCP had aided the acting mediator in the armistice negotiations, for the most complex questions were saved for the CCP.

Second, the Arab governments had received no security from their own people. Having manipulated public opinion to an anti-Israel fervor during the Palestine war, and having negotiated the armistice agreements in secret, the Arab governments found it extremely difficult to negotiate a formal and public peace with Israel. Each government was wary of coming to terms with Israel, regardless of how beneficial that settlement might be to an Arab nation as a whole through UN and US financial and technical assistance, because such a settlement might contribute to a coup d'état. Each government feared that admission of the failure of its Palestine policy would result in the overthrow of the government by disappointed and frustrated citizens.

Third, the Arab governments could not maintain hopes of controlling Palestine in the future and yet bargain on the refugee question. The Arab governments realized that the claim to full repatriation was accepted by a number of other governments as legally or morally valid. Despite long and heated arguments on this subject, the basic fact remains that in the view of many, Israel did have some responsibility for the flight of Arabs from predominantly Arab Palestine. Whatever the extent of voluntary Arab withdrawal from Palestine and withdrawal at the urging of local Arab politicians, the fact remains that Zionists did at times undertake various acts of terrorism against Palestinian Arabs, then publicize those acts in order to frighten more Arabs into leaving—the most notorious of such events being the massacre at Deir Yasin.[80] Thus the Arab governments realized they had at their disposal a widely accepted legal-moral argument that could be put forward in the hopes of returning a predominantly Arab population to Palestine.[81] Any compromise settlement of the refugee question, one not entailing large-scale resettlement, would

---

And since Israel, like Bunche, presumed that the agreements were a transitional step toward a permanent peace treaty, Israel was content to bargain on military matters as a separate group of issues rather than relate them to the more explosive questions such as recognition, responsibility for refugees, and the future of Jerusalem.

[80] See the objective article by Georgiana G. Stevens, "Arab Refugees: 1948–1952," *Middle East Journal* 6, no. 3 (Summer 1952): 281–98.

[81] See further, *ibid.*

98

mean that the last potentially effective measure short of coercion against Zionist-controlled Palestine was being given up.[82] Termination of the refugee question without major repatriation, although not erasing Arab hatred toward the Zionists, would remove the last major physical example of Arab resistance to Jewish control of Palestine.

Fourth, Arab deficiencies in the Palestine war produced an Arab trauma, a national crisis of identity, which led to an overemphasis on status and prestige.[83] The debacle of the Arabs in 1947—48, coming at a time when Arab nationalism was gaining momentum, made a profound impact on many Arabs who had visions of a new Arab empire in the Middle East—one that would be respected as in the days of past Arab glories. To compensate for the 1948 defeat and the resultant collective inferiority complex, at times the Arabs stressed matters of prestige, dignity, and status at the expense of reality. Such an attitude impeded realistic negotiations based on bargaining, particularly when the Arabs preferred advocation of an obsolete right to acknowledgment that the right would not be implemented in practice.[84]

Israel, by contrast, did indeed desire a settlement to the Arab-Israeli conflict. But, like the Arabs, Israel did not want to bargain on what it considered major issues. It "had won the war

---

[82] This argument assumes that propaganda attacks and emphasis on the words of past Assembly resolutions will be relatively ineffective in producing changes in Israeli policy. Such an assumption seems verified by the history of the Arab-Israeli conflict, 1947 to the present.

[83] See Musa Alami, "The Lesson of Palestine," *Middle East Journal* 3, no. 4 (October 1949): 373—405; John C. Campbell, *Defense of the Middle East* (New York: Harper & Bros., 1960), pp. 325—26; Cremeans, *Arabs and the World*, pp. 60, 126, 130; Polk, *United States and the Arab World*, p. 191; Safran, *United States and Israel*, p. 286; Constantine K. Zurayk, *The Meaning of the Disaster*, trans. R. B. Winder (Beirut: Kashaf Press, 1956). That the CCP could have perceived this factor is seen by the early dates of the Alami and Zurayk works, and also by the conclusions drawn by Azcárate to the same effect (*Mission in Palestine*, p. 203). Azcárate's manuscript was written in 1952.

[84] This factor, however, should not be overemphasized itself, since the Arab quest for prestige did not prevent private meetings with the Israelis during the Lausanne conference and in Jordan, not to mention at Rhodes. The first UN Secretary-General had found the Arabs realistic in private, despite unrealistic public pronouncements. Lie, *In the Cause of Peace*, p. 189.

and saw no reason why [it] should have to lose the peace."[85] In short, Israel wanted the Arabs to recognize the territory it controlled, the sector of Jerusalem it controlled, and resettlement as the primary solution to the refugee question.

This general disposition brought the Israelis into inevitable conflict with the CCP. The CCP represented, inherently, a barrier to Israel's exacting the fruits of its military victory. The Commission's mandate represented international interest in the Palestine question and was based on principles of law and equity. Therefore, the CCP's presence was inimical to Israel's *realpolitik* and was to the advantage of the Arabs who were trying to regain through words what they had lost through force. Over time, the Israelis became more and more dissatisfied with the roles played by the CCP. They tended to forget their responsibility in rejecting the principle of repatriation, the key to a general settlement. Israel had understandable reasons for hesitation on the repatriation issue, in the aftermath of war and in the context of talk of a second round of that war. And there is no denying that thinking in UNRWA, CCP, and US circles was tending toward resettlement. Yet, Israel, in marshaling arguments against undertaking repatriation, used the bellicose public pronouncements of Arab spokesmen at face value while privately knowing the unreliability of such posturing. Israel was also aware of the nature of Arab domestic public opinion and the dangers to an Arab government negotiating with Israel. In the final analysis, Israel seemed unwilling to take risks for peace, unwilling to risk taking one step backward in order to take two steps forward over time, unwilling to accept the principle of repatriation and to repatriate a limited but unspecified number of refugees in order to obtain some resettlement and a general settlement.[86] Israel also came to have an unqualified faith

---

[85] J. C. Hurewitz, *The Struggle for Palestine* (New York: W. W. Norton, 1950), p. 330.

[86] Arab belligerency thus gave Israel both a reason and an excuse to reject the principle of repatriation. An excuse was desired since the raison d'être of the Jewish state was the gathering in of the diaspora, the opening of the state to mass immigration. Repatriation worked counter to immigration because scarce land and housing, desired for Jewish immigrants, would be claimed by Arab refugees.

in the efficacy of direct talks per se. The Israelis tended to dismiss from memory the unproductive direct talks held privately in towns around Lausanne, held later with Jordan, and held formally in the presence of the CCP with regard to blocked accounts.

Given these attitudes by the parties, the CCP tried almost every role with the exception of trying to mobilize force. The role of initiating policy recommendations appears well carried out in terms of the substance of the recommendations, the criticisms of the disputants notwithstanding. Very early in its existence, the Commission perceived that lesser forms of involvement would not be productive, and the CCP did not shrink from making substantive suggestions to the parties directly concerned—which is more than can be said for some governments. On the refugee question the CCP adopted the most realistic approach when it endorsed limited repatriation and large-scale resettlement. Such an approach sought a maximum agreement on principle with a minimum of conflict over the crucial actual movement of persons. The subcommittee on refugees and the Clapp Mission provided sound recommendations, and the CCP's later emphasis on compensation and resettlement was a realistic alternative for an international agency without effective government support. The proposals presented at Paris comprise one of the better general blueprints for settlement, given the CCP's lack of support and the facts of Israeli control over certain territory. In particular, the tenth progress report contained numerous trenchant observations, among them the need for compromise on the part of the parties, mutual respect for state security, understanding of the Assembly resolutions *in toto* rather than in self-serving parts, rectification of the dislocations caused by Israel's creation, and adjustment to changed facts in the Middle East.

The effect of the substance of these policy recommendations, however, was lessened by inappropriate tactics by the CCP, a deficiency related in turn to the Commission's lack of liaison with other UN field organs and to its composition. There was an early lack of goal-orientation and drive on the part of the CCP which became pronounced during the Lausanne conference. This characteristic also applied to CCP activities during most of 1950. Thus

101

many of the CCP's policy recommendations were made after the conflict had "hardened" in the post-1949 period. This lack of early goal-orientation stemmed in part from the nature of the CCP's composition, particularly since the United States had a hands-off policy on the Palestine question. In addition, because of a lack of familiarity with Middle East politics, a second tactical error was made by the CCP: it relied excessively on diplomacy by conference at a time when the Arab states required quiet diplomacy—if not a tacit, rather than a formal, agreement. Given the insecurity of the Arab governments and the inferiority complex with the concomitant emphasis on public posturing in pursuit of dignity, the CCP's search for a formal peace treaty via conference diplomacy was ill-suited to the Arabs' needs. Finally, in treating the Arab delegations *en bloc,* the CCP missed an early opportunity to facilitate a separate Israeli-Jordanian settlement. Eventually, treating the Arabs *en bloc* failed to shield the states disposed to a compromise settlement—Jordan and Lebanon—from the more intransigent influence of Egypt and Syria. This tactical deficiency stemmed directly from the lack of CCP liaison with the acting mediator, who had successfully employed separate (and quiet) negotiations. Further lack of liaison between the CCP and UNRWA caused the two organs to work at cross-purposes: the CCP in 1951 sought to reopen the issue of repatriation while UNRWA was trying to implement de facto resettlement.

A closing word is in order with specific regard to the composition of the CCP. No power and authority accrue automatically to a UN subsidiary organ because it is comprised legally of governments. Effectiveness, based on power and authority, may or may not be present in UN involvement, depending on the execution of the roles undertaken. In these peacemaking roles, power and authority may be employed to reduce the efficacy of the UN organ. Such was the case with the CCP, particularly with regard to the US threat to apply pressure on Israel in 1949. The threat of pressure was hastily applied and hastily withdrawn without positive results. Because the CCP was involved in that process, the inconsistent US effort weakened the CCP. On the other hand, it cannot be assumed that a subsidiary

102

organ of government members will be so automatically hamstrung by its internal politics that it cannot function. In the early years of the CCP, France and Turkey clearly deferred to the United States, thus making for a friction-free, if less international, peacemaking field organ.[87]

[87] Some writers have argued that internal dissension impeded the CCP's peacemaking efforts. See Earl Berger, *The Covenant and the Sword* (London: Routledge & Kegan Paul, Ltd., 1965), pp. 41–43 for a case in point. See also, *New York Times,* 5 May 1949, p. 2; and *Palestine Post,* 10, 26 May and 8 June 1949, p. 1. On the basis of the present study, there is no doubt that Turkey was unimportant and that France was cooperative in the US-led work of the CCP. There were times when the French appeared to give reporters the impression that the faults of the CCP were those of the United States. But the French, like the British, were content to let the United States run the show. It is to be recalled that the French delegation to the CCP was relatively independent of the Quai d'Orsay, and that the British were delighted to be off the Palestine hot seat.

IV

THE CCP AND QUASI-FUNCTIONALISM

After the 1949–51 period, the CCP had one further period of intensive diplomatic activity. The Commission established a Special Representative in 1961-62 to make inquiries about, and ultimately to submit a plan for, possible changes in the configuration of the refugee problem. This mission is dealt with in the following chapter. But for most of the 1950s and 1960s the CCP merely symbolized UN hopes for rapprochement between the Arabs and Israelis. Other UN field organs were more active than the CCP during these two decades, but UNRWA, UNTSO-MAC, and UNEF did not acquire responsibility for peacemaking. The CCP, while on "ice," remained responsible for facilitating a peaceful settlement. Some accord was achieved through the CCP in the 1950s on the issue of individual bank accounts "frozen" in the various countries, but most of the Commission's time was occupied by the effort to identify and evaluate Arab refugee property in Israel.

In regard especially to the 1952-60 technical effort of identification and evaluation of, as well as the work on, blocked accounts, it has been said that the CCP was engaged in a functional approach to the Palestine question—that "nonpolitical" problems were being treated in the hope that progress in this realm would lead to progress in the "political" sphere. The Commission itself contributed to this evaluation, for, in its twelfth progress report, it stated that it was working on the issues of blocked accounts and compensation in the hope of generating "sufficient good will" among the parties so that the negotiations could be resumed.[1] And a leading student of the refugee problem has concluded that the CCP was indeed following a functional approach after 1951.[2] It would seem more accurate to say, however, that the CCP was using a quasi-functional approach in its efforts: it was mainly wasting time, doing the necessary "paper work" while looking for some change in the configuration of the Arab-Israeli conflict which would allow it to play an important diplomatic role once more. All involved in the Commission's work in the period would have been ecstatic if the CCP's activities on the subjects of frozen bank accounts and property identification and evaluation had resulted in a breakthrough to a negotiated settlement, but virtually no one involved expected this to happen. The CCP itself reported in 1958 that it was working on "concrete problems which might be of direct benefit to a great number of refugees ... independently of the readiness of the parties to reach over-all agreement."[3] And one CCP representative told the seventh session of the General Assembly that the Commission was concerned with compensation because there was an absence of opportunities to deal with more general questions; therefore, the CCP was collecting technical data for the time when such information might be used in settlement talks.[4] Hence in pursuing these technical aspects of the Palestine question, the CCP was undertaking work that *did* have to be completed prior to a general settlement. But there was little hope from the CCP or from the parties involved that such efforts themselves would lead to a meaningful resumption of the settlement negotiations—apart from some alteration, militarily or psychologically, in the variables of Middle East politics.

[1] UN Doc. A/2216, 8 October 1952, p. 7.

[2] Don Peretz, *Israel and the Palestine Arabs* (Washington, D.C.: The Middle East Institute, 1956), pp. 1, 243–44.

[3] UN Doc. A/3835, 18 June 1958, p. 1.

[4] GAOR: 7th Sess., Ad Hoc Political Committee, pp. 161–62.

It is an understatement to say that much transpired in the Middle East in the 1950s and 1960s while the CCP worked on property figures and bank accounts. But little occurred to alter the Commission's marginal diplomatic position. Both the Suez crisis of 1956 and the 1967 Arab-Israeli war changed a number of factors in the Arab-Israeli confrontation. Yet in the wake of both events, the CCP remained on the sidelines while the Secretary-General, in 1956, or his representative, after 1967, carried the brunt of UN peacemaking efforts.[5] At the end of the 1950s, the CCP was reporting that in its view the overall situation with regard to the Palestine question remained "substantially the same" as in 1951.[6] This view was not without foundation, for the parties continued to adhere to previous policy rather than engage in compromise— both before and after the interlude of Suez. Thus it was the Commission's opinion that the parties' attitudes precluded peace-making for most of this 1951-67 period; quasi-functionalism seemed the only role available.

No doubt Israel regarded peace as unobtainable via negotiation, and, as much as it could, it concentrated on pressing domestic problems after 1951.[7] Of course the Arab boycott of Zionist goods and shipping and the Arab raids into Israel were major antagonistic elements in Israeli-Arab relations. The psychological gulf that eventually separated Israel from the rest of the region can be seen in attitudes toward the 1956 Suez episode: the Israelis saw their thrust southward and westward as a great achievement, one that would bring them respect; the Arabs saw it as an example of Zionist aggressiveness, which "further magnified the resentment of the Arab states toward Israel and made the chances of acceptance of [Israel's] existence in their midst even more remote."[8] The same analysis could be applied to the post-1967 period. Having argued during 1950 and 1951 that it

[5] See Nadav Safran, *From War to War* (New York: Pegasus, 1969), for an overview of the conflict.

[6] A/3835, p. 1.

[7] Nadav Safran, *The United States and Israel* (Cambridge, Mass.: Harvard University Press, 1963).

[8] *Ibid.*, p. 257.

could negotiate with the Arabs more effectively in the absence of an active third party, Israel found in the 1950s and early 1960s that it could make no progress toward an overall settlement even with the CCP in the background. Moreover, as time went on, not only did the boycott, border raids, and retaliations intensify mutual fears and hates, but the Israeli public and government took an increasingly "hard line" on the key issue of repatriation. The point was reached where it could be said that Israeli attitudes constituted "a unified resistance against an Arab return."[9]

Whatever changes occurred in the Arab world during the nine years under discussion, there was no change in basic Arab attitudes toward Israel. The most important events were the rise of Jamal Abd al-Nasir in Egypt and the increased backing that the Soviet Union gave to the Arab nationalists. Nasir was in general a shrewd diplomat, an articulate spokesman, and a popular symbol of Arab nationalism; his rise caused the prospects for an Arab-Israeli settlement eventually to recede farther into the background. Gradually anti-Zionism came to be an integral part of Arab nationalism, and as Nasir articulated the tenets of that nationalism, he spoke out against accepting the presence of Israel again and again. Given the contents of an anti-Zionist Arab nationalism, Nasir could not claim to be leader of the Arab world and yet take a conciliatory approach toward Israel. With increased financial, technical, and military aid from the Soviet Union and its satellites after the mid-1950s,[10] Nasir and the Syrian leaders derived a two-fold return. Not only was such direct aid welcomed, but Arab courting of the communists resulted for a time in increased US assistance to the Arab world as the West sought to counteract the Soviet aid. Hence the Arabs were supported in their anti-Israeli diatribes by a Soviet Union that reversed completely during 1951-53 its pro-Israel policy, and at the same time the Arabs became even less susceptible to Western pressure since the Arab bargaining position was noticeably improved by Soviet favor.

[9] Peretz, *Israel and the Palestine Arabs*, p. 86.

[10] See Walter Z. Laqueur, *The Soviet Union and the Middle East* (London: Routledge & Kegan Paul, 1959), pp. 136–38, and *passim*. See further J. C. Hurewitz, *Middle East Politics: The Military Dimension* (New York: Frederick A. Praeger, 1969).

Despite increasing Soviet activity in the region, for most of the 1950s the United States continued to comprise the third leg of a triangle of parties directly involved in the Palestine question: American, Arab, Israeli.[11] The threesome had to be broadened into a foursome to include the Soviets in negotiations after 1967—a sign of their increased presence in the area. But, prior to 1967, the United States was the most influential outside nation operating in Middle East politics. The United States was the major donor to UNRWA, and a number of observers believed any solution of the refugee problem would entail US financial and technical assistance. Moreover, the United States consciously sought involvement to protect what it saw as its national interests in the region. The changeover from a Democratic to a Republican administration in 1952 and back to Democratic in 1960 did not alter the basic American approach to the Palestine question that had been present in 1949: if the Arabs and Israelis refused compromise, then the United States was content to let matters drift as long as the Soviet Union was contained and regional violence limited. To be sure, the Republicans were less sympathetic toward Zionist aspirations than the Democrats under Truman.[12] As one author has commented: "The fact that the four lean years of Israel's foreign relations corresponded with the first term of the Eisenhower Administration was not entirely coincidental."[13] And that administration did apply effective pressure on

[11] Use of the concept of a triangle of parties when referring to the Palestine question is employed to good advantage in Erskine B. Childers, "Palestine: The Broken Triangle," *Journal of International Affairs* 19, no. 1 (1965), pp. 87–99. The author makes the point that the West, concerned for the moral implications of Western anti-Semitism against Western Jews, sought to make up for the past by granting the Zionists a homeland in the Middle East at the expense of the Arabs, who were not guilty of anti-Semitism. The author goes on to argue that this background has broken the Western-Arab dialogue and that only the Western-Zionist dialogue continues. It would seem that Childers's analysis of the moral implications in the Palestine question, while basically accurate, does not necessarily mean that a breakdown in Western-Arab communication has to follow.

[12] See J. C. Hurewitz, ed., *Diplomacy in the Near and Middle East, A Documentary Record: 1914–1956* (New York: D. Van Nostrand Co., 1956), pp. 337–98.

[13] Safran, *United States and Israel,* p. 231.

Israel.[14] But strategic changes made in the Eisenhower-Dulles period are difficult to define, despite rhetorical claims to the contrary. The Eisenhower doctrine of 1958 was simply the public exposition of the basic assumptions that had long guided American policymakers: containment of communism was the primary objective; specific regional issues were less important.

In this context, characterized by lack of initiative for significant change especially from Arab and Israeli sources, the CCP and other third parties concentrated on the refugee problem without noticeable gain. Eric Johnston, dispatched by the Eisenhower Administration, sought to negotiate an agreement among the four states bordering the Jordan River that would facilitate the economic and industrial development of the area (and thus also facilitate refugee resettlement—particularly in Jordan). Working diligently during the early years of Eisenhower's first term, Johnston succeeded in gaining tacit agreement among Syria, Lebanon, Jordan, and Israel on numerous points, but there was no signed document. Although some of these points of agreement were upheld for some time by the parties, for example in regard to the percentage of water that could be diverted by each party from the Jordan River and its origins, a number of points were never agreed upon and continued to be sources of friction. Johnston's total plan was never implemented, although his mediatory effort seems one of the more capable ones in the history of the Palestine conflict.

Secretary-General Hammarskjold made a study trip to the region in the late 1950s, but his report failed to provide a way out of the fixed pattern—at least in the view of the parties directly concerned. And during this period UNRWA continued its program of direct relief to the refugees but was not able to make progress toward large-scale resettlement. UNRWA's activities pursuant to

[14] See William R. Polk, *The United States and the Arab World* (Cambridge, Mass.: Harvard University Press, 1965), pp. 266–67. In 1953, the United States used its economic leverage on Israel in order to get that country to stop its work toward the construction of a hydroelectric plant on the Jordan River. The United States acted through the channels of the Security Council and UNTSO.

resettlement were still dependent upon the CCP's work—then in progress—on identification and evaluation of refugee property as a basis for compensation. More importantly, after tending toward some settlement during 1950-51, the Arab policy hardened on this issue with the coming of a better-led nationalistic movement. With a well-articulated and more dynamic nationalism containing anti-Zionism as one element, resistance to de facto resettlement under UNRWA auspices increased in the Arab world, just as opposition to repatriation increased in Israel.[15]

The General Assembly provided few alternatives to the post-1951 and 1956 status quo. Arab delegations used the Assembly as a forum for propaganda attacks on Israel; and token, symbolic efforts were made to change the composition of the CCP (which indicated both a dissatisfaction with the member governments of the Commission and a desire to place the blame for the continuation of the conflict on the UN organ). Each time that the Arab delegations stressed refugee rights, Israel stressed its state security. In the mid-1950s the Soviet delegation entered the debates with some vigor after a long silence, a reflection of renewed Soviet interest in the Middle East in the wake of the Czech-Egyptian arms deal of 1955.

In the later 1950s the Arabs sought to reactivate the CCP on the refugee question. This initiative was supported by a large number of member states—including the United States, which said it welcomed ideas pertaining to the CCP, a new commission, or any other approach.[16] Israel opposed the reactivation strongly,

[15] CCP-UNRWA relations in the 1952—60 era were slight to nonexistent. There was consultation from time to time on matters such as the progress being made by one organ or the other and on the filing of reports. On several occasions during the mid-1950s various Arab delegations raised the question with UNRWA officials of the status of Arab refugee property in Israel. UNRWA informed the delegates that such matters belonged under the jurisdiction of the CCP. It would thus seem that the existence of the CCP helped UNRWA to avoid delicate issues that it did not want to handle, although UNRWA's reply is legally well founded. There were few, if any, contacts between the CCP and UNTSO or between the CCP and UNEF.

[16] GAOR: 14th Sess., Special Political Committee, p. 126.

110

but it failed to find support for its position.[17] Finally the 1959 Assembly instructed the Commission to make further efforts to secure the implementation of paragraph 11 of A/Res/194(III), the paragraph concerning refugee rights. During 1960, however, the CCP did virtually nothing to carry out this directive, and the Arab delegations were vociferous in their criticism of the CCP at the following Assembly session.

The Arabs then sought to invest the Commission with custodial functions over Arab refugee property in Israel, and a draft resolution to this effect, *inter alia*, passed in committee voting. The United States, despite earlier statements supporting an active CCP, became the leading defender of the CCP's record and leading opponent of custodial functions for the Commission—a stand vigorously endorsed by Israel. Israel threatened noncooperation with the CCP if that organ were given custodial functions, and the United States implied clearly that it would not work to carry out such a mandate. At one point, in a final effort to head off passage of a resolution that would have created a UN organ to control refugee property, the US spokesman resorted to a thinly veiled threat of economic pressure: "If other Members see virtue in actions that may tend to prolong the refugee dilemma, we trust that those Members will be prepared to assume an increased responsibility for that burden."[18] That phase of the resolution was deleted, and the Assembly requested the CCP to "intensify" its efforts pursuant to paragraph 11 of A/Res/194(III).[19]

The role of the CCP in the field, until the General Assembly issued the specific directives of 1959 and 1960, was determined by

[17] See *ibid.*, pp. 110, 165. Israel's was the only negative vote in committee voting on the draft resolution to reactivate the CCP and the only abstention in plenary voting. The final resolution was A/Res/1456(XIV).

[18] GAOR: 15th Sess., Plenary Meetings, pt. 2, p. 447.

[19] The vote on the paragraph pertaining to custodial functions was 44—38—12, short of the necessary majority. The final vote on the resolution as a whole was 37—17—38, with Israel and Jordan voting in opposition and Arab and communist states abstaining.

This request for intensification of efforts pursuant to paragraph 11 was one reason for the Joseph E. Johnson mission of 1961—62, treated in the following chapter.

111

the continuation of the 1951 configuration of policies that even the Suez crisis failed to change. Debates in the Assembly during this 1952—60 period had little effect on the CCP primarily because, whatever was being said in the Assembly, the states concerned continued to display largely status quo behavior—except in 1956. In 1952 a CCP spokesman indicated that the Commission had received no requests for assistance during this year,[20] and the CCP reported it had received exactly one communiqué during that same year—from Yemen.[21] The CCP did try to persuade Israel in the mid-1950s to agree to make compensation payments outside a general settlement, but it was unsuccessful in this effort.[22]

The CCP served in a limited way as a channel of communication when the Arab states first indicated an interest in the status of Arab refugee property in Israel, prior to their raising the issue in the Assembly itself.[23] A more successful process of communication and negotiation involving the CCP occurred on the subject of blocked accounts. Early in 1952 Israeli and US officials began to confer on this subject. Since the CCP had dealt with this subject previously, and since Israel was interested in the Arab reaction to its unfreezing of Arab refugee accounts, the CCP was involved in the process. Ambassador Palmer received the authorization of the Commission to make personal contacts on this issue, and the result of his efforts was an Israeli message to the United States in June 1952, that stated Israel's favorable attitude toward the unfreezing of accounts. This attitude was then relayed by the United States to the Commission.[24] Both the United States and Israel tried to

---

[20] GAOR: 7th Sess., Ad Hoc Political Committee, p. 153.

[21] A/2216, Annex II, p. 11.

[22] See UN Doc. A/3199, 4 October 1956, p. 6. The CCP, in a rare statement of criticism, termed Israel's policy "negative" and "inconsistent" with previous statements.

[23] In March 1953 the Arab states, via the CCP, charged that Israel was disposing of Arab refugee property and using the income from such disposals to finance the settlement of immigrants into Israel. The CCP made inquiries of Israel, and that government's reply in August 1953, confirmed the Arab accusation. There was no CCP follow-up or report, and the matter was dropped—except for Arab criticism of Israel and the CCP at the 1954 Assembly. (See UN Doc. A/2629, 4 January 1954, pp. 7—10; and GAOR: 9th Sess., Ad Hoc Political Committee, p. 149.)

[24] UN Doc. A/2216, 8 October 1952, p. 2; and *United States Participation in the*

give the impression to those concerned that this Israeli policy was a unilateral concession designed to promote an improvement in Arab-Israeli relations. Israel's primary reason for agreeing to the release of the blocked accounts, however, was to develop a quid pro quo with Iraq, which had frozen the assets of Iraqi Jews who had registered for immigration to Israel. Israel indicated subsequently that Iraqi unfreezing would have to take place prior to Israel's release of any accounts, although this condition was later withdrawn.[25]

It was the Commission's belief that Israel, in agreeing to an Israeli-Jordanian banking transaction supervised by the CCP, had agreed to an unconditional release operation. But Israel's opinion was that it had agreed only to renew its offer to release up to one hundred Palestinian pounds (P£) on each account frozen.[26] This misunderstanding was cleared up in the actual negotiations for the release operation which began in the fall of 1952, in accordance with the CCP's view. Actual release of funds started in 1953, but a procedural problem arose soon thereafter.[27] The CCP dispatched a troubleshooter to help erase the controversy, and his successful mediation again resulted in the release of funds.[28]

United Nations: Report by the President to the Congress for the Year 1952, Department of State Publication 5034 (Washington, D.C.: Government Printing Office, 1953), pp. 77–78.

[25] Peretz, *Israel and the Palestine Arabs,* p. 227.

[26] The clearest statement of this controversy is found in *ibid.,* pp. 226–27.

[27] The Arab states complained to the CCP that the paper work involved in a refugee's obtaining his funds required a tacit recognition of Israel. The Arab states also objected to an Israeli tax on the banking operation. See *ibid.,* p. 232; cf. Rony E. Gabbay, *A Political Study of the Arab-Jewish Conflict: The Arab Refugee Problem (A Case Study)* (Geneva: Droz, 1959), p. 451.

[28] Israel was persuaded to drop the tax; and the troubleshooter, John Reedman, worked out to the satisfaction of the disputants alternative wording on the forms involved.

There has been controversy over the relation of the release of blocked accounts to a judicial proceeding in Jordan involving Barclay's Bank, the primary bank involved in the release operation. Residents of Jordan sued Barclay's in 1954 in order to obtain release of their funds. There is speculation that this suit did much to initiate the release operation: if Barclay's had lost the case and still failed to release the funds, the bank could have lost its right to operate in various locales. Full-scale release of blocked accounts did not occur until 1955, or until the suit had been brought. Peretz concludes

This subject of blocked accounts was the one bright spot in the CCP's work at this time, and in the mid-1950s the Commission reported that the release scheme "has clearly demonstrated the way in which international action, coupled with the cooperation and good-will of the parties directly concerned, can assist in solving some of the many problems which beset the region, thereby gradually reducing the area of disagreement."[29] But there was no "spill-over" from the progress in this technical or economic sphere into the diplomatic or political realm. The negotiated solution on blocked accounts did not result in further solutions to other problems. It did not even result in mutual unfreezing by Iraqi authorities, which had been the object of the Israeli policy. Israel continued to refuse to pay compensation outside of the terms of a general settlement; and the Arabs, at the start of the release operation, opened the controversy over CCP custodial duties and the status of Arab refugee property in Israel. Nevertheless, the release operation continued to proceed smoothly, and by 1957 the bulk of the funds held in Barclay's Bank—circa P£4,000,000—had been unfrozen.[30] In 1959 Israel indicated to the CCP that it was prepared to release accounts held in banks other than Barclay's. The principal secretary of the CCP initiated negotiations with the appropriate banks, and this further release operation began.[31]

While these negotiations on blocked accounts and the more limited exchange with regard to the status of Arab refugee property in Israel were taking place, the CCP was carrying out its effort to identify and evaluate refugee immovable property as a basis for compensation. The Israeli government, using a system of its own, was also at work on this same task.

---

that the greatest beneficiary from the release scheme was the bank since it was freed from further legal action (*Israel and the Palestine Arabs*, p. 246; cf. Earl Berger, *The Covenant and the Sword* [London: Routledge & Kegan Paul, 1965], pp. 15–16). There seems to be little doubt that Israel's primary motivation in agreeing to the release operation was the development of quid pro quo with Iraq.

[29] A/3199, p. 11.

[30] Peretz, *Israel and the Palestine Arabs,* p. 245.

[31] UN Doc. A/4225/Add. 1, 12 November 1959, p. 1.

As a starting point, the CCP had before it the estimate of 100 million Palestinian pounds by the Commission's own Refugee Office, which had worked on the problem preparatory to the 1951 Paris conference. This figure had been rejected by both camps at the Paris conference, and subsequently the Arabs had argued that the figure was no less than twenty times smaller than what it should be.[32] Israel had considered the global estimate "academic"[33] because of other, nontechnical factors that figured into the negotiations—such as reparations.[34]

With some knowledge of the criticism that had been directed toward its earlier evaluation effort, the CCP in 1952 started on a more detailed and comprehensive attempt to identify and evaluate each piece of Arab immovable property in Israel. The massive scope of this undertaking can be seen in the fact that of the private property within the nation of Israel after 1948, Arab refugee ownership accounted for at least eighty percent.[35] The CCP technical experts made an attempt to account for trees and other cover on each piece of property, to list each addition to every building, and in other ways to provide as accurate a record as possible of refugee holdings in Israel. The CCP was aware that "the passage of time would render the understanding of a project such as this increasingly difficult."[36]

[32] UN Doc. A/1985, 19 November 1951, pp. 20–22. See also GAOR: 7th Sess., Ad Hoc Political Committee, 25th mtg. Cf. Peretz, *Israel and the Palestine Arabs,* p. 207. According to some Arab spokesmen, the figure should have been at least two billion pounds sterling.

[33] Peretz, *Israel and the Palestine Arabs,* p. 208.

[34] The 1951 estimate was also criticized by Sami Hadawi, an Arab technical expert of the CCP and former official in the mandatory government. For example, Hadawi claimed that the 1951 estimate of the value of Arab refugee property in the Israeli sector of Jerusalem was exactly half of what the mandatory government had said it was in 1946. The 1951 estimate was, however, at least two and one-half times greater for each classification of property than the estimate by the government of Israel. See Sami Hadawi, *Palestine: Loss of a Heritage* (San Antonio: Naylor Co., 1963), esp. pp. 74–77, 144–45.

[35] See, *inter alia,* Don Peretz, "Problems of Arab Refugee Compensation," *Middle East Journal* 8, no. 4 (Autumn 1954): 403. Cf. the numerous sources listed in Khouri's bibliography relating to this subject. (*The Arab-Israeli Dilemma* [Syracuse: Syracuse Unversity Press, 1968]).

[36] A/4225, 22 September 1959, p. 8.

The CCP, identifying property from its Jerusalem office and evaluating it from New York, adopted a basic, two-fold principle as a foundation for its work: (1) ownership of property was sought as of 15 May 1948, the date that the state of Israel was proclaimed; (2) evaluation was sought on the basis of the market values prevailing as of 29 November 1947, the date of the partition resolution.[37]

Regarding identification, the CCP followed the principle of including doubtful cases rather than excluding them on the grounds that it would be comparatively easy to exclude such cases at a later stage. The CCP avoided relying on hearsay evidence or on other forms of evidence without official documents. In this work the CCP officials were assisted not only by the parties directly concerned but also by the United Kingdom which released appropriate records.

As far as settled land was concerned, according to the CCP, identification could be said to be "positive and definite." The basic source for this assurance was the complete forms of the Registers of Title. But with regard to nonsettled land the CCP concluded that identification was "not so definite." The basic problem was that the tax lists showed who paid the tax, not who was the actual owner. Hence the CCP was not always able to obtain "absolute proof" of ownership. For example, in several Bedouin villages the land was used in common and was not listed according to private owners. Other problems arose with regard to nonsettled land because of the absence of the relevant records. The most noticeable example of this problem was the entire district of Beersheba.[38] The Commission concluded that its

[37] Unless otherwise indicated, statements of fact and quotations in this section are drawn from UN Doc. A/AC.25/W.84, 28 April 1964. This is the *Working Paper Prepared by the Commission's Land Expert on the Methods and Techniques of Identification and Valuation of Arab Refugee Immovable Property Holdings in Israel.*

[38] The records needed for identification were never located. Moreover, the area was inhabited primarily by Bedouin who cultivated different pieces of property at different times. The CCP made some informal contacts to try to rectify the problem, but it cannot be said that a concerted effort was made. Subsequently, some Arabs obtained an old military map of the area in which some indication of property cultivation was given, a fact leading to some private criticism of the CCP.

identification effort in Beersheba "cannot be regarded as in any way complete." The same lack of needed records hindered identification for several other smaller areas and for some villages. The largest area, other than Beersheba, was Ramle, and with regard to this town the CCP stated flatly that "identification may be incorrect."

With regard to evaluation, once identification had been completed, the CCP had access to both the owner's declared worth of the property as of mandate days and the "true value" worth as assessed for tax purposes by the mandatory registrars. The CCP also studied buying and selling trends on the open market for the two years prior to the passage of the partition resolution. Thus in the Commission's opinion, the use of this data resulted in an evaluation of the "true market value in the hands of the owner and not its value to the State of Israel. On the other hand, it does not necessarily represent the capital sum which would be required to produce an income on investment, equivalent to an income issuing out of such property."[39] Hence the CCP was indicating that it had made no effort to transform 1947 values into then-current values. In giving what it termed the "true market value in the hands of the owner," the CCP was establishing a base figure which could be adjusted according to formulas arrived at through negotiation of the parties. At this time the CCP did not attempt to say publicly what would constitute a fair adjustment of the 1947 values.

This base figure of property evaluation was not released by the Commission, for in the 1960s—even prior to the 1967 war—the CCP believed such a release would simply become the focal point for further controversy. It became increasingly known, however, that the UN estimate of immovable refugee property, as of the mid-1960s when the CCP's Land Office was closed, was more than twice the figure previously released by the Commission back in 1951. That is to say, whereas the CCP had originally placed the

---

[39] Details of the methodology for evaluation can be found starting on p. 13 in A/AC.25/W.84. It is of interest to note that the CCP occasionally found errors in the tax records of the mandatory governments. In these instances the CCP tried to make a fair adjustment of the figures so that its own evaluation would be equitable.

value, in 1947 terms, of that property at some $240,000,000, it now privately suggested approximately $480,000,000 as the basic figure. Furthermore, several UN officials experimented with various means of adjusting this base figure to account for changing land values, currency values, and possible income from the property had it been in use by Palestinian owners during the time after 1947. The minimum figure arrived at after adjustment in UN circles was around $1,500,000,000. Other estimated adjustments ran from twice to seven times that amount, depending, of course, upon what type of adjustment equation was employed.[40] Whatever the range for the base figure and the adjusted figure, the latter was altered by the 1967 war and the former remained controversial.

From the Paris conference of 1951 to the third Arab-Israeli war, the CCP's quasi-functionalism achieved little—as might have been expected—from both the nature of the political context and the nature of the Commission's undertakings. The most obvious feature of the CCP's existence during this period was the lack of progress toward peacemaking on the basis of the Commission's technical efforts. The quasi-functionalism had succeeded in wasting time, and it had "kept the door open" for further UN involvement in the Palestine question. But neither the work on blocked bank accounts nor identification and evaluation created a foundation for Arab-Israeli agreement.

Efforts toward "unfreezing" accounts did give a preview of the form of future CCP activity: the use of single diplomats in the place of the three-government Commission. Palmer worked alone on the question of accounts, although he obtained and retained the formal backing of the CCP as a whole. When conflicts arose over the release operation, troubleshooter Reedman worked alone to alleviate the problems. When a new stage of unfreezing was reached, the principal secretary of the CCP handled the technical negotiations with the banks involved.

---

[40] The author wishes to emphasize that these figures are unofficial and that they pertain to refugee property as identified and evaluated prior to the 1967 Arab-Israeli war. These figures are based on interviews with officials involved in the evaluation effort.

Efforts at identification and evaluation met with even less success than efforts regarding blocked accounts. Not only were the evaluation data withheld from public knowledge for fear of further conflict, the CCP's methodology in the identification process was subjected to criticism as well.

Some four years after the identification and evaluation were largely completed and two years after the CCP published the methodology used, the Arab states challenged the validity of the CCP effort. In April 1966, the Arab states concerned sent a letter to the Commission designed to "draw attention to the fact that the work needs more adequate examination."[41] To the Arabs, the CCP's treatment of identification did not "fully and truly represent the situation with regard to Arab property" because of a number of factors. Among those listed were the absence of mandatory records for several types of property, the lack of coverage of Arab rights to grazing land and to uncultivatable land, and the CCP's identification method for the district of Beersheba. In addition to these technical arguments, the Arab states asserted three politico-legal arguments of a more general nature regarding identification. According to these Arab states, since the mandatory government had large property holdings, these holdings should revert to the population; therefore the Arabs who lived in Palestine had a right to that property in direct proportion to their numerical strength in 1947. Moreover, the Palestinian Arabs had a right to the movable property of the mandatory government such as vehicles, office furniture, telephone equipment, and the like, "which was seized *in toto* by Israel." Finally, the Arabs charged that many Arab villages, buildings, and plantations were destroyed by the Israelis and that their identity was thus destroyed; yet the CCP's report did not mention them.

As far as evaluation was concerned, the Arab states likewise rejected the CCP's work in this area. In general, the Arabs charged that CCP estimates would necessarily be too low because the tax

---

[41] Statements from the April 1966 letter are drawn from UN Doc. A/AC.25/W.85, 16 May 1966, pp. 1–6.

data used for evaluation did not list the fair value of the different forms of property. The Arab states concluded that for the reasons cited, " . . . the report of the Land Expert of the United Nations Conciliation Commission is found to be unacceptable for its inconsonance with reality and its unfairness to Arab rights." The Arabs went on to stress that Arabs accounted for ninety-eight percent of property owners in Palestine at the start of the mandate, and that as of 1947 Jewish ownership still amounted to only six percent of the total. In the Arabs' opinion, the formulation of estimates by the CCP as reported did not give the Arabs sufficient rights in keeping with their status in Palestine, and as a result of this belief the Arab states asserted that the CCP's work contradicted the spirit and letter of past General Assembly resolutions.

The comments of the Arab states and the lack of a public policy statement from the Israeli government on the Commission's identification and evaluation notwithstanding, it would seem that the work of the CCP on identification and evaluation of Arab refugee property in Israel was one of the more difficult technical undertakings of the United Nations and one that in general was performed capably. In reply to the Arab letter of April 1966, the CCP's technical officials prepared a rebuttal for the private reading of the Commission's members, and the CCP as a whole was satisfied with the statement. Several of the Arab objections were directed toward issues which were outside the CCP's chosen frame of reference. In particular, the Arab claims to former mandatory property, whether well-founded or not, pertained to issues which would have to be decided through legal rulings or negotiated solutions, not through the CCP work on private property holdings. Moreover, the Commission stated frankly that in some areas of its work the data were incomplete; it would follow from this that where better proof of ownership and cultivation rights, *inter alia*, could be presented, the CCP would be willing to alter its findings. And it would appear that some of the more extreme demands of the Arab states would be offset by Israeli claims, such as for reparations, thus bringing the CCP's conclusions to the forefront as a reasonable compromise.

The CCP tried to engage the Arab states in negotiations after the Arabs had submitted their letter of criticism in April 1966. In May of that year the CCP wrote to the Arab states: "In response to what it feels is the spirit of this letter, the Commission would welcome consideration, by its Technical Representative and by the delegations or land experts of the host governments, of the technical aspects of these observations, leaving aside the broader issues which they raise, in order to clarify any technical problems which may arise from misunderstanding or misapprehension." The CCP went on to say that it has always been concerned with Arab property rights in Israel within the terms of its mandate, especially paragraph 11 of A/Res/194.[42] The Arab states did not respond to this letter, nor did they respond favorably to initiatives carried out privately by some technical officials without the authorization of the CCP per se. Thus the CCP, and the CCP's technical officials operating on their own, made an attempt to keep the Arab letter of April 1966 from becoming a rejection of their efforts. But these efforts were to no avail.

Despite the long and involved work of the CCP and the reasonableness of its conclusions, at least on identification, the fact remains that there was little progress from its efforts. A few individual refugees have diposed of their holdings within Israel, using the CCP appraisals as a guide in making claims vis-à-vis Israeli officials, who have made their own evaluations. Other refugees have checked with the CCP regarding their property in order to settle a family dispute or just to inquire about the CCP's figures. The Commission's technical work could constitute a starting point for reasonably fair compensation to Palestinian refugees, far superior to the global estimate of 1951, given a change of view of the parties. But the technical work itself has not provided a stimulus for changing those views.

It cannot be stressed enough that the CCP was dealing with a massive problem and that occasionally official records were lacking. It appears that the Commission compensated for these documentary gaps with reasoned judgments. The CCP's report on

[42] See *ibid.*, p. 7.

identification and evaluation does not constitute absolute proof of all refugee property holdings, nor does it give an unchallengeable system of valuation. But the CCP appears justified in concluding that "everything possible short of physical inspection was done to take into account the various factors which affect the value in the open market of any particular parcel of land."[43] The CCP also seems to be on firm ground in saying that the results obtained from the application of the published methodology "would be fair and reasonable" to the refugees, subject to better proof of ownership presented to the Commission.[44]

[43] A/AC.25/W.84, p. 29.

[44] *Ibid.*, p. 31.

V

THE "SPECIAL REPRESENTATIVE" APPROACH

As the United Nations moved toward completion of its effort to identify and evaluate Arab refugee property in the early 1960s, efforts were made to rejuvenate the CCP through use of a Special Representative. This little-known mission proved to be significant for numerous reasons. It was, of course, the last effort to ameliorate the Arab-Israeli conflict, through alteration of the refugee problem, prior to the Six-Day War of 1967. The mission also more clearly illuminated the real—as opposed to the publicized—policies of the parties directly involved. And the Special Representative approach provided a point of comparison for analysis of the earlier CCP efforts in 1949-51. To be sure, the contexts for UN involvement were not identical in 1949 and 1961. By the 1960s, attitudes had hardened, the refugee problem had increased in dimension, and Israel had gained increased acceptance among non-Arab states. Yet the comparison remains useful. Advantages to the United Nations from the use of nongovernmental personnel become evident, as do the limitations inherent in that approach.

That the refugee question had increased in dimension from the late 1940s to the 1960s was an all-too-evident fact.[1] The

---

[1] For an overview of the changing refugee problem, see Fred J. Khouri, *The Arab-Israeli Dilemma* (Syracuse: Syracuse University Press, 1968).

number of refugees had grown through natural increase from some 750,000 to well over one million. Individuals grew up as second-generation Palestinians, never knowing any life but that of the refugee camps. They were easily mobilized into hate campaigns, a natural enough development given their daily frustrations, as the growth of the Palestinian commando organizations after 1967 was to demonstrate.

UN assistance to the refugees through UNRWA, based chiefly on US contributions, remained crucial but at the subsistence level. An early effort by UNRWA to resettle the refugees had been abortive,[2] and the number of refugees assimilated into either Jordan or Lebanon declined rapidly after the skilled laborers were taken. This left UNRWA with the prospect of providing direct relief ad infinitum. The same politico-psychological considerations that blocked resettlement, in addition to some economic factors, also operated to limit the impact of UNRWA educational programs. Both refugees and Arab governments limited UNRWA's effort to provide vocational training that might lead to further de facto resettlement by making refugees into productive and therefore desirable citizens for one of the Arab nations. Thus UNRWA was not able to contribute to resettlement, directly or inadvertently. Despite impressive accomplishments for UNRWA in the most trying of circumstances in terms of providing for the basic physical needs of the refugees, the refugee question continued to grow and fester.

The Kennedy Administration viewed this state of affairs as both a pressing humanitarian problem and as a possible stepping stone toward the amelioration of fundamental tensions in the region. Some US officials thought that yet another effort to do something about the refugee question, although it might fail, would still have the merit of pinning the responsibility for that failure directly on the Arabs or Israelis; this would then free the Assembly from further polemics on the issue. Hence, the Kennedy Administration moved to have the CCP use a Special Represen-

---

[2] See Don Peretz, *Israel and the Palestine Arabs* (Washington, D.C.: The Middle East Institute, 1956), chap. 3.

tative to seek a solution to the refugee question. On the one hand, the United States hesitated to use the existing CCP as a format for diplomacy, since it was wary, if not suspicious, of French intentions in the Middle East. But, on the other hand, use of the United Nations offered the United States a useful forum for the attempt to mobilize the interest of other states in the project. Moreover, the United States would not be directly responsible for the outcome of the mission and thus would not be publicly risking its prestige by overtly supporting a particular policy.

The US government eventually secured the cooperation of France and Turkey for the Special Representative approach; and using the 1960 Assembly request for an "intensification" of CCP efforts to implement paragraph 11 of A/Res/194(III) as a mandate for action, President Kennedy began to try and encourage the parties concerned to reevaluate their positions. He first sought to build bridges to the Arab world by writing to President Nasir of the United Arab Republic, among others, that US policy "will continue to be anchored in the firm bedrock of support for General Assembly recommendations concerning refugees. . . . We are determined to use our influence toward a just and peaceful solution."[3] Later he sent one of his advisers, Myer Feldman, to Israel with the promise of US military support in the event of Arab aggression.[4]

In the meantime, the Commission sought a man for its mission and finally selected Joseph E. Johnson, president of the Carnegie Endowment for International Peace.[5] An American and former member of the State Department, Johnson was to spend more time negotiating with US officials than with Israel or the Arab states, since he believed only the United States was in a

[3] *Middle East Record* (Jerusalem, Israel: Israel Program for Scientific Translations, 1961), 2: 197–99.

[4] *New York Times*, 16 June 1968, p. 5.

[5] The CCP first asked A. R. Lindt of Switzerland, formerly UN High Commissioner for Refugees. Lindt deliberated several months and at last declined the nomination because: his own "soundings" did not indicate much likelihood of progress, he did not expect much support from the Assembly, and he did not consider the CCP an appropriate base from which to operate.

position to underwrite the financial burden of a settlement and bring effective pressure to bear on Israel should that be necessary. Yet Johnson was in no way taking instructions from the US government. The outcome of his efforts was to demonstrate how separate was his position from that government's. For most of his two years as Special Representative, Johnson also operated rather independently of the Commission. He preferred it that way, for he was aware of the close liaison between France and Israel during the early 1960s; the United States preferred the mission that way for the same reason; and the French and Turks were at least content for Johnson to proceed without close supervision, perhaps so they could absolve themselves of responsibility for anything that might happen.[6]

Johnson spent the first three weeks of September 1961, in the Middle East. Regional politics were relatively tranquil during this period, and it appeared to be a propitious time to tackle the refugee question. Johnson did nothing to inflame public opinion in the region and described his talks with the parties as "friendly and frank" or "interesting and useful."[7] Relatively vague discussions with the separate Arab leaders took place in a realistic and quiet tone with few Arab public statements. Johnson then went to Israel where he encountered more overt resistance to his mission. The Israeli leaders proved very difficult to deal with, and the antagonistic attitude of Israel's Prime Minister produced an early crisis in the mission. The Israelis were skeptical of the Johnson mission from the start. They did not have a high regard for past UN involvement on the Palestine question, and they thought Johnson was working for something which, ipso facto, was detrimental to their interests. Johnson proceeded along general lines, as he had in the Arab countries, and tried to discover what

[6] A spokesman for the Quai d'Orsay played down the importance of the Johnson mission. He gave the United States responsibility for initiation of the mission and stressed that it was a fact-finding mission only. *Jerusalem Post,* 29 August 1961, p. 1.

[7] At the time the disputants had agreed to receive the Johnson mission, the Secretary-General had requested a news blackout on the substance of the talks. This request was observed for the most part in 1961. Violation of this request in 1962 was to lead to serious difficulties.

avenue might lead to some progress. He proposed no particular settlement outline but rather indicated he was there to listen. Despite the general nature of the discussions, Israel began to read into the mission an effort to give a "free choice" to the refugees. Johnson had made no such proposal, but Prime Minister Ben Gurion told the Knesset:

> Israel categorically rejects the insidious proposal for freedom of choice for the refugees, for she is convinced that this proposal is designed and calculated only to destroy Israel. There is only one practical and fair solution for the problem of the refugees: to resettle them among their own people in countries having plenty of good land and water and which are in need of additional manpower.[8]

The Knesset later adopted a resolution which stated "that the Arab refugees should not be returned to Israel territory, and that the sole solution to the problem is their settlement in the Arab countries."[9] Israeli Foreign Minister Meir was quoted as saying that some further repatriation might be possible via the family reunification scheme.[10]

After these talks but prior to submitting a report to the CCP, Johnson gave draft copies of a proposed report to the parties involved and invited their comments. The changes made pursuant

---

[8] *Jerusalem Post,* 12 October 1961, p. 1. In a detailed exposition of Israeli policy, the Prime Minister listed six reasons why Israel rejected repatriation, in addition to reasons of security. (1) The refugees from World War II had been resettled, and the same process should be applied to the Palestinian refugees. (2) "Almost all the Arab refugees" had left Israel prior to the creating of the state. (3) Thirty thousand refugees had already been repatriated through the family reunification scheme. (4) The Arabs left because of the orders of the Mufti to do so. (5) Israel had accepted Jews from Arab lands, and this represented an exchange of populations since equal numbers were involved. (6) Israel already had a number of refugees from the Palestine war (for example, the Jewish refugees from the old city of Jerusalem). Ben Gurion went on to say that compensation was dependent upon an overall settlement and was further tied to compensation for Jewish land left behind in the Arab states by immigrants to Israel. If the Arabs agreed to enter into direct talks pursuant to a peace treaty, Israel would "give all possible assistance towards the settlement of the refugees among their own people. . . . "

[9] Knesset resolution of 6 November, reprinted in the *Jerusalem Post,* 7 November 1961, p. 1. The vote on the resolution was 68–7.

[10] *Jerusalem Post,* 19 November 1961, p. 1.

to these suggestions further worsened Johnson's relations with Israeli officials; particularly annoyed was the Israeli Foreign Minister.[11] In revising his report, Johnson had made numerous changes on the basis of suggestions received from the Arab states. He rejected other Arab suggestions. Israel offered no suggestions. When the final report was presented, Foreign Minister Meir became piqued that an earlier reference to the Arab rejection of the partition resolution and subsequent use of force was omitted in the final copy, as was a reference to the Arab rejection of the Hammarskjold report of the late 1950s. Other Israeli diplomats were impressed by Johnson's report, particularly the part where he spoke of the need to consider the total Palestine question for a proper treatment of the refugee issue, but they were not able to persuade Mrs. Meir to alter her view of the changes.

The CCP expressed support for Johnson's report, and in introducing his findings, the Commission praised Johnson for reopening channels of communication; the CCP stated that it "warmly" endorsed his report.[12]

Johnson's basic finding after his preliminary conversations was that all parties wanted peace in a general way but were not willing to make the specific sacrifices necessary to attain that peace in reality. The passage of time had hardened "public positions on some issues." Moreover, Johnson had found mutual fear present, which "underlies, and to a certain extent probably explains, governmental policies. . . ." This factor Johnson cited as a major barrier to progress. Johnson concluded that the parties viewed the refugee problem as part of the larger Palestine question, but that there was some possibility for a step-by-step handling of the refugee question as an isolated issue. In reaching these conclusions, Johnson stated that he was aware that national interests were intertwined with a humanitarian concern for the plight of the refugees. He did not believe that those national

[11] Findings of this study confirm the general accuracy of the story appearing in the *Jerusalem Post* on this friction; 29 November 1961, p. 1.

[12] UN Doc. A/4921/Add. 1, 22 November 1961. All quotes relating to Johnson's report are from this document unless otherwise stated.

interests should be surrendered, but he thought it was possible for them to be "harmonized" with the other relevant interests. Johnson saw a long period of international assistance to the refugees under any settlement, and he thought that an overall settlement would be required for the complete solution of the refugee problem. He finished by quoting Hammarskjold to the effect that when the United Nations failed to gain support for its decision, frequently it was the member states who were at fault and not the organization itself.

Johnson's first report was passed along by the CCP to the Assembly where it fell under attack by Arab delegations participating in the annual debate regarding UNRWA and the refugees. An isolated personal attack on Johnson[13] was accompanied by the expected attacks on the CCP,[14] and the core of Arab public statements continued to center on the right of unqualified repatriation as the only solution to the refugee question.[15] Despite these public criticisms of the Johnson mission from Arab delegations, and despite continued efforts to change the composition of the CCP and invest it with custodial functions over refugee property in Israel, the Assembly ultimately requested the CCP to continue its efforts pursuant to paragraph 11 of A/Res/194(III).[16] The Commission also went through the motions of formally reappointing Johnson, and this time the CCP asked him to make recommendations concerning the implementation of paragraph 11 of A/Res/194(III).

[13] GAOR: 16th Sess., Special Political Committee, p. 243.

[14] See the statements by the Syrian and UAR spokesmen in *ibid.*, pp. 269–81. See also pp. 283–84 and 287–90 for Tunisian and Jordanian statements following this same trend.

[15] See the statements by Emile Ghory, a spokesman for the Mufti, and by the Lebanese delegate, in *ibid.*, pp. 262–96.

[16] The proposals to enlarge the CCP and to invest it with custodial functions over Arab property in Israel once again received a majority vote in the Special Political Committee but failed to receive the necessary majority vote in plenary session. Regarding continuation of CCP work pursuant to paragraph 11, the Arabs voted in opposition in committee, then abstained on the plenary vote. Israel defended the traditional composition and mandate of the CCP, abstained on the committee vote to continue work on the refugee question, then voted affirmatively in plenary session.

The regional political context was not as good in 1962 as it had been in 1961. In addition to an Israeli-Syrian crisis in late March, which resulted in a Security Council censure for Israel, the Arab world was caught up in exacerbated intra-Arab rivalries. The turmoil culminated in an Egyptian-Syrian conflict during one of the sessions of the Arab League, meeting in August at Shtoura, Lebanon.[17] One of the charges levied by Syria was that Nasir was becoming "soft" on Israel. In this context, as in 1949, it could be politically dangerous for an Arab leader to reach a settlement with Israel on the refugee question since such a leader might be subjected to the charge that he was dealing with "the enemy." In Nasir's case, he might lose his claim to being leader of the Arab world if such a charge were repeated too often.

Going to Israel first this time, Johnson began to speak in general terms of a pilot project involving a relatively small number of refugees at first, after an initial determination of preferences by the refugees about their future residence. Johnson set no precise figures, although Israeli officials wanted to talk in terms of specific numbers. At one point Johnson mentioned the figure of fifty thousand families as a possible repatriation project, but this suggestion was not well received. Israeli authorities still viewed any repatriation as a threat to the state's security, and they were skeptical of allowing a determination of preferences for the refugees. They feared a large number would want to be repatriated and therefore they wanted to set in advance a definite and small limit to those that might be repatriated.

In the Arab countries the clearest opposition to the pilot project came from Jordan. The Jordanian officials were quite articulate in expressing their policies; their main concern as expected was the protection of the Hashimite regime. They stated explicitly that their speeches in the General Assembly were to be discounted: Jordan did not want paragraph 11 of A/Res/194(III) implemented separately from an overall settlement or as a prelude

---

[17] The dispute became so heated that the records of that session of the Arab League Council have been removed from the rest of the League records. See Robert W. MacDonald, *The League of Arab States* (Princeton: Princeton University Press, 1965). See also *Al-Ahram*, 22 August–21 September 1962.

to any other diplomatic action. It was the Jordanian position that the refugee question had to be approached simultaneously with territorial and other aspects of the Palestine question in order to be resolved. As long as Israel maintained its current territory and desired more immigration, Jordan would not feel secure. It viewed Israel as an aggressive state because of the Jewish capture of Palestine, its Suez venture, and its potential for action vis-à-vis Jordan in 1962.

A second series of fears underlined this first Jordanian fear of insecurity. It was the Jordanian officials' opinion that under any program permitting a listing of desired alternatives, most of the refugees would choose not to return to Israel and would remain in Jordan as dissatisfied troublemakers. Moreover, the Jordanian authorities believed that a sizable number of those who did opt for and receive repatriation would become unhappy with life in Israel, would dispose of their holdings there, and would return to Jordan full of bitterness for the regime that had waited so long to send them back to their homes. And a gradual approach, according to the Jordanian leaders, would take too long for the regime to execute without its losing the confidence of the Palestinians. Thus Jordanian officials opposed a gradual pilot project, since they feared a threat to the regime's stability from domestic repercussions.

Nevertheless, Johnson continued to try to persuade the parties to accept some form of a pilot project involving a limited but open-ended start on repatriation. The Israelis continued to ask for specific numbers and clearly defined limitations.[18] In general the Arabs seemed noncommittal, although Johnson pointed out that by accepting his recommendation they could bypass direct talks and public treaties. Johnson also warned that certain Western states might be reexamining their contributions to UNRWA and reexamining their tolerance of Arab propaganda attacks in the

[18] The Israelis wanted a specific, if indirect, dialogue to develop among the disputants. They recalled the tactics of Eric Johnston, who related specific statements from one party to the other. The Israelis particularly wanted this type of specific dialogue on the refugee question, since the security risks seemed great to them.

131

General Assembly.[19] But Jordan began to lead an active opposition to the Johnson mission by stirring up public and government opinion against an inaccurate version of the substance of the negotiations.[20] By leaking a story to a Beirut newspaper,[21] Jordan tried to put itself on public record as rejecting a pilot project involving the repatriation of 250 thousand refugees. The story reported Jordan as saying, *inter alia,* that such an approach involved the selling of Palestine to Israel.

Johnson, back in New York, was dismayed by the disclosure of this inaccurate version of his talks with Jordan and of the Jordanian opposition to any pilot project. He considered terminating his efforts since there seemed to be little hope of achieving the implementation of limited repatriation and limited resettlement on a trial basis, in the light of the Jordanian early public rejection. Nevertheless, Johnson decided to try to find an alternative approach based on the two rounds of conversation completed. He worked on this new approach for the duration of the summer of 1962, maintained contact with US officials and the representatives of the parties in New York, but did not make another trip to the Middle East. Some bilateral contact on the issue took place between the United States and Israel.

Having completed an alternative plan by the end of the summer, Johnson then faced a decision regarding his tactics that was to prove important. Three alternatives seemed available: to seek further negotiations with the parties on the basis of the plan; to seek CCP and perhaps Assembly endorsement of the plan

---

[19] Johnson was not supported by government persuasion at this time. The United States intentionally did not enter the negotiations. Rather it asked the United Kingdom to support Johnson. The United Kingdom declined since it was not optimistic regarding Johnson's ultimate success and thus wanted to do nothing to jeopardize its relations with the Arabs. Unimpeachable source.

[20] This effort was led by a group of Arabs meeting informally in Amman: Prime Minister Tall and Foreign Minister Nasaybah of Jordan, the ubiquitous Shuqayri, Dr. Tannlus of the Palestine Higher Committee, *inter alios.* Subsequently, Jordan sent communiqués to other Arab governments in order to build opposition to a pilot project, and Shuqayri was dispatched to Arab capitals to explain Jordan's position. For partially accurate commentary, see *Mideast Mirror: A Review of Middle East News,* vol. 14, nos. 17, 18, 19.

[21] See *Beirut Daily Star,* 29 May 1962, p. 1.

without further negotiations; to seek Arab and Israeli comments on the plan without further field negotations and without any offical endorsement of the plan. After some indecision, the last alternative was elected by Johnson and the member governments of the CCP, in the hope that the series of proposals would eventually be endorsed by the Assembly and implemented by the parties without a formal declaration or treaty.

In the Johnson plan,[22] the Special Representative stated explicitly that he did not think a negotiated settlement could be obtained on the basis of paragraph 11 of A/Res/194(III), which, of course, called for repatriation, resettlement, and compensation for the refugees. Moreover, Johnson stated that he saw no likelihood of any early settlement of the larger Palestine question. Nevertheless, Johnson went on to make a series of proposals that, in his opinion, could lead to progress on the refugee question.

According to Johnson, there were several fundamental considerations upon which progress could be made. First, the wishes of the refugees must be given priority. Second, the legitimate interests of the states concerned must be safeguarded. Third, the United Nations could play the role of harmonizer when these first two considerations conflicted. Johnson went on to explain in some detail what he meant by these three fundamentals in his approach. In particular he stressed that Israel's existence could not be allowed to be threatened by the return of any refugees. Johnson reasoned that Israel was recognized as a state by many other states, even though Israel was not a member of the United Nations when A/Res/194(III) was passed; thus it had a legitimate interest in protecting its security. Because of this, it was necessary, said Johnson, to include the following qualification on the repatriation of the refugees: any state to which a refugee

---

[22] The complete plan has never been made public. The *Chicago Daily News* on 1 October 1962 published part of the contents of the plan; this version was accurate but not complete. The *Boston Globe* and *Washington Post* picked up the story on 2 October, the *New York Times* on 3 October, and the *Christian Science Monitor* on 4 October. These latter articles were likewise incomplete but were accurate in what was printed. Some of the basic concepts involved in Johnson's plan are contained in his article, "Arab v. Israeli: A Persistent Challenge," *Middle East Journal* 18, no. 1 (Winter 1964): 1–13. The present account is based on an unimpeachable source.

expressed a desire to go was to have the final say as to whether or not permission was to be granted for that refugee to enter. This provision also applied to the Arab states or to states outside the Middle East. Johnson went on to state that the United Nations had an obligation to use every legitimate means at its disposal to urge and assist the parties concerned to implement paragraph 11 as interpreted. The states concerned, said Johnson, had an obligation to cooperate with the United Nations in this effort in good faith.

Johnson next indicated the specific elements drawn from the fundamental considerations. (1) The wishes of the refugees were to be ascertained confidentially by the United Nations. (2) The refugees were to be shielded by the United Nations from external influence as they made their decisions. (3) The refugees were to be told what choices were available to them, that their first choice might not be granted, and that their first choice was not necessarily the final option that they could exercise. The refugees were to be given the right of choosing any country they wished for their future domicile. (4) The refugees were to be told as exactly as possible what their choice would entail for their future, particularly with regard to their return to a Jewish state. (5) With regard to repatriation, the United Nations was to exercise oversight of that operation, and the supervisory machinery was to have the authority to report directly to the General Assembly. (6) With regard to payment of compensation, the base-1947-value obtained by the CCP was not to be the only factor considered, since the refugees had not had the use of their property since their departure and since exchange standards had been altered. From communal Arab property in Palestine, a special fund was to be created that was to be used for the erection of communal facilities for nonrepatriated refugees. A general compensation fund was to be established by the United Nations, to which Israel was expected to contribute. The United Nations was also to establish a reintegration allowance which was to be used to help settle the refugees and help compensate for the dislocation and hardship that they had endured since 1947–48. In addition, Israel was to pay compensation for those homes which were no longer available to those returning. (7) The United Nations was to oversee

134

resettlement operations and aid in that undertaking as needed. (8) The new UN administrative organ foreseen was to exercise leadership in all phases of this plan and was to be advised by the parties concerned.

In addition to his fundamental considerations and specific elements, Johnson spoke of four concepts entailed in his proposals. The parties concerned were to grant their acquiescence in this undertaking. They were to be expected to indicate their willingness to allow the stated operations to go forward and to cooperate in good faith with the responsible UN officials. These officials would require the normal privileges and immunities, would need to be able to supply accurate information to the refugees, and would need to be able to be available to the refugees for confidential conversations. Second, repatriation and resettlement were to be undertaken simultaneously in order that mutual fear by the parties might be dispelled. Third, any party was to have the right to disengage from the process, so that the initial acquiescence would not be binding if, for example, a state's security became endangered. Fourth, the entire process would be gradual. The undertaking would be initiated slowly, with small but unspecified numbers of refugees involved. The parties concerned would want to observe how matters were progressing, and the United Nations would want time in which to gain experience.

Within a relatively short period of time Israel indicated to Johnson that his proposals were unacceptable.[23] The main Israeli objection concerned the provision of a listing of preferences by the refugees, for Israel still thought that the greatest number of refugees would opt for repatriation.[24] In addition, the Israelis did not believe that the United Nations would be able to conduct a

[23] Unimpeachable source.

[24] There is no indication that Israeli officials took much notice of the Jordanian attitudes expressed through the Beirut papers in late May, and there is no indication that Israeli officials reevaluated their opinion of refugee desires on the basis that if Jordan was against Johnson's pilot project then Israel should have some reason to be for it. The Jordanian leak to the Beirut press was reported in Israeli papers, but there were no editorials pursuant to that report. There is no indication that the Israelis considered the possibility that many of the refugees would not want to be repatriated.

fair tabulation; they did not think that the United Nations would be able to shield the refugees from Arab propaganda or be able to counteract the effects of the propaganda that had been directed toward the refugees during the period since 1947–48. Moreover, some Israeli officials reacted adversely to what they viewed as the relative suddenness with which the proposals were presented to them.

Shortly thereafter the Arab states concerned presented a uniform statement to Johnson indicating that while their comments should not be taken as a rejection of the plan, they did not consider it a suitable framework for a fruitful discussion since Israel had not given assurance of its clear and unconditional acceptance of paragraph 11.[25] The Arabs were in an uncomfortable diplomatic position at this time, by their own admission. They had long argued publicly for the implementation of paragraph 11 as based on the preferences of the refugees, and now an effort had been made that was difficult to reject—because it was consistent to a large degree with their past public statements. But the Arab states, particularly Jordan, did not want that paragraph as a basis for actual UN action, apart from the other aspects of the Palestine question. Syria had never been inclined toward reaching agreement with Israel on the refugee issue, and the United Arab Republic was content to follow Jordan's lead on the matter. Lebanon, as usual, had a coattail approach and also deferred to the stand expressed by Jordan. Hence the Arab states gave an indefinite reply to Johnson and hoped that while they waited Israel would reject the plan publicly and "take them off the hook." Ambasador Rifa'i of Jordan apparently drew up such a rejection, but it was not presented at this time.

After these first reactions of the parties were made known, relations among Israel, the four Arab states, the United States, the CCP, and Johnson drifted—that is, they were indeterminate. Israel avoided taking a public stand on the proposals, but it continued to express to US officials its opposition to the plan. Israel, too, was waiting for the other side to reject the plan publicly. For its part,

[25] Unimpeachable source.

136

the United States did not give any official reply to these informal comments by Israel; and the more Israel gave an informal "no," the more it seemed that the United States might take this answer to be an informal "yes." In any event, Israel felt the need to continue stating its opposition, and talk of support for the proposals continued to be heard in various quarters around the United Nations in the early fall of 1962. The Arabs also avoided giving a public statement on their position regarding the proposals, and the CCP took no further action, either to back Johnson or to table his plan.

Then, for the second time, a press leak occurred which affected the Johnson mission.[26] On 1 October the *Chicago Daily News* printed a story on the proposals, and it was apparent that the reporter had had access to the actual plan. The State Department on 3 October confirmed the accuracy of the printed version; but on the following day the Department's spokesman shied away from supporting Johnson and said that neither the CCP nor the United States had taken an official position on the entire subject.[27] Then Syria rejected Johnson's plan publicly[28] in a unilateral move that took the other three Arab governments by surprise. Israel continued to give no public statement on the subject except to say that it had already indicated its rejection at the time the plan became known,[29] but on 12 November Foreign

[26] See note 22 above.

[27] For a concise account of events on 3 and 4 October, see the *Jerusalem Post,* 5 October 1962, p. 1.

[28] The Syrian rejection was published later in *Al-Sada al-'Amm,* 6 October 1962. Foreign Minister Al-'Azm was quoted as saying that Johnson should have worked on the total question, not just on the refugee issue. Johnson's plan was said to "conflict with the spirit and text" of A/Res/194(III). The crux of the Syrian argument was that the plan "paves the way for the liquidation of the Palestine problem in a final manner and in favor of Israel." Johnson's efforts were termed "a Zionist-imperialist conspiracy," and a plea was made for concern for "humanitarian values and the principles of right and justice." Syria then called on the other Arab states to "save Palestine," and it indicated that it "firmly and determinedly rejects the Johnson plan."

[29] *Jerusalem Post,* 4 October 1962, p. 1. But by late October Foreign Minister Meir was still refusing to give an official statement of Israel's policy on the Johnson plan (*ibid.,* 23 October 1962, p. 1). Meir and Rusk had been having talks on the plan, and

Minister Meir told the Knesset that resettlement was the only possible solution to the refugee problem. According to Mrs. Meir, this did not mean that Israel's policy was "no not a single refugee" but that the solution to the refugee problem was to be found in the Arab lands. The refugee question had to be considered in the context of Arab belligerency, the chief example of which at this time was Nasir's intervention in Yemen.[30] Subsequently, the Knesset adopted a resolution in which it reiterated its resolution of November 1961 "to the effect that the Arab refugees should not be returned to the territory of Israel and that the only solution to their problem is their resettlement in the Arab states."[31]

Despite all the rejections and denunciations, the outcome of the Johnson mission remained in doubt throughout the fall of 1962—chiefly because of the undetermined policy of the United States. The United States had thus far hesitated to press for CCP endorsement as a step toward Assembly endorsement of Johnson's approach. Likewise, France and Turkey made no move to have the CCP take a stand on Johnson's plan. Both of these states appeared "uncomfortable" about the prospects of having to participate in some decisive action pursuant to the Johnson mission. These states were thus a restraining rather than a stimulating influence in the United States.

But the United States remained undecided about whether or not to use persuasion and pressure in support of Johnson. On the one hand, it did not want to antagonize the Arab world; on the other hand, it was aware of the Jewish vote in the approaching congressional elections. It therefore sought to delay action until after those elections. Its effort to delay in making a final decision

---

there had been press speculation in Israel that there was support for the implementation of the plan over a two-year period (*ibid.*, 7 October 1962, p. 1).

[30] *Ibid.*, 13 November 1962, pp. 1, 3. It is of interest to note that the United Arab Republic had made relatively few public statements against either Israel or Johnson in the fall of 1962. In this context Israel still was skeptical of Nasir's intentions and cited his intervention in Yemen as a cause for alarm.

[31] *Ibid.*, 14 November 1962, p. 1.

on the Johnson mission was stimulated by Zionist lobbying against the Johnson plan.[32]

After those elections President Kennedy met with top officials from the State Department in early December in order to determine policy with regard to the Johnson mission. It was decided at that meeting, on the basis of two primary factors, not to seek the implementation of the Johnson plan at that time. The primary reason for this decision was the rejection of the plan by all parties. State Department personnel had been looking for some official acceptance "somewhere along the line." Without this acceptance by at least one or two of the states concerned, the State Department did not believe that the probability of success for a supporting diplomatic effort was great enough to run the risk of incurring possible damage to other US interests in the area. Had one or more of the Middle Eastern states accepted the proposals, it appears that the United States would have attempted to use that entrée to reason with the other parties and perhaps take other measures designed to secure a wider acceptance of Johnson's ideas. But without at least this small indication of likelihood for progress, the President and the State Department officials agreed that the plan should not be "pushed" at that time. President Kennedy's first question had been to this effect: if we seek to implement this plan, are we going to succeed? The chances for success did not appear good to US officials, especially since the United States had other interests in the region—such as access to communication channels and to oil supplies and the limitation of the Soviet Union's influence—that could be involved in an attempt to persuade or influence the parties to accept Johnson's proposals.

The second factor that led to a dropping of the Johnson plan was Jewish influence in the American political process. President

[32] In these lobbying activities in both UN and US political processes, there was an attempt to distort Johnson's recommendations. It was said that Johnson had proposed a free choice for the refugees and that Israel did not have the right to reject refugees for security reasons. See Johnson's reference to this distortion in "Arab v. Israeli," p. 9, n. 5. Later in the General Assembly, a US spokesman requested the delegations "not to give credence to distorting rumors which had been circulated" about the Johnson plan (GAOR: 17th Sess., Special Political Committee, p. 206).

Kennedy was aware that an attempt to persuade Israel to accept the Johnson plan against its stated opinion would cause a political feedback in the United States, led by the Zionist groups. The recent lobby activities by the American Zionist groups and by the individual supporters of Israel had reached the President, partly through the President's adviser, Myer Feldman. Moreover, the President was aware of the Jewish support and vote that were important to the Democratic party. Therefore, while the major national interests of the United States—to US decisionmakers—appeared to stand against any exertion of pressure on the Arab states, a desire to avoid political repercussions appeared to impede exertion of pressure on Israel.

The decision was also made not to publicize the Johnson plan. This was designed to avoid criticism of Johnson himself and to avoid pointless acrimony that would only exacerbate already present hostilities. It was also an attempt to preserve the integrity of Johnson's plan so that in the future the plan might be used when the context was more propitious to its implementation. There was still some hope that, like the Eric Johnston plan on the Jordan waters problem, the Joseph Johnson plan on the refugee question might be implemented to some degree in a quiet, de facto process. Subsequently, the CCP presented a bland report to the Assembly in which it was stated that the "most significant" aspect of the CCP's recent work had been the Johnson mission, but it gave no important details of that mission and bypassed the subject of his proposals.[33]

Member governments of the General Assembly did not try to obtain more information from the CCP about its Special Representative approach. Most were content to let the matter drop without extensive debate.[34] The disputants engaged in the now-expected

---

[33] UN Doc. A/5337, 7 December 1962, p. 4.

[34] Johnson had found that most governments wanted to avoid having to take a decisive stand on the refugee question. It is of interest to note that in the early 1960s USSR policy on this question did not seem to be an important factor in the situation. There is no indication that the USSR sought to influence the Arab states on the question, and Johnson did not involve the USSR in any negotiations. This, of course, is in marked contrast to the mediation of Gunnar Jarring after the 1967 Middle East war, which involved the USSR repeatedly because of its ties in the Arab world.

recriminations on the floor of the Assembly. The United States sought to pin the responsibility for lack of progress on the refugee question directly on Israel and the Arabs: "As the years passed, each side adhered to the same rigid attitude, hoping, in the face of all logic, that the arguments of the adversaries would be miraculously destroyed and that it would be possible to solve the problem in accordance with its own wishes."[35] France, less critical of the disputants, nevertheless also tried to relieve the CCP from the responsibility for lack of progress. According to the French spokesman, Johnson "had shown great perseverance and an exceptional understanding of the different sides of the question . . . but the Commission had had to recognize that in the circumstances and in view of the reservations of the parties directly concerned, discretion would better serve the purposes of its mission of conciliation."[36] The General Assembly ultimately adopted a nondescript resolution calling on the CCP to continue its efforts pursuant to paragraph 11.

Johnson was disappointed that the CCP and the United States in particular had not supported him by exerting influence on the disputants, and shortly thereafter he submitted his resignation. In doing so he criticized, in diplomatic language, the CCP and the United States for not backing him in his efforts vis-à-vis recalcitrant parties. A second theme was his conclusion, stated in his unpublished report, that paragraph 11 as written in 1948 could not be implemented in the 1960s:

> It may be appropriate to state now that the experiment of a Special Representative of the Commission has, in my view, proved a worthwhile method for beginning a new effort to facilitate implementation of paragraph 11. As Special Representative I was free to study afresh and in depth this paragraph first adopted in 1948, and to examine and evaluate the attitudes of all concerned. I sought to isolate and develop some basic considerations and specific elements that I believe require consideration in any approach to the implementation of that paragraph in the 1960s. There is reason to think, however, that the role a single individual representing the Conciliation Commission can play in trying

[35] GAOR: 17th Sess., Special Political Committee, p. 205.
[36] *Ibid.*, pp. 265–66.

to move beyond analysis into the actual achievement of progress on this complex problem has at least for the time being been carried as far as is practicable.[37]

The Johnson mission on the refugee question, "the thorniest and most tragic aspect of the Arab-Israeli conflict,"[38] appears in retrospect as a capable effort resulting in reasonable policy recommendations. Johnson's series of proposals struck a balance between humanitarian concerns and legitimate *raisons d'état*. The proposals continued to be the preferred policy of several third parties. As the Assembly requested further efforts by the CCP, the United States in 1963 made several contacts in the Arab world—at the ambassadorial level but without much vigor—pursuant to the Johnson plan. But there was no affirmative response, and thereafter the plan was shelved.[39]

The recommendations were derived in spite of, rather than because of, the Special Representative's mandate. Paragraph 11 of A/Res/194(III), a specific principle, was at variance with the desires of the disputants. Even the Arab states, which had emphasized the paragraph repeatedly, did not really desire action on the basis of this separate issue alone. The issue of repatriation had been stressed precisely because Israel had always refrained from acknowledging the validity of the principle per se. This refusal by Israel gave the Arabs an excuse not to recognize or negotiate directly with Israel: by demanding that Israel first accept the principle of repatriation in general, and anticipating that Israel would refuse, the Arab states could then argue that Israel's recalcitrance was blocking settlement of the conflict. When Johnson made a practical attempt to implement paragraph 11 on the basis of a determination of preferences by the refugees, a preference that might or might not be qualified in any given instance, the Arabs rejected the plan. Egypt and Syria desired to keep the refugee question as a politico-legal weapon useful for the

[37] UN Press Release PAL/925, 1 February 1963, p. 3.

[38] Nadav Safran, *The United States and Israel* (Cambridge, Mass.: Harvard University Press, 1963), p. 290.

[39] See UN Doc. A/5545, 1 November 1963, p. 1.

domestic and international policies of each. Jordan believed the refugee question could not be treated apart from territorial considerations without great danger to Jordanian political stability. Lebanon tagged along.

Israel's viewpoint had not changed since 1949. The Arab refugees were not desired. It is clear that Israel thought it could get along better without the refugees, any number of them, than with them. Israel wanted a population with the highest possible proportion of Jews, and it wanted land and housing for future Jewish immigrants. It wanted to reject the refugees for security reasons; and when it was not able to do so under the Johnson plan, Israel tried to distort the plan so that it would be able to make that traditional claim. In short, repatriation remained anathema to Israel.

Johnson's effort to persuade the disputants to accept his mixture of repatriation, resettlement, and compensation was not successful, but this was due to the adamant views of the parties rather than to errors by the Special Representative. Johnson's field tactics of quiet and informal contacts were well suited to the problem at hand.[40] He maintained the respect of the parties throughout his mission. But his appeals to logic and national interest, and his occasional threats vis-à-vis the Arabs, were to no avail.[41]

The use of a Special Representative *had* allowed the CCP to carry out several roles beyond compiling technical reports and serving as a symbol of UN interest in the Arab-Israeli conflict. It is extremely doubtful that the CCP could have intervened qua Commission with any degree of effectiveness in the early 1960s. Its membership was characterized by mutually conflicting policies with regard to the Middle East. There was a lack of trust between

[40] It seems that Johnson might have maintained more direct and more constant contact with the disputants during the summer of 1962 when he was drafting his proposals. It appears that the changeover from a pilot-project scheme to the approach finally chosen took some Israeli officials by surprise. There is some indication that Israel may have overreacted to the relative suddenness of the presentation of the Johnson plan.

[41] In addition to the threats used on the Arabs, Johnson was aware that he had an issue to use as a threat on Israel—namely, a change in the composition of the CCP that would not be favorable to Israel. Johnson elected not to resort to this threat.

the United States and France, and between France and Turkey. The Special Representative approach had permitted capable and impartial involvement.

The use of a Special Representative, however, is not a substitute for political action—that is, the exertion of influence. If the third party's recommendations and attempts at persuasion remain ineffective, the only alternative to the failure of the mission is mobilization of governmental persuasion or pressure on the disputants. If a solution to a problem cannot be negotiated on the basis of persuasion, it may still be solved in a relatively peaceful process through a combination of negotiation and pressure. Johnson was very much aware of this potential for the application of governmental pressure in conjunction with his diplomatic effort. He was also aware that in the long history of the Arab-Israeli conflict the disputants had agreed on very little through a voluntary meeting of minds. Thus he sought support from the United States. In this regard it perhaps can be said that Johnson's tactics in seeking to mobilize pressure on the disputants were defective. He agreed not to have the CCP endorse his plan as a first step toward Assembly endorsement. When the disputants did not agree to let the plan be implemented, Johnson was not in a strong bargaining position, for he had no committed allies. If he had pressed for CCP endorsement—including, of course, the United States—the United States would have found it more difficult to abandon the Johnson plan as it later did.

In his resignation statement, Johnson indicated he was disappointed that he did not receive US support. He later wrote: "... the United States is by all odds the most important member of the Conciliation Commission, and ... any progress on the refugee question must depend in very large measure on the government of the United States. ..."[42]

[42] Johnson, "Arab v. Israeli," p. 2.

VI

UNITED NATIONS PEACEMAKING

The CCP had exhausted most of its utility in the Arab-Israeli conflict by 1968. After the Johnson mission in 1961-62, the CCP again became merely a symbol of UN interest in the conflict—although in 1963 it did try to clarify the disputants' positions with regard to the Johnson plan, and in 1966 it tried to clarify the Arabs' policy with regard to the Commission's identification and evaluation of Arab refugee property in Israel. Several factors indicated that the CCP would not be resurrected from this symbolic role, as it had been in the early 1960s.

First, the CCP itself reported candidly in both 1965 and 1966 that it could not affect the configuration of the conflict.[1] As if further proof of the CCP's marginality were needed, the 1967 Middle East war indicated the extent to which UN peacemaking had failed. Moreover, the CCP's main focus of interest since 1951, the refugee question, was changed by the 1967 war: new Arab refugees were present outside Israeli-controlled territory; old Palestinian refugees found themselves within Israeli-controlled territory; new destruction of property was sometimes heaped upon previous destruction; territory such as Jerusalem and the West Bank changed hands, affecting the future of both repatriation and resettlement.

[1] See UN Docs. A/6225, 28 December 1965, and A/6451, 30 September 1966.

145

Perhaps most significantly, the inactivity of the CCP in the wake of war and the appointment of a United Nations Middle East Mission (UNMEM) by the Secretary-General at the direction of the Security Council indicated an intentional bypassing of the CCP. Rationales for such a move were ample: the long history of unproductive CCP involvement; lack of confidence by the disputants in the Commission; charges of bias in the composition of the CCP by various member governments of the Assembly; fear of exacerbated conflict among the member governments of the CCP (especially after France adopted a pro-Arab foreign policy in 1967 and the United States remained an ally of Israel). Yet the United Nations left the CCP in existence, thus placing itself in a somewhat illogical position. The Council gave UNMEM a comprehensive, general mandate; the Assembly, at approximately the same time, instructed the CCP to continue its efforts pursuant to paragraph 11 of A/Res/194(III). On the one hand, UNMEM represented a fresh approach to peacemaking. On the other hand, the CCP's mandate on the refugee question, found to be dated by the Johnson mission, was endorsed once more.

The Assembly's 1967 request for further efforts on the refugee question, however, was not taken seriously by a number of involved parties; this thus increased the likelihood that the CCP would remain symbolic. The Assembly, contrary to usual past practice, did not specify *when* the CCP should report back to the Assembly on its efforts. And even when the Assembly had done so in the past, the CCP's post-1963 meetings had remained an "academic exercise" directed toward drawing up the "appropriate piece of paper." For some time the Assembly and the CCP had played a time-wasting game: the CCP would report that it could make no progress on the refugee question on the basis of paragraph 11; the Assembly would then request the CCP to make further efforts on the refugee question pursuant to paragraph 11; whereupon the CCP would repeat its report, and the Assembly would repeat its request.

The CCP's data on identification and evaluation of Arab refugee property in Israel remained available to any peacemaking mission, as did the basic concepts of the Johnson plan. But as of the early 1970s it seemed highly improbable that the CCP would become an active third party in the Arab-Israeli conflict again. Hence it appears an appropriate time to seek generalizations about UN peacemaking, with the CCP's 1948-68 efforts as a focal point.

There can be no doubt that generalizations are difficult to derive regarding UN peacemaking. Not all conflicts stand an equal chance of being resolved; there are differing degrees of psychological hostility, differing degrees of outside intervention, differing degrees of military capability. But while a rigorous theory of UN peacemaking in conflict situations must await some breakthrough in the accumulation of knowledge, there remains a "middle-range" area of limited generalization. Just as UN peacekeeping differed in the Gaza, Congo, and Cyprus operations, so UN peacemaking differs in its various contexts. But just as one can generalize about the structures and functions of the various peacekeeping operations,[2] so one can generalize about UN peacemaking. The following discussion considers UN peacemaking in terms of composition, mandate, tactics, and field relationships. This structural framework permits an orderly discussion of functional roles.

First, however, several general trends can be noted concerning peacemaking. The major policy organs of the United Nations are likely to remain too large, too fragmented, and too public for effective peacemaking. Thus there is reason to believe that delegation of authority to subsidiary organs will continue. The question of which policy organ, the Council or the Assembly, will emerge as the primary parent body for peacemaking missions is likely to be decided—if it is decided at all—by the changing needs of influential governments. Past UN practice does not prove one parent body generally more effective than the other in providing oversight and instruction to the subsidiary organ. For example, the Assembly in 1949 debated the status of Jerusalem ad nauseam when the crucial issues in the CCP field negotiations were territorial boundaries and refugees. But the United Nations

---

[2] See, for example, David P. Forsythe, "United Nations Intervention in Conflict Situations Revisited: A Framework for Analysis," *International Organization* 23, no. 1 (Winter 1969): 115–39.

UNITED NATIONS PEACEMAKING

Commission for Indonesia (UNCI) received equally inadequate oversight from the Council, which "demonstrated a disinclination to adopt strong measures even when its previous resolutions had been unsatisfactorily implemented, or even disregarded."[3] The political considerations of such governments as the United States, and their preferences for the Security Council and its veto as compared with a not-easily-manipulated General Assembly, may lead to the reemergence of the Council and a fulfilling of its role as the organ primarily responsible for "peace and security"—whatever its record of efficacy.

A second general trend is that peacemaking organs have usually been created on an ad hoc basis by the United Nations, with little regard for the lessons of past experience.[4] There has been little or no systematic reference to the success and failure of past operations. Moreover, contrary to certain academic typologies, it does not appear that the United Nations takes into account—or needs to take into account—the *type* of conflict that it tries to pacify. It is suggested here that neither the breakdown of conflicts into cold war, colonial wars, wars within a new state, and wars among new states; nor the breakdown into colonial wars, internal conflicts, and proxy wars, sheds much light on the nature of UN involvement.[5] Although such typologies are useful devices for organizing analytic description of political events, it seems valid to state, as a general conclusion, that "the Organization's primary concern with threats to international peace and security

[3] Alastair N. Taylor, *Indonesian Independence and the United Nations* (Ithaca: Cornell University Press, 1960), p. 401.

[4] See Leland Goodrich and Anne Simons, *The United Nations and the Maintenance of International Peace and Security* (Washington, D.C.: The Brookings Institution, 1957), pp. 294–318; and Elmore Jackson, "Mediation and Conciliation in International Law," *International Social Science Bulletin* 10, no. 4 (1958): 535.

[5] See Yashpal Tandon, "The Peaceful Settlement of International Disputes," *International Relations* 2, no. 9 (April 1964): 569–76; and Linda B. Miller, *World Order and Local Disorder: The United Nations and Internal Conflicts* (Princeton: Princeton University Press, 1967). As Miller herself notes: "The line between internal and international conflicts has become increasingly difficult to draw" (p. 35).

has resulted in . . . international preoccupation with outcomes, regardless of the immediate origins of conflict."[6]

A third trend is that UN peacemaking organs usually become deeply involved in the negotiation and execute roles such as submitting policy recommendations and mobilizing persuasion, if not pressure. This is not surprising. Frequently UN peacemaking is undertaken after a period of violence or after communication between the disputants has broken down. In such situations it is logical for lesser degrees of involvement such as playing a symbolic role, making procedural suggestions, and asking for clarification of policy to be ineffective. In short, the intensity of conflict is such that intensive involvement is required to alter the confrontation. The greater degrees of involvement may occur after a prolonged period of policy clarification by the third party, but nevertheless that greater involvement does occur as the rule rather than the exception. The use of the title "Good Offices Commission" does not seem to be a clear indication that only minor degrees of involvement will be undertaken.[7]

Whatever the composition of the UN peacemaking organ, the process of composing the mission can affect its later role-execution. UN peacemaking is facilitated when there is consultation among the parties concerned with regard to composition,[8] and when there is an attempt by UN officials to meet the desires of the disputants. A selection process in keeping with the desires of the disputants contributes to the early prestige of the subsidiary organ and helps reduce the likelihood that in the future the mission's composition would become a point of friction. A negative case in point is that of the CCP. The disputants were not consulted with regard to its composition, and they were not satisfied with its

[6] Miller, *World Order*, p. 63. This statement was made in the context of comparing colonial and post-colonial conflicts. It is suggested here that the statement has wider applicability.

[7] For a general review of UN practice, see Goodrich and Simons, *United Nations*.

[8] Elmore Jackson, *Meeting of Minds* (New York: McGraw-Hill Book Co., 1952), p. 126.

member governments. Thus they had less reason to be favorably predisposed to the CCP. Moreover, particularly the Arab states challenged the composition of the CCP in later years when they became dissatisfied with the organ's inability to implement resolutions on the refugee question.

Subsidiary organs of multiple membership can be composed in several ways in order to maintain a favorable atmosphere for early roles. The Indonesian Good Offices Commission had three members, one chosen by each disputant and the third selected by the two so chosen.[9] In the case of the United Nations Commission for India and Pakistan (UNCIP), each disputant selected one member, the Council selected two, and the president of the Council one.[10] Both processes proved efficacious.

From time to time the argument has been made that the United Nations could compose peacemaking missions with greater rapidity and effectiveness if it constantly had ready a "corps of mediators."[11] The fact remains, however, that the United Nations has made little use of the International Panel of Inquiry and Conciliation, created in 1949 and composed of five persons named by the Assembly. And a 1950 Yugoslav proposal for a permanent UN good offices commission was never adopted. Moreover, different conflicts necessitate different fields of expertise by the intervenor. Hence the United Nations needs recourse to a broad spectrum of individuals because of the varied issues it tackles. There is no denying the need for rapid action by the United Nations in many conflict situations. Thus perhaps what has been termed a "crisis directory"[12] is apropos to its needs: a listing of individuals with specific fields of competence who are willing to work with the United Nations and who have shown an ability or potential for mediation.

[9] The Secretary-General could select the third in the event that agreement could not be reached by the first two representatives.

[10] See Josef Korbel, *Danger in Kashmir* (Princeton: Princeton University Press, 1954), p. 118.

[11] Miller, *World Order,* p. 207. Cf. Tandon, "Peaceful Settlement of International Disputes," p. 580.

[12] Oran R. Young, *The Intermediaries: Third Parties in International Crises* (Princeton: Princeton University Press, 1967), p. 344.

Role-execution by the UN peacemaking mission can be affected not only by the composing process but also by the organ's composition per se. A government-comprised peacemaking organ runs a high risk of producing impediments to peacemaking. This hypothesis can be substantiated despite the fact that as of the mid-1960s forty-two of sixty-nine UN subsidiary agencies—of all types—had been comprised of governments as legal members.[13]

With a subsidiary organ of governmental membership, the probability is increased that complicating national influences will be introduced into the negotiations at a premature time. There is a need in peacemaking to isolate the conflict, to as great a degree as possible, from the short-range influences of nation-states not directly involved. Such isolation helps the third party to emphasize factors that benefit the long-range interests of the disputants and of the entire international political system. Long-term interests stemming from the avoidance of force and the benefits of cooperation can be stressed with less attention given to short-range demands of interested governments. Such isolation also affords the disputants maximum opportunity to reach a voluntary meeting of minds. In addition, unnecessary complexity is avoided that might otherwise arise from a multiplicity of cross-cutting national interests being introduced into the basic conflict. After all, there is little point in using a subsidiary organ to bypass the fragmentation of the parent body if the mutually incompatible inputs to peacemaking are reintroduced in the field negotiations through the presence of governments on the subsidiary organ.

The isolation of the conflict through UN efforts to seal off the confrontation is only relative. Some extra-disputant national interests may be present from the start of UN involvement, expressed through the field organ's terms of reference. These interests may be introduced at a later stage through review of, and instruction for, the organ's efforts. And of course it is likely that bilateral diplomacy will continue between a given disputant and another government. The peacemaking mission itself may seek to

[13] Yashpal Tandon, "Consensus and Authority behind United Nations Peacekeeping Operations," *International Organization* 21, no. 2 (Spring 1967): 259.

mobilize persuasion or pressure from interested governments at some juncture in the negotiations, as will be discussed below. One of the primary functions of UN peacemaking is, however, to ensure that such extra-disputant influence is not incompatible with the settlement terms desired initially by the disputants or subsequently by the United Nations as spokesman for international society.

Second, peacemaking through subsidiary organs of governmental membership increases the probability that UN involvement will be impeded by the organ's own internal politics. Not only may the interests of member governments be at variance with the interests of the disputants or of the international society, but the interests of member governments may also be mutually conflicting. A clear example of this phenomenon is the UNCIP, whose work with India and Pakistan was disrupted by the presence of the communist delegation from Czechoslovakia after the 1948 change of governments in that nation.[14] Another example is the Conciliation Commission for the Congo (UNCCC), which was badly fragmented by competing national conceptions of the issues under discussion.[15] The CCP was able to function in the Arab-Israeli conflict in the early 1960s only by circumventing mutual government suspicion through use of a Special Representative; in the later 1960s, the CCP was considered unreliable for any role beyond serving as a symbol because of the global and regional tension between the United States and France.

It is not true, however, that the presence of subsidiary organs of governmental membership ipso facto results in ineffectiveness from internal politics. Neither the UNCI nor the CCP during 1949-51 was impeded in its efforts by internal factors, because other member governments on the two organs deferred to the leadership of the United States. But it is to be noted in this regard that the United Nations, and the General Assembly in particular, is no longer dominated by the United States—led Western states—as was true at the time of the creation of the UNCI and CCP. It is

[14] See Korbel, *Danger in Kashmir*, p. 154.
[15] See Miller, *World Order*, p. 90.

probable that future field organs of governmental membership could not be created along a pro-Western axis on the basis of consensus. Thus the likelihood of conflict among government members of subsidiary organs has increased with the increased application of the principle of equal geographic representation.[16]

Third, the probability of use of excessively formal rather than flexible tactics is increased through the presence of a government-comprised field organ. There seem to be three main reasons for this. First, formal tactics seem to inhere in the operation of a peacemaking mission of government members because of the need for bureaucratic communication. Governmental instruction may be fixed in such a way that it becomes at variance with the trend of negotiation in the field. The time it takes to clear new policies with the administration "back home" may result in missed opportunities for agreement. Second, a need for coordination because of the number of parties involved in the negotiations may produce excessive formality. The greater the number involved, the greater the likelihood that conference diplomacy will be used. And in conference diplomacy there is a low probability that an informal, relaxed, and frank exchange of views will occur.[17] These first two reasons for excessive formality can be exemplified by the United Nations Truce Commission for Korea I and II (UNTCOK),[18] and by the CCP.[19] It is to be noted

[16] It would seem possible to reduce the potential for conflict among government members by selecting UN members termed "neutralist": Sweden, Canada, India, etc. A problem still inheres in the fact that a usually neutralist state may not be neutral on a particular conflict; for example, India, partly because of its large Muslim community, has been other than neutral on the Arab-Israeli conflict.

[17] This general conclusion is well substantiated by the 1968 Paris negotiations between North Vietnam and the United States. Sessions of the conference were characterized by reading of formal statements and adherence to publicly stated policies. Early progress, even though minimal, came through quiet, informal conversations during "tea breaks" and other recesses in the conference.

[18] An in-depth study of UNTCOK I and II concludes that success in peacemaking requires "flexibility unusual for a body of instructed delegates" (Leon Gordenker, *The United Nations and the Peaceful Unification of Korea* [The Hague: Martinus Nijhoff, 1959], p. 257).

[19] "It has been maintained in this respect that the work of the Palestine Conciliation Commission might have proceeded more rapidly if it had followed a more flexible plan of operation" (Jackson, *Meeting of Minds*, p. 104).

153

once again, however, that this trend toward formality is not *always* detrimental to peacemaking. Despite the generally unproductive record of conference diplomacy—one can cite the UN 1961 attempts at conference diplomacy in the Congo crisis as yet another example—the UNCI in the Dutch-Indonesian conflict executed well a variety of peacemaking roles via both conferences and less structured contacts.[20] Finally, governmental concern for prestige and status may lead to rigidity rather than flexibility. Government members may become overly zealous in defense of the organ's record and oppose change in the organ's composition or mandate in order to avoid the implication that the organ's member governments had not carried out the terms of reference well. This is particularly true for organs such as the CCP that exist over a long period of time. Member governments of that organ fought change—even when change seemed justified in the hopes of securing better cooperation from one or more of the disputants—because of fear that unfavorable implications would be directed toward the original member governments.[21] For perhaps inexplicable reasons, nongovernmental personnel appear more ready to make themselves expendable in hopes of securing progress in peacemaking: particularly good examples can be cited regarding mediators Plaza Lasso in the Cyprus conflict and Bernadotte in the Palestine conflict. Also perhaps proving this is UNCIP's request for a mediator to replace itself in the Kashmir conflict.

The disadvantages to subsidiary organs of governmental membership appear to outweigh the advantages stemming from such field organs. In some cases there may be a continuity of approach to problems because governments comprise the subsidiary organ dealing with a protracted conflict, and this was the case in the Indonesian dispute.[22] In the Arab-Israeli conflict, however,

[20] See Taylor, *Indonesian Independence,* esp. pp. 410–11.

[21] UN peacemaking may frequently result in use of the UN organ as a scapegoat by the disputants. See Goodrich and Simons, *United Nations,* pp. 295–96. This may not be an altogether unwelcome pattern, especially if such usage results in change of policy by the disputant conducive to attaining a settlement. A problem does arise if the disputant blames the third party for failure rather than reexamining its own adamant position.

[22] Taylor, *Indonesian Independence,* p. 422.

there was a rapid turnover in government-appointed personnel on the CCP during the 1949-51 period. A variety of personnel was also characteristic of UNTCOK.[23] This variety of personal membership does not necessarily affect the continuity of government policy unless that policy is initiated to a significant degree by field personnel. Such field initiative was present in the CCP's operations; it was not present in the activities of the UNCI.[24] Therefore, if there is a variety of governmental representatives on the field organ, and if specific policy is generated in the field within the general outlines formulated in the national capital, government membership for a field organ does not necessarily result in continuity in the field organ's efforts.

It has also been argued that governmental membership increases the authority of the subsidiary organ. Like continuity, authority may or may not be conveyed through government members. In the Indonesian case, the authority of the UNCI was great partly because the member governments exercised their political power and exerted influence on the disputants.[25] But government influence in support of UNCIP was not applied to any significant degree in the Kashmir conflict. In the case of the CCP, despite the presence of the United States and France on the Commission, the authority of the Commission remained low almost from the beginning of 1949. This was due initially to lack of consultation during its formation, tactical mistakes, personnel problems, and its relatively inferior performance compared with that of Bunche. And the power of the United States, instead of increasing the authority of the CCP, was used so intermittently and inconsistently that it further reduced the authority of the CCP. The power of France was virtually absent from the early life of the CCP.

[23] Gordenker, *Peaceful Unification of Korea*, p. 256.

[24] Taylor, *Indonesian Independence*, p. 409. As for Korea, very little policy was being made anywhere in regard to UNTCOK. The Commissions became "elaborate time wasting" devices (Gordenker, *Peaceful Unification of Korea*, p. 242).

[25] Tandon, "Peaceful Settlement of International Disputes," p. 557; Taylor, *Indonesian Independence*. Other factors contributing to the high authority of the UNCI were its successful tactics and its reputation for impartiality. See Taylor, *Indonesian Independence*, pp. 410–11.

The fact that disadvantages involved in the operation of field organs of governmental membership do outweigh the limited advantages is reflected in the practice of the United Nations,[26] which tends to use single individuals.[27] UN involvement in the Arab-Israeli conflict provides the clearest example: a government commission was replaced by a single representative, who was in turn replaced by a mediator unconnected with the commission. There is every indication that UN practice will continue in the same direction.[28]

There are definite advantages in the use of a single representative as opposed to a commission of governments. Present in this form of peacemaking is a high probability for flexibility in decisionmaking. Speed in making decisions is facilitated in this approach, and the prestige of the mediator is frequently high because of the quality of men selected by the United Nations. Not only did the United Nations send men like Bernadotte, Bunche, and Johnson to the Middle East, but also Dixon and Graham were sent to work on the Kashmir dispute and Hammarskjold himself worked on the Congo problem. In addition, it is easier to hold quiet talks and maintain secrecy during the negotiations through the efforts of a mediator. Finally, and perhaps most importantly, the conflict frequently becomes more isolated from the short-range policies of interested governments when a mediator is used, thus allowing more time for supra-national and long-range interests to come into play. Of course this isolation cannot ever be complete, and, as noted earlier, the mediator himself may seek to involve some of the governments which support his approach at a later time.

The use of an uninstructed individual, however, is not a panacea for all the difficulties involved in peacemaking.[29]

[26] Even where UN practice relied upon government members, scholarly opinion suggests that uninstructed intermediaries would have been more efficacious. See Gordenker, *Peaceful Unification of Korea*, p. 266, with regard to Korea.

[27] Jackson, "Mediation and Conciliation," pp. 535–37.

[28] For a suggestion that multi-individual third parties be employed, see Jackson's 1952 work, *Meeting of Minds*, pp. 150, 155–57.

[29] See further Gordenker, *Peaceful Unification of Korea*, pp. 262–64.

Flexibility in the approach of a mediator or "special representative" may be negated by the desire of the disputants to reject the result of his flexible approach. Speed in decisionmaking may be vitiated by the immaturity of the decisions made. Initial prestige may be offset by tactical or strategic errors. Secrecy and informality in the negotiations may be countered with a carefully timed press release by the disputants or by a concerted effort to discredit in public what has taken place in private.

The most basic limitation involved in peacemaking by an individual is that the parties frequently have the political capability to reject his approach to the problems involved. Despite every effort on the part of the mediator to remain impartial, to seek the mutually compatible interests of the disputants, and to further the interests of international society, the parties directly concerned—because of emotionalism, nationalism, fear, or hate—may reject his overtures. As Johnson stated in his resignation, there are definite limitations to the role of an uninstructed individual when it comes time to move from analysis and suggestions to action—by which he meant the implementation of his suggestions. Such limitations show up particularly well in the Cyprus conflict. The differences between the Greek-speaking majority and the Turkish-speaking minority were mediated by different third parties using different recommendations. But neither British personnel, the NATO representative, nor UN representatives were able to obtain agreement on the substantive issues.[30]

The independence of a UN mediator is indeed a "mixed blessing."[31] As representative of the United Nations, his roles *are* facilitated by the probable characteristics discussed above: flexibility and speed in decisionmaking, prestige, and relative freedom from complicating national interests. But the execution of his peacemaking roles may be hindered by the fact that the forms of influence at his disposal are generally restricted to means of persuasion. If persuasive influence proves insufficient to bring

[30] See Miller, *World Order*, pp. 120–48.
[31] See Young, *Intermediaries*, pp. 274–75.

157

about a settlement, the only alternative to failure of the peacemaking mission is the mobilization of governmental persuasion and pressure on the disputants. Governmental influence was successfully mobilized in the Dutch-Indonesian conflict, as the United States filled the hiatus left by inadequate support from the Security Council.[32] Governmental influence was also mobilized successfully by Bunche during the armistice negotiations, as the United States responded with an ultimatum to Israel demanding withdrawal from Egyptian territory and with other means of influence.[33]

To be sure, the mobilization of governmental influence is a complex and delicate operation. On many complicated issues, nondisputant governments may not desire to become involved—preferring, like individual politicians, to avoid taking an official stand on a given issue. There has always been a hesitancy to "go to war to protect the peace," or, in other words, to expand the conflict in order to resolve it.[34] On other issues, costs as well as benefits may be involved in applying governmental influence. The United States clearly thought, *inter alia*, that the cost of supporting the Johnson mission in 1962 entailed unacceptable costs in terms of an increase in domestic political opposition to a policy of support. In the Cyprus conflict, the United States exerted persuasion through Presidential initiative in 1964; but the risks of applying pressure were thought to be too great, since in part the United States feared that Makarios, the leader of the Greek-speaking majority, would turn to the Soviet Union for support. Or it may be true that the attempt to apply persuasion or pressure will be so handled as to provoke antagonism on the part of the disputant rather than a change of policy conducive to settlement of the conflict. US threats of deprivations vis-à-vis Israel in 1949 are a prime example.

[32] Taylor, *Indonesian Independence,* pp. 410–11.

[33] See further Pablo de Azcárate, *Mission in Palestine 1948–1953* (Washington, D.C.: Middle East Institute, 1966), pp. 111–12.

[34] A reflection of this attitude is found in the arguments of those who interpret the Charter narrowly and say that the United Nations has a major responsibility in peacekeeping but not peacemaking. See the discussion above, in the Introduction, n. 21.

A final argument against the mobilization of influence is that some problems have to be lived with rather than solved.[35] There is a great deal of merit in this argument, for there is no doubt that some such conflicts do exist. In the 1960s such symbols of tension as divided Berlin and divided Germany, the Sino-Soviet rift, and the basic Arab hate of Israel are probably not susceptible to any solution in the present political context. But the danger in relying upon this approach to conflict resolution is that opportunities to solve conflicts may be missed on the assumption that an attempt at conciliation backed by government support would do no good. It is a great deal easier to say in retrospect that a problem has to be lived with rather than to make that judgment with any assurance at the time of the first crisis. Moreover, in several conflicts—Kashmir and Palestine among them—the attitudes of the parties have hardened over time so that whatever entrée was present for peacemaking at the outset of the conflict has been lost. Arab versus Israeli is one of the conflicts most often cited as a dispute that has to be endured. But before Arab nationalism gained its leader in Nasir, anti-Zionism was not a firm tenet of that nationalism. And the present study has indicated the extent to which the Arab states were interested in the terms of a general settlement in 1949 in their private contacts with Israel. No less an expert on this conflict than Bunche believes that a settlement was possible in the early months of 1949 if government pressure had been applied in support of the CCP.[36] Although it must be recognized that some conflicts are not likely to be solved, there is a concomitant need to recognize that in some conflicts—even complex ones—the problems will yield to a concerted effort and that such an effort will bring better results when applied before attitudes become fixed. There is no simple answer about which conflicts can or cannot be solved.

[35] In general, see Inis L. Claude, Jr., *The Changing United Nations* (New York: Random House, 1967), p. 217. On the Arab-Israeli conflict in general, see Charles D. Cremeans, *The Arabs and the World* (New York: Frederick A. Praeger, 1963), p. 180. On the refugee problem, see Don Peretz, "The Arab Refugees: A Changing Problem," *Foreign Affairs* 41, no. 3 (April 1963): 558–70.

[36] The same thesis can be found in Nadav Safran, *The United States and Israel* (Cambridge, Mass.: Harvard University Press, 1963).

The classic example of the overall complexity and delicacy of the exertion of influence in support of UN peacemaking is the Arab-Israeli conflict. Israel desired to hold every major gain made during the 1948 war; significant concessions were not desired. The Arab states, Jordan included, did not want to try to make the best of the de facto situation and admit that Palestine had been irrevocably lost as an Arab state.[37] The West, which dominated the General Assembly and the CCP at the outset of peacemaking, had interests in Arab oil and in maintaining good ties with the dominant people of the region. Moreover, the Arabs could be offended by influence exerted on them, since such exertions were frequently regarded as manifestations of neocolonialism.[38] But influence exerted by France, the United Kingdom, or the United States on Israel would result in an unwanted feedback in the domestic political system of each nation because of Jewish influence therein. Thus the West tried unsuccessfully to freeze the 1950 status quo and let time per se ameliorate the conflict. Violence erupted frequently, however, culminating in the 1967 Middle East war which brought the United States and the Soviet Union perilously close to a direct military confrontation. Nevertheless, most governments continued to avoid the costs of supporting UN peacemaking efforts, even though many core interests continued to be threatened. In this milieu, the Special Representative approach of 1961—62 on the refugee question was more capably executed than the CCP's involvement qua Commission in 1948—51; but neither peacemaking mission was able to obtain a settlement without supporting government influence.

It has been written that it is relatively easy to create peacemaking missions,[39] and in a sense it *is* easier to name a

[37] For an excellent but little-known exposition of Arab attitudes. see Abdelmanim Zanabili, *Les Etats Arabes et les Nations Unies* (Aurillac, Suisse: Imprimerie de Cantal, 1953). For the insightful thesis that the Arabs are a problem-perpetuating people while the Israelis are a problem-solving people, see Aubrey Hodes, "Signpost to a Solution," *New Outlook* 7 (March—April 1964): 32—39.

[38] For an interpretation of more recent Arab views regarding foreign influence, see John S. Badeau, "Development and Diplomacy in the Middle East," *Bulletin of Atomic Scientists* 22, no. 5 (May 1966): 5—10.

[39] Tandon, "Peaceful Settlement of International Disputes," p. 580.

mediator or the members of conciliatory instruments than it is to make a peacekeeping unit operational. But the establishment of the terms of reference for a subsidiary organ in the realm of peacemaking is an intellectually and politically demanding task. Is a settlement facilitated if the organ's mandate is general or specific? Is the parent body facilitating a settlement by attempting to spell out the procedure and goals of the organ, or is it preferable to leave these matters to the organ's competence as it negotiates with the parties? What type of mandate will facilitate a peaceful settlement, and what type will prove an impediment?

Two assumptions are frequently articulated regarding how a subsidiary organ's terms of reference facilitate UN peacemaking. It is said sometimes that a general mandate promotes flexibility in the field negotiations and that such flexibility is conducive to conflict-resolution. It is also said that a specific mandate facilitates peacemaking since it indicates the presence of a consensus in support of a particular settlement. The argument is then made that successful peacemaking depends upon a strong consensus. It is difficult to find fault with either of these assumptions as stated in the positive sense, especially if, in the latter case, one understands "strong consensus" to mean a willingness on the part of governments to take *action* consonant with verbal policy. There are, however, several negative effects stemming from both specific and general mandates in actual peacemaking attempts.

A specific mandate for a UN peacemaking organ increases the probability that the disputant with the stronger bargaining position will oppose the UN's recommendations. The more powerful disputant or disputant-in-possession usually views with disfavor third-party efforts at conflict-resolution.[40] De facto settlement works to the advantage of such a disputant. By comparison, UN peacemaking is usually based on principles of law and equity, which is a barrier to the exercise of *realpolitik* by the stronger disputant. The more specific the mandate of the peacemaking organ, the greater the probability of antagonism between that organ and the stronger disputant. India, for example,

---

[40] See Arthur Lall, *Modern International Negotiation* (New York: Columbia University Press, 1966), pp. 84–90.

the state in possession, has consistently opposed specific directives to the UN peacemaking organ to implement a plebiscite among the people of Kashmir.

Relatedly, a specific mandate increases the probability that the mandate will become dated by events and that a sense of failure and frustration will characterize the peacemaking effort. Given the probable initial recalcitrance of the stronger disputant discussed above, and given what must be termed the normal hesitance of interested governments to exert significant influence on the disputants in a conflict, specific terms of reference tend to become dated very quickly. There is less room provided for the third party to find a meeting of minds, since its leeway for decisionmaking is circumscribed. This situation is exacerbated by a frequent tendency of the parent body to repeat previous resolutions or parts thereof in an effort to maintain consistency and a proper concern for law and justice. And given these usual difficulties and complexities in peacemaking, one result of involvement under a specific mandate is a decline in the sense of progress and accomplishment. Frequently there is a resulting decline in the general prestige and status of the parent *and* subsidiary body because of the difficulties of implementing a specific mandate.

Finally, once again given the normal complexities of conflict-resolution, there is a tendency for the third party to interpret rather broadly the specific terms of reference in an attempt to find some sort of modus vivendi among the disputants, a tendency frequently resulting in the third party's being subjected to charges of acting *ultra vires.* Such attacks on the third party, whether legally well founded or not, frequently become useful escape points for disputants who wish for some acceptable way to reject a third-party recommendation that is otherwise well reasoned. The ability of the disputant to make a logical case for rejection on grounds that the third party had exceeded its mandate would be reduced in proportion to the generality of the mandate.

Each of these impediments stemming from a specific mandate can be found in the General Assembly's directives to the CCP on the questions of the status of Jerusalem and the future of the

Palestinian refugees. There was an especially strong consensus, measured in terms of votes, within the Assembly, for an international regime for the city of Jerusalem. The consensus held together on a number of specific points, yet the CCP was unable to obtain the cooperation of either of the states in possession, Jordan and Israel, even for a compromise plan that maintained the Arab and Jewish sectors of the city. The Assembly continued to request a *corpus separatum* for Jerusalem under international direction even when it was clear that member governments of the Assembly who voted for that measure were not inclined to take action supporting the resulting resolution. The Assembly's instructions to the CCP concerning the refugees revolved around a specific principle: the right to repatriation or to resettlement with compensation for those who wanted to live at peace. Once again Israel as the state in possession of territory to which refugees would be returning refused to acknowledge the validity of the principle. Eventually Israel became convinced that repatriation was impossible given the Arab bellicose public statements, and unofficial international recommendations on the refugee question from as early as 1950 look to resettlement as the primary if not sole solution to the problem. Yet the Assembly continued to endorse the principle of repatriation, even after the Special Representative reported to the CCP in the early 1960s that the 1948 guideline was inapplicable as a basis for settlement. That same representative was charged by the Arabs with acting *ultra vires* for trying to make a practical implementation of his mandate.

It seems clear that a general mandate to a peacemaking organ does provide relief from these negative effects of a specific mandate. And most diplomats endorse the need for flexibility in successful negotiation. Unfortunately, it cannot be said that a general mandate to a UN agent always results in effective peacemaking. The main liability in employing a general mandate is that the UN subsidiary organ may seek to lead a consensus rather than follow one, and failing to build that consensus, it may find itself subjected to a crippling barrage of government criticism.

The obvious example of such a phenomenon is the entire UN

involvement in the Congo crisis–peacekeeping, peacemaking, and peacebuilding. The Secretary-General had at best an "uncertain mandate,"[41] and in trying to restore order amid domestic anarchy and competing foreign influences he found at one point that he was the guest of a host government which, in fact, did not even exist. It was only through UN peacemaking, via the procedural and policy recommendations of the UNCCC, that a government was brought into being to act as host for the United Nations. When that government proved too Western-oriented for a number of member governments of the United Nations, a politico-legal-financial crisis resulted which kept the entire Assembly in limbo for about a year.

Yet because of the negative effects frequently stemming from specific mandates and–more importantly–because a specific consensus in support of a particular settlement is at times extremely difficult to obtain,[42] general mandates are likely to continue as those most often used if not preferred.[43] Given the fragmented and mutually conflicting inputs to the UN peace-making process, the United Nations is likely to retain two unappealing options: to play little or no role at all in the resolution of a conflict, or to try to play a more significant role despite probable opposition from various quarters and in various degrees of exerted influence. General mandates are frequently necessary to allow UN subsidiary organs to exist at all–for example, the United Nations Force in Cyprus (UNFICYP).[44] Once in existence, the subsidiary organ may have to determine its own limitations to effective action through trial and error, constant reporting back to the parent body for instruction, or political acumen with regard to changed contextual factors.

[41] See, *inter alia,* Ernest W. Lefever, *Uncertain Mandate: Politics of the UN Congo Operation* (Baltimore: Johns Hopkins Press, 1967). Cf. Stanley Hoffmann, "In Search of a Thread: The UN in the Congo Labyrinth," *International Organization* 16 (Spring 1962): 331–61.

[42] See Tandon, "Consensus and Authority," pp. 256–59.

[43] This does not rule out, of course, the possibility of terms of reference being both general and specific in part. See Goodrich and Simons on this point, *United Nations,* p. 236.

[44] See Miller, *World Order,* p. 209.

It would appear that a general mandate would be in keeping with the trend toward the use of such nongovernmental personnel as third parties, a subject discussed in the section regarding composition. Use of a general mandate permits the subsidiary organ to discover the attitudes of the disputants through quiet diplomacy prior to establishing the recommended framework for settlement. Thus flexibility in the origin of the peacemaking mission would be added to the flexibility of the nongovernmental third-party's efforts to facilitate agreement on specific points within the framework once established. There is nothing to prevent the subsidiary organ from requesting from the parent body, at a later time, specific guidelines for its own direction or to demonstrate to the disputants that its actions are supported by the parent body. Delayed adoption of specific guidelines also helps to restrain the parent body from establishing terms of reference that stand little chance of being implemented; delayed adoption would thus protect the status of both parent and subsidiary organ. The primary goal of both organs is the promotion of a durable settlement through measures short of force, not the levying of specific moral and legal responsibility.

The tactics of a subsidiary organ in the realm of peacemaking are more important for role execution than has been generally recognized. Because the United Nations frequently deals with disputes of great emotional intensity, the tactics employed by the field organ to alleviate bitterness and avoid charges of partiality are significant. The simple fact is that in many conflicts the disputants do not negotiate in good faith with each other. This state of affairs negates to a great extent the assumption that the tactics of the field organ are insignificant, because the faith and good will of the parties is the only important factor. If this were true, there would be little reason to attempt peacemaking in any number of conflicts where any party, at the time of UN involvement, did not display good faith toward another. Thus the tactics used to try to overcome this psychological gulf between the disputants merit attention. This, of course, is not to deny that peacemaking tactics are more likely than not to result in successful role-execution when good faith *is* displayed by the disputants. Moreover, the efficacy of tactics is also affected by another contextual factor—the presence or absence of a relative balance of power among the disputants. On the one hand, a disputant clearly in a superior bargaining position will usually see little need to make concessions pursuant to a compromise settlement. On the other hand, a disputant in a clearly disadvantageous position may have little to lose by holding to an extreme bargaining position. Since he is already disadvantaged, there may be little reason to fear further setbacks, provided his basic security is not endangered. Thus a relative balance of power among the disputants seems to facilitate the impact of appropriate tactics. The successful tactics of the UNCI in the Dutch-Indonesian conflict are a case in point.[45]

One of the primary conclusions with regard to peacemaking tactics—one not yet realized by national and international officials—is that "time counts."[46] Not only in the study of international conflicts but also in the study of domestic labor disputes is the conclusion reached "that the 'cooling-off' concept as originally propounded has very little validity."[47] The passage of time does not usually result in a lessening of tension but rather in the reinforcement of mutually exclusive approaches to problems. Tensions tend to heat up over time, and policies become more fixed.[48] Yet most government officials tend to avoid crisis

[45] Taylor, *Indonesian Independence*, pp. 410–11, 421.

[46] Lord Hankey, *Diplomacy by Conference* (London: Ernst Benn, 1946), p. 171. See also Gordenker, *Peaceful Unification of Korea*, pp. 256–59, 262–64.

[47] Jackson, *Meeting of Minds*, p. 163; Robert O. Mathews, "The Suez Canal Dispute: A Case Study in Peaceful Settlement," *International Organization* 21, no. 1 (Winter 1967): 79–101.

[48] Claude argues that delay can prove useful in peaceful settlement efforts by the United Nations, and he cites the examples of Trieste, the Anglo-Iranian oil dispute, the question of an Austrian peace treaty, and the issue of West Irian (*Changing United Nations*, p. 218). In arguing that the United Nations can "nurse" disputes to a stage of "maturity," Claude presents a reasoned hypothesis. His examples, with the exception of Trieste, pertain to those cases that were largely ignored by the United Nations, not those where there was an intensive UN effort at settlement. This suggests two things. First, the examples given do not represent the most disruptive type of conflict, as evidenced by the lack of effort to solve them. Therefore the examples are of conflicts more likely than not

decisionmaking, and as recently as the 1967 war in the Middle East the Secretary-General sought unsuccessfully to avoid the conflict by playing for time and calling for a cooling-off period. The CCP was notably lacking in making time count, as it showed little sense of purpose, urgency, and drive for a goal during the early months of 1949 when a settlement was perhaps possible. CCP statements on a number of occasions endorsed cooling-off periods, yet there is no indication that such periods ever facilitated the work of the CCP. Despite the fact that the signing of the armistice agreements had lessened the need for a rapid settlement in the minds of the parties, the record of the CCP in making decisions quickly is much inferior to that of Bunche—who literally wore out the delegates of the parties with continuous meetings directed toward rapid attainment of specific goals.[49] It is quite true that the CCP was dealing with a variety of complex issues whereas Bunche was handling military matters of a limited nature. It can be stated, without casting any reflection on Bunche, that the most difficult problems were left for the CCP. Nevertheless, a start on solving complex problems is important to their more complete resolution in the future—even if that more complete treatment requires an extended period of research and administration. Part of the sound reasoning behind the Johnson approach to the refugee problem was his attempt to obtain a start on the solution while reserving the right of the parties to disengage from the process at a later date.

In this regard it can be said that the initial tactics of the subsidiary organ are of great importance, not only because of the need to treat the conflict prior to a hardening of attitudes but also because early tactical success is important to the early prestige of the organ and to the creation of a sense of progress and forward momentum in the negotiations. Initial tactical success increases the confidence of the disputants in the third party and in each

---

to solve themselves eventually. Second, it would appear that once the United Nations becomes intensively involved in a conflict, the concomitant emphasis on the problem necessitates that the third party "make time count" in order to counteract a fixation of policy on the part of the parties as a response to increased publicity.

[49] See further Azcárate, *Mission in Palestine*, p. 114.

other—which is then conducive to further lessening of tension and further agreement.

Maturity of judgments, in addition to speed in making those decisions, is important in conciliatory efforts. It would appear that generalizations are especially difficult to formulate on this subject because of the varying contexts and the multiplicity of substantive disputes with which the United Nations deals. It does appear that flexibility of decisionmaking structures promotes mature judgment[50] in that the field organ's accurate perception of needs of the parties and of the appropriateness of its own role is facilitated. The CCP had a fixation with use of conferences. Even after the lack of success with this tactic in 1949, the Commission intended to resume its efforts in 1950 with the same approach. It was not until the parties directly concerned changed the size and authority of their delegations to the CCP that the Commission resorted to the mixed-committee idea, and in 1951 it returned to the use of a formal conference. After this early period of diplomacy by conference, the CCP did use the "single individual" approach, even prior to Johnson's mission. But in the 1949–51 period, the CCP's highly structured approach impeded its perception that the Arab delegations were "hiding behind" the Commission and that the conferences were ill-suited to the Arab need to bypass domestic public opinion and interstate opinion through quiet diplomacy.[51]

It is also an important tactic in peacemaking to make every effort to facilitate clear communication and to keep communication lines open.[52] A number of UN field organs—including the CCP—have had difficulty in getting the disputant parties together

---

[50] See Jackson, *Meeting of Minds,* p. 146.

[51] In attempting to change its approach from diplomacy by conference to the Clapp Mission in August 1949, however, the CCP tried to pursue a negotiated solution at the same time that the research mission was underway. Thus the establishment of a study mission seeking economic solutions undercut the CCP's attempt to obtain a negotiated solution to the refugee problem. In the maintenance of a flexible approach, it is important not to pursue conflicting tactics at the same time or to change approaches so frequently that the field organ appears to vacillate in its decisions.

[52] See Stuart Chase, *Roads to Agreement* (London: Phoenix House, Ltd., 1952), pp. 235–40; Young, *Intermediaries,* esp. p. 39; and Mathews, "Suez Canal Dispute."

so that direct communication could be initiated.[53] By meeting with the Arab states *en bloc* and by not pressing diligently for some form of direct negotiations, the CCP did not make a vigorous effort to obtain effective communication among the parties to the Palestine question. The Lausanne conference was characterized more by a restatement of views by each party than by an exchange of views. Given the private contact among the parties, the direct meeting between the Egyptians and the Israelis on the issue of blocked accounts, and the indirect communication that went on through the CCP, it does not appear that the lack of tête-à-tête talks in the presence of the CCP was among the most influential factors impeding a settlement. But it is true that there could be little hope for improving the attitudes of the parties toward each other as long as they did not meet together in some fashion and learn of the mutual humanity and life in the Middle East that they shared. As Johnson stated in his 1964 article, the communication gulf between Israel and the Arabs operated to reinforce erroneous conclusions that each party maintained regarding the other—and to reinforce the confidence of each that it understood the other, despite having no contact across the gulf.[54]

A final conclusion about the tactics of peacemaking organs suggests that if the negotiations are secret, the attitudes of the parties are less likely to become fixed. If the talks are quiet, the policies of the parties are less likely to be based on prestige factors and more likely to be based on more concrete state interests. The more flexible the attitudes of the parties and the more concern expressed for factual situations rather than nebulous and subjec-

[53] See Jackson, "Mediation and Conciliation," pp. 538–39. Neither the United Nations Commission on Korea (UNCOK) nor the United Nations Special Committee on the Balkans could get the parties together. The Indian-Pakistan Commission was also unable to obtain communication during the early phases of that conflict.

[54] What seemed to be needed in the Arab-Israeli conflict was not formal, direct talks since the Arabs had understandable psychological reasons and *raisons d'état* for avoiding this process. What was needed in this conflict was either informal direct talks, perhaps "behind the back" of the third party, or the type of mediation carried out by Eric Johnston on the Jordan waters problem—characterized by the transmission of specific ideas and policies from one party to another.

tive values, the more likely a settlement becomes.[55] As noted previously, the CCP's formal conferences, widely reported on by the Middle East press, were not conducive to the needs of the Arab states. And the study of the Johnson mission, encompassing the two press stories that damaged the outcome of his efforts, strongly validates the hypothesis that "premature publicity . . . may be fatal." [56]

There would appear to be, however, a role for publicity in peacemaking efforts. Publicity can be used by a third party as a means of exposing a party's reason for maintaining a policy opposed by the third party. The CCP threatened to submit a detailed report of the parties' policies to the General Assembly on several occasions. In addition, publicity can be employed by the third party to counteract some tendency within the negotiations that the third party believes to be detrimental to the solution of the conflict. In this regard, there is reason to argue that Johnson's final report should have been made public in order to counteract future Arab emphasis on the letter of paragraph 11 of A/Res/194(III), and to counteract Israel's distortion of his proposals. While secrecy is needed in the actual negotiations, there may be a need for an appropriately timed blending of publicity and privacy.

The execution of UN peacemaking roles is facilitated by close liaison among various field organs working on related problems and by direct supervision by one organ over the others.[57] Peacemaking seems to be especially enhanced by coordination of peacemaking and peacekeeping operations.[58] In conflicts characterized by the use of force, there is an understandable tendency

---

[55] On the need to emphasize facts, see Chase, *Roads to Agreements,* pp. 235–40.

[56] Hankey, *Diplomacy by Conference,* p. 36.

[57] Peacebuilding organs are included under this maxim. UNRWA's programs of vocational training for Palestinian refugees and ONUC's civilian operations directed toward state-building in the Congo are examples in point.

[58] "The operation of the subsidiary bodies in these fields has shown that the functions of bringing about a termination of hostilities and of assisting the parties to reach a substantive agreement are closely intertwined" (Jackson, *Meeting of Minds,* p. 116).

for the United Nations to place primary emphasis on ending the fighting, then in a secondary consideration turn to an attempted settlement of the problems underlying the fighting.[59] The justifiable primary emphasis of the United Nations has been to try and save lives. There are, however, possible disadvantages for peacemaking involved in this sequence of emphases. While some of these disadvantages are perhaps unavoidable, their negative impact on peacemaking can in some cases be reduced.

First, an overly narrow emphasis on peacekeeping may result in an unintentional and contentious attempt to resolve some of the substantive issues of the conflict. Law and order are not inherently neutral and value-free. Certain values and certain elites are protected by any system of order. Thus all peacekeeping is policy-oriented rather than neutral, to some degree. Hence a problem arises when UN peacekeeping operations are based on the assumption that large-scale order can be obtained first and the issues of the conflict treated later. A related problem arises when the United Nations cannot build a consensus in support of the system of order it has tried to create—that is, in support of its attempt to resolve some of the basic issues of the conflict. The probable outcome in such situations is increased conflict and complexity rather than increased order. The classic example is UN peacekeeping in the Congo crisis. The United Nations, through the actions of the Secretary-General, sought the removal from the area of Belgian personnel—in anticipation of "holding operation" for UN peacekeeping forces. But subsequently the Secretary-General discovered that UN forces were deeply involved in unintended peacemaking through assistance to the central Congolese government in opposition to the leader of secessionist Katanga province and its leader Tshombe. In short, the Secretary-General discovered that a "rigorous order of priorities" between peacekeeping and peacemaking was unobtainable.[60] Further UN peacekeeping involved ONUC in further conflict-resolution, but much of this initially unintended peacemaking was intensely opposed by a

---

[59] This is not to suggest that any of the three types of involvement naturally occurs first.

[60] Miller, *World Order,* pp. 76–77.

number of nonaligned and communist states. The tenuous order that was obtained after some four years of confusion was achieved at a heavy price by the United Nations, measured in terms of loss of men, money, prestige, and future utility in conflict situations. A clearer conception of the inherent relationship between peacekeeping and peacemaking would probably have led to more limited but less contentious intervention.

Second, the political relations among the disputants at the time that peacekeeping occurs may be solidified, thus reducing the probability of success for peacemaking. Reduction in the level of violence and concomitant gain in limited security may lessen the desire of the disputants to move beyond a cease-fire to negotiation of the more fundamental problems of the conflict. As the Secretary-General said in his 1965 Annual Report: "The very fact that [these unresolved conflicts] have become an accepted and semi-permanent part of the way of life in the areas has tended to . . . reduce the sense of urgency which might stimulate a search . . . for a basic and peaceful solution. . . . "[61] The Cyprus and Palestine conflicts provide specific examples of this general rule. Particularly in the latter case it can be said that peacekeeping, in the form of the negotiation of the armistice agreements, reduced the desire of some of the parties to negotiate a settlement; the Arabs obtained relief from Israeli military force without having to negotiate on nonmilitary matters.

Relatedly, it does not appear that a cease-fire agreement or other success in peacekeeping inherently leads to an expansion of the scope of agreement. The converse appears to be true: the peacekeeping success is usually so fragile, tenuous, and prone to violation, that the security and mutual respect derived from the termination of general hostilities tend to decrease rather than increase. It is too soon to make this judgment with regard to successful peacekeeping in Cyprus, but it is obviously the case in the Arab-Israeli and Indian-Pakistani conflicts.[62]

[61] Quoted in Lincoln P. Bloomfield, "Peacekeeping and Peacemaking," *Foreign Affairs* 44, no. 4 (July 1966): 677.

[62] On the decline of security derived from the Middle East Armistice Agreements, see J. C. Hurewitz, "The UN and Disimperialism in the Middle East," *International*

Third, a full and complete settlement of military matters in conjunction with peacekeeping may reduce the number of malleable factors with which the peacemaking organ can deal, thus lessening the maneuverability of the organ in the settlement negotiations. In both the Kashmir and Indonesian conflicts, efforts to secure a durable peace were combined with immediate efforts to stop the fighting.[63] In the Indonesian case, the presence of negotiable factors pertaining to military matters aided the field organ in obtaining a more general settlement. And in both these cases, the suggested terms of a general settlement aided the efforts to secure an end to the fighting. In the case of Palestine, not only did the signing of the armistice agreements remove bargaining points concerning military matters from the purview of the CCP, but also those agreements tended to legitimize, in a de facto process, the territorial situation existing at the end of the war. It is true that the agreements stated explicitly that they did not constitute the final settlement of the territorial question. But it is also true that after those agreements were signed, Israel had little motivation to make territorial concessions when the Arab states had already agreed—in a permanent and formal agreement—to stop fighting and leave Israel in control of the territory listed.

On the other hand, there remain two reasons for seeking an immediate cease-fire. First, lives are being lost; second, there is the possibility that peacemaking negotiations can be interrupted and pushed into a position of secondary importance because of some new outbreak of hostilities. Without a consistent limitation on the use of force, the instability of the conflict situation is likely to be an impediment to prolonged concentration on a more general settlement. On several occasions Count Bernadotte had to interrupt his attempts to gain a general settlement on the Palestine question and work toward the pacification of some renewed hostilities. The same was true of Bunche's efforts to negotiate the armistice agreements. Thus primary emphasis to peacekeeping should be given in a reaction to a crisis.

Organization 19, no. 3 (Summer 1965): 755; and David Brook, _Preface to Peace_ (Washington, D.C.: Public Affairs Press, 1966), p. 30 and _passim_.

[63] Jackson, _Meeting of Minds,_ p. 117.

Yet there remains a need for the third party, whether peacekeeper or peacemaker or both, to be aware of the peace-making roles inherently involved in trying to establish order when the disputants themselves have not agreed upon the type and degree of order desired—and when the parent body has not agreed upon the type and degree of order it is prepared to enforce. One of the most important differences between UNEF in the Sinai and ONUC in the Congo was that UNEF's basic task in 1956-67 was to keep the minimum degree of order that the disputants had reached agreement on, while in the Congo there was no such minimum agreement among the competing factions—and no agreement among the influential member states of the United Nations. There also remains a need for the third party not to formalize and solidify the cease-fire positions of the disputants any more than necessary. In this regard, it would appear to facilitate the work of the peacemaking organ to proceed directly from cease-fire negotiations to settlement negotiations, without the intervening negotiation of a formal armistice. Likewise, it would appear to facilitate the role-execution of the peacemaker for the cease-fire to be of an indeterminate nature rather than one imposing a permanent cessation of force. Such measures would tend to keep the general situation somewhat flexible—and there-fore negotiable—and to keep the disputants from becoming overly satisfied with the limited security derived from the cease-fire. It is not yet clear to what extent a division of structures helps or hinders the appropriate coordination of peacekeeping and peace-making interventions. In the aftermath of the Congo morass, characterized by a confusing overlap of peacekeeping and peace-making efforts, the United Nations resorted to a precise division of labor and structure in the Cyprus intervention: the peace-keeping was clearly separated from the peacemaking (indeed, at one juncture there was a mediator to handle day-to-day problems and another mediator to handle more long-range subjects). But in the Arab-Israeli conflict the lack of liaison between Bunche as peacekeeper and the CCP as peacemaker was detrimental to the overall resolution of conflict.

174

The UN peacemaking record over the last two decades is not very impressive. There is no point in trying to avoid the basic truth that "settling disputes is an even more demanding task than pacifying them."[64] The peacemaker frequently faces parochial if not chauvinistic attitudes on the part of the disputants, and in seeking to mobilize influence vis-à-vis the disputants, the subsidiary organ finds itself dealing with a fragmented global political system in which effective support is obtained only with the utmost effort.

In many conflict situations, minor roles by the UN subsidiary organ can be expected to produce little progress in peacemaking. Procedural recommendations and requests for policy clarifications are not likely to change attitudes toward highly valued issues. In conflicts of intense antagonism, which unfortunately are prevalent rather than scarce, the only realistic approach to resolution of the conflict is the successful mobilization of governmental influence on the disputants pursuant to a settlement which will prove itself durable. The probabilities of a UN subsidiary organ recommending such a settlement are enhanced by the disinterested origin of the organ and the expertise of the personnel chosen. The probabilities of a UN subsidiary organ being successful in mobilizing governmental influence in support of its recommendations depend in part upon the execution of the various peacemaking roles, which in turn depends upon the composition, mandate, tactics, and relations to other parties involved in the conflict. In part, the successful mobilization of influence also depends upon a growing awareness of interdependence, mutual vulnerability, and a common destiny on behalf of the actors in the global political system.

In the foreseeable future UN peacemaking will be a difficult operation, for the United Nations remains half way between being its own master and being the spokesman for a fragmented world. States still ask it to do more for them than they are willing to do

---

[64] Bloomfield, "Peacekeeping and Peacemaking," p. 677.

for it.[65] UN peacemaking is likely at times to be "subjected to the most severe attacks, but these may serve roughly to measure the usefulness of the UN in making politically possible a renunciation which might otherwise cost much more bloodshed and travail."[66]

[65] See Stanley Hoffman, "In Search of a Thread: The UN in the Congo Labyrinth," *International Organization* 16, no. 2 (Spring 1962): 331–61.

[66] Whitney T. Perkins, "Sanctions for Political Change—The Indonesian Case," *International Organization* 12, no. 1 (Winter 1958): 42.

APPENDIX A

GENERAL ASSEMBLY RESOLUTION 194(III), 11 DECEMBER 1948

The General Assembly,

Having considered further the situation in Palestine,

1. *Expresses* its deep appreciation of the progress achieved through the good offices of the late United Nations Mediator in promoting a peaceful adjustment of the future situation of Palestine, for which cause he sacrificed his life; and

Extends its thanks to the Acting Mediator and his staff for their continued efforts and devotion to duty in Palestine;

2. *Establishes* a Conciliation Commission consisting of three States Members of the United Nations which shall have the following functions:

(a) To assume, in so far as it considers necessary in existing circumstances, the functions given to the United Nations Mediator on Palestine by resolution 186(S—2) of the General Assembly of 14 May 1948;

(b) To carry out the specific functions and directives given to it by the present resolution and such additional functions and directives as may be given to it by the General Assembly or by the Security Council;

(c) To undertake, upon the request of the Security Council, any of the functions now assigned to the United Nations Mediator on Palestine or to the United Nations Truce Commission by resolutions of the Security Council; upon such request to the Conciliation Commission by the Security Council with respect to all the remaining functions of the United Nations Mediator on Palestine under Security Council resolutions, the office of the Mediator shall be terminated;

3. *Decides* that a Committee of the Assembly, consisting of China, France, the Union of Soviet Socialist Republics, the United Kingdom and the United States of America, shall present, before the end of the first part of the present session of the General Assembly, for the approval of the Assembly, a proposal concerning the names of the three States which will constitute the Conciliation Commission;

4. *Requests* the Commission to begin its functions at once, with a view to the establishment of contact between the parties themselves and the Commission at the earliest possible date;

5. *Calls upon* the Governments and authorities concerned to extend the scope of the negotiations provided for in the Security Council's resolution of 16 November 1948[1] and to seek agreement by negotiations conducted either

[1] See *Official Records of the Security Council,* Third Year, No. 126.

177

with the Conciliation Commission or directly, with a view to the final settlement of all questions outstanding between them;

6. *Instructs* the Conciliation Commission to take steps to assist the Governments and authorities concerned to achieve a final settlement of all questions outstanding between them;

7. *Resolves* that the Holy Places—including Nazareth—religious building and sites in Palestine should be protected and free access to them assured, in accordance with existing rights and historical practice; that arrangements to this end should be under effective United Nations supervision; that the United Nations Conciliation Commission, in presenting to the fourth regular session of the General Assembly its detailed proposals for a permanent international regime for the territory of Jerusalem, should include recommendations concerning the Holy Places in that territory; that with regard to the Holy Places in the rest of Palestine the Commission should call upon the political authorities of the areas concerned to give appropriate formal guarantees as to the protection of the Holy Places and access to them; and that these undertakings should be presented to the General Assembly for approval;

8. *Resolves* that, in view of its association with three world religions, the Jerusalem area, including the present municipality of Jerusalem *plus* the surrounding villages and towns, the most eastern of which shall be Abu Dis; the most southern, Bethlehem; the most western, Ein Karim (including also the built-up area of Motsa); and the most northern, Shu'fat, should be accorded special and separate treatment from the rest of Palestine and should be placed under effective United Nations control;

Requests the Security Council to take further steps to ensure the demilitarization of Jerusalem at the earliest possible date;

Instructs the Conciliation Commission to present to the fourth regular session of the General Assembly detailed proposals for a permanent international regime for the Jerusalem area which will provide for the maximum local autonomy for distinctive groups consistent with the special international status of the Jerusalem area;

The Conciliation Commission is authorized to appoint a United Nations representative, who shall co-operate with the local authorities with respect to the interim administration of the Jerusalem area;

9. *Resolves* that, pending agreement on more detailed arrangements among the Governments and authorities concerned, the freest possible access to Jerusalem by road, rail or air should be accorded to all inhabitants of Palestine;

Instructs the Conciliation Commission to report immediately to the Security Council, for appropriate action by that organ, any attempt by any party to impede such access;

10. *Instructs* the Conciliation Commission to seek arrangements among the Governments and authorities concerned which will facilitate the

economic development of the area, including arrangements for access to ports and airfields and the use of transportation and communication facilities;

11. *Resolves* that the refugees wishing to return to their homes and live at peace with their neighbours should be permitted to do so at the earliest practicable date, and that compensation should be paid for the property of those choosing not to return and for loss of or damage to property which, under principles of international law or in equity, should be made good by the Governments or authorities responsible;

Instructs the Conciliation Commission to facilitate the repatriation, resettlement and economic and social rehabilitation of the refugees and the payment of compensation, and to maintain close relations with the Director of the United Nations Relief for Palestine Refugees and, through him, with the appropriate organs and agencies of the United Nations;

12. *Authorizes* the Conciliation Commission to appoint such subsidiary bodies and to employ such technical experts, acting under its authority, as it may find necessary for the effective discharge of its functions and responsibilities under the present resolution;

The Conciliation Commission will have its official headquarters at Jerusalem. The authorities responsible for maintaining order in Jerusalem will be responsible for taking all measures necessary to ensure the security of the Commission. The Secretary-General will provide a limited number of guards for the protection of the staff and premises of the Commission;

13. *Instructs* the Conciliation Commission to render progress reports periodically to the Secretary-General for transmission to the Security Council and to the Members of the United Nations;

14. *Calls upon* all Governments and authorities concerned to co-operate with the Conciliation Commission and to take all possible steps to assist in the implementation of the present resolution;

15. *Requests* the Secretary-General to provide the necessary staff and facilities and to make appropriate arrangements to provide the necessary funds required in carrying out the terms of the present resolution.

Hundred and eighty-sixth plenary meeting,
11 December 1948

At the 186th plenary meeting on 11 December 1948, a committee of the Assembly consisting of the five States designated in paragraph 3 of the above resolution proposed that the following three States should constitute the Conciliation Commission:

France, Turkey, United States of America.

The proposal of the Committee having been adopted by the General Assembly at the same meeting, the Conciliation Commission is therefore composed of the above-mentioned three States.

A CHRONOLOGY OF THE DIPLOMATIC
HISTORY OF THE CCP

December 1948	CCP created via A/Res/194(III); comprehensive mandate given; "Big Five" names three government members (France, Turkey, United States).
	Egyptians request negotiations through United Nations to end Palestine war; Security Council urges CCP to complete organization and supervise talks; acting mediator (Bunche) meets Egyptians and Israelis at Rhodes.
February 1949	CCP completes organization after delays; agrees not to intervene in Egyptian-Israeli armistice negotiations; later decides to let Bunche also negotiate three other armistice agreements.
	CCP declines to facilitate separate Israeli-Jordanian settlement; decides to seek more general Arab-Israeli treaty; finds that Arab states (except Jordan) want Israel to agree to repatriation of Palestinian refugees prior to talks.
March 1949	CCP assembles delegations from interested Arab states in Beirut; persuades Arabs to drop demand for precondition to talks; persuades Arabs to agree to a meeting in Lausanne for "an exchange of views"; Israeli delegation to be present.
April–May 1949	Lausanne conference initiated by CCP; Israel's application for membership in United Nations debated by General Assembly; Israel, via CCP, offers family reunification plan for limited repatriation of refugees; Arabs, acting *en bloc*, make no immediate comment on Israel's offer, but concentrate on trying to make Israel's UN membership conditional upon concessions in peace negotiations; Assembly admits Israel to membership.
12 May 1949	Lausanne protocol signed by disputants; CCP initiative results in linking of territorial and refu-

gee questions; boundaries of partition resolution accepted as a basis for negotiations; stalemate ensues as Israel advocates settlement on basis of post-bellum status quo; Arabs indirectly advocate return to territorial provisions of partition resolution with immediate limited repatriation.

29 May 1949   United States exerts diplomatic threat vis-à-vis Israel; formal note threatens changes in US policies toward Israel if UN resolutions not accepted as guidelines for Israeli policy; CCP aware of US action; Israel refuses to change policy; United States declines to carry out threat; CCP indirectly discredited by US vacillation.

June 1949   Israel, persuaded by CCP, offers to take control of Gaza territory, including refugees therein; Arabs reject offer.

July—August 1949   Israel, persuaded by CCP *inter alia*, offers to repatriate 100,000 if refugees can be relocated in Israel according to security-economic needs; Arabs, saying all refugees have right to original homes, reject offer; Arabs make repatriation proposal, linked to territorial provisions of partition resolution; Israel rejects proposal.

August 1949   CCP establishes mixed committee on blocked accounts; tête-à-tête talks ensue between Egyptians and Israelis in presence of CCP official; no agreements reached despite realistic negotiation.

CCP asks disputants to clarify policies; *inter alia*, Jordan and Syria offer to resettle some refugees; Egypt hedges, implies resettlement could be linked to border adjustments; Israel agrees to drop restrictions on 100,000-scheme; CCP fails to follow up on policy statements of disputants; concentrates instead on creation of Clapp Mission to study refugee question.

September 1949   Israel asks for reduced CCP role in negotiations.

October—November 1949   General Assembly focuses on status of Jerusalem; CCP compromise draft statute for international regime for city rejected by disputants; CCP defends its draft, but Assembly votes to establish a *corpus separatum* for the city and turns subject over to Trusteeship Council; issue subsequently beomes dead-letter, as Council reports back to Assembly in 1950 and Assembly takes no action.

17 November 1949   Clapp Mission reports circa 725,000 Arab Palestinian refugees outside Israel; reports that negotiated settlement necessary for economic improvement of refugees.

December 1949   General Assembly creates UNRWA to administer relief to Palestinian refugees; asks CCP to continue efforts with same composition and same mandate —minus the Jerusalem question.

January—February 1950   CCP suggests creation of one mixed committee for peace negotiations; Arabs insist Israel first agree to principle of repatriation; Israel refuses.

March 1950   CCP suggests creation of several mixed committees for discussion of various issues; Arabs make same demand; Israel still refuses.

25 May 1950   Tripartite Declaration issued by France, United Kingdom, United States; endorses existing boundaries in Middle East; thus solidifies Arab-Israeli stalemate; CCP aware of this effect.

August 1950   CCP makes tour of Arab capitals; only area for progress seen to be issue of compensation to Palestinian refugees; CCP seeks compensation payment by Israel without general settlement, as catalyst for resettlement; conflict with UNRWA develops regarding which agency is responsible for resettlement.

October 1950   CCP reports to General Assembly; urges Assembly not to accept "negative peace" now present but urges further Assembly directives, especially on refugee question.

December 1950	General Assembly creates Refugee Office under CCP aegis; work of office to be directed toward matter of compensation.
Spring 1951	Refugee Office organized; CCP pursues no diplomacy; conflict again arises with UNRWA regarding status of office; UNRWA fears office will usurp its duties.
August 1951	Refugee Office estimates value of Arab refugee property in Israel to be circa $240,000,000.
September 1951	Paris conference begins at CCP initiative; Arabs refuse to sign CCP draft nonaggression pact; CCP skirts issue and submits comprehensive outline for settlement; disputants criticize outline, and stalemate continues.
November 1951	CCP reports to General Assembly; says it cannot execute its mandate; says UN organs in Middle East need to be coordinated.
December 1951	General Assembly debates future of CCP; finally decides not to change CCP composition or mandate; but United States and Secretariat decide to reduce CCP role to that of symbolizing UN interest in conflict; CCP gets low budget outlay and moves headquarters to New York.
1952–57	Subject of blocked accounts treated; negotiations start in 1952; limited release obtained in 1953; difficulties alleviated by CCP official, and release operations continue; by 1957, circa $9,000,000 unfrozen from state banks and returned to owners; mutual agreement to unfreeze accounts does not lead to agreement on political questions.
1952–64	Subject of value of Arab refugee property in Israel treated; massive identification and evaluation effort undertaken; United Kingdom provides information from mandate days; CCP seeks to obtain base figure of value according to 1947 standard; base figure could then be adjusted to account for demands of disputants in negotiations; CCP evalu-

| | ates property, as of 1947, at approximately $480,000,000, but keeps figure secret; no negotiations undertaken on basis of identification and evaluation work. |

May 1961   CCP decides to use "Special Representative" approach on refugee question; United States initiates move; France and Turkey hesitant; United States and France mutually suspicious of each other's intentions; mission is labeled a fact-finding inquiry.

August 1961   Joseph E. Johnson named Special Representative; Hammarskjold and Kennedy seek to facilitate mission.

Fall 1961   Johnson spends September in Middle East; finds Arab policies ambiguous; finds Israeli leaders difficult to deal with and almost terminates mission; Israel implies Johnson is trying to give "free choice" to Arab refugees; Israel's Foreign Minister upset by Johnson's revision of his report to CCP.

November 1961   Johnson mission and report endorsed by CCP; report indicates some hope for step-by-step approach to refugee question, although report acknowledges question to be part of overall Palestine question; Arab public statements critical; Israeli statements also critical, but privately.

December 1961   General Assembly requests CCP to continue its efforts on refugee question; no change in nature of Assembly debates; traditional recriminations and subjects arise.

March 1962   Johnson reappointed and instructed to give CCP recommendations on how to treat refugee question.

April—May 1962   Johnson goes to Middle East; seeks agreement on "pilot project"; wants parties to agree to accept limited number of refugees for repatriation and resettlement in simultaneous, open-ended process;

184

Israel asks for specific limitations; Jordan fears eventual threat of domestic repercussion.

May–June 1962
Jordan tries to mobilize opposition to pilot project; fears coup d'état by dissatisfied Palestinians; leaks inaccurate story to Beirut paper; sends communiqués to other Arab states; seeks to put itself on public record as opposing project.

Summer 1962
Johnson considers terminating mission again; finally decides on alternative approach; does not return to Middle East; does not believe disputants will reach agreement inter se voluntarily.

September 1962
Johnson's report presented to parties for comments, without CCP or Assembly endorsement; report advocates listing of preferences by refugees regarding repatriation or resettlement in any nation; preferences subject to veto by receiving state for security reasons; compensation part of process; gradual start foreseen; unilateral disengagement allowed. Israel indicates privately that plan is unacceptable. Arab joint statement says plan is not suitable framework for discussion. Disputants wait for adversary to make public rejection.

October 1962
Johnson plan disclosed by *Chicago Daily News;* Syria gives public rejection quickly thereafter; US policy remains noncommittal, publicly and privately; pro-Israel pressure groups and individuals lobby against Johnson plan in United States and United Nations; attempt to distort contents of plan.

12 November 1962
Israeli Knesset approves declaration that only solution to refugee question is resettlement.

Early December 1962
White House decides not to exert influence in support of Johnson plan; prospects for implementing plan via US persuasion-pressure not seen to be good; prospects of domestic political feedback via Jewish voters taken into account; plan not to be made public.

7 December 1962	CCP submits bland report to General Assembly; does not mention Johnson plan. General Assembly later instructs CCP to continue efforts on refugee question.
February 1963	Johnson resigns as Special Representative; statement implies criticism of CCP and United States for not giving support; also implies paragraph 11 cannot be implemented as written; United States subsequently makes weak follow-up on Johnson mission; no belated acceptance of plan by disputants.
1964	CCP publishes methodology used in identification and evaluation work.
Spring 1966	Arab states challenge validity of identification and evaluation methodology; CCP tries to initiate negotiations on technical aspects of its work, but Arabs do not respond further.
Fall 1966	CCP reports to General Assembly that it is not able to effect any change in the configuration of the Arab-Israeli conflict.
June 1967	Third Arab-Israeli war.
Post-June 1967 to present	CCP inactive; Secretary-General bypasses CCP and appoints Jarring as mediator in conflict; France changes sides and endorses Arab policies; US-Israeli ties remain close.

BIBLIOGRAPHY

On the United Nations Conciliation Commission for Palestine

Primary data from United Nations and government sources

General Assembly debates from the third session to the present, and Supplements to those debates as appropriate. Tedious reading, but helpful in understanding the bitterness of the Arab-Israeli conflict. Glimpses given of dissatisfaction with the CCP by various member governments of the Assembly. Patterns of interests over time revealed, such as Arab emphasis on refugee property within Israel. Problem is unreliability of government public statements, especially Arab.

Progress Reports of the CCP. Particularly informative in providing official outline of Arab-Israeli conflict. Useful guideline for raising questions about why and how something was done. Frequently uninformative on the specifics of crucial decisions.

A/819,	15 March	1949
A/833,	5 April	1949
A/927,	21 June	1949
A/992,	22 September	1949
A/1252,	14 December	1949
A/1255,	29 May	1950
A/1288,	17 July	1950
A/1367,	2 September	1950; and Rev. 1, 2 October 1950; and Add. 1, 24 October 1950
A/1793,	10 March	1951

A/1985,	19 November	1951
A/2121,	2 May	1952
A/2216,	8 October	1952; and Add. 1, 24 November 1952
A/2629,	4 January	1954
A/2897,	3 March	1955
A/3199,	4 October	1956
A/3835,	18 June	1958
A/4225,	22 September	1959
A/4573,	14 November	1960
A/4921,	15 October	1961; and Add. 1, 22 November 1961
A/5337,	7 December	1962
A/5545,	1 November	1963
A/5700,	5 November	1964
A/6225,	28 December	1965
A/6451,	30 September	1966

Other CCP records remain restricted, with the exception of the select list presented below.

A/AC.25/W.81/Rev. 2, *The Question of Reintegration by Repatriation or Resettlement*, 1961.

A/AC.25/W.82/Rev. 1, *The Question of Compensation*, 1961.

A/AC.25/W.84, *Working Paper Prepared by the Commission's Land Expert on the Methods and Techniques of Identification and Valuation of Arab Refugee Immovable Property Holdings in Israel*, 1964.

Final Report of the United Nations Economic Survey Mission for the Middle East: An Approach to Economic Development in the Middle East, Lake Success, 1949, 2 vols.

Also relevant are several background papers prepared by F. E. Jarvis, Technical Representative of the CCP, on his own authority. These have not been adopted by the CCP but are available through that organ.

Jarvis, F. E. "Financial Aspects." Mimeographed, n.d., 5 pp.

————. "The Meaning and Amount of Compensation." Mimeographed, n.d., 9 pp.

————. "The Meaning of the Term 'Refugee' in the Context of the Palestine Question." Mimeographed, n.d., 3 pp.

————. "The Payment of Compensation—Three Outline Plans." Mimeographed, n.d., 4 pp.

————. "The Relationship between Compensation and Rehabilitation." Mimeographed, n.d., 7 pp.

————. "The Status of Expropriated Property in International Law with Special Reference to the Palestine Refugees." Mimeographed, n.d., 18 pp.

————— . "The Status of Refugees in the Context of the Palestine Question." Mimeographed, n.d., 13 pp.

Government publications of special note:

Department of State Publication 3765, *United States Participation in the United Nations: Report by the President to the Congress for the Year 1949.* Washington, D.C.: Government Printing Office, 1950.

Department of State Publication 5034, *United States Participation in the United Nations: Report by the President to the Congress for the Year 1952*, Washington, D.C.: Government Printing Office, 1953.

Howard, Harry N. *The Development of United States Policy in the Near East, 1945-1951.* Reprint from *Department of State Bulletin*, 19 and 26 November 1951. Washington, D.C.: Government Printing Office, 1952.

United States Senate Committee on Foreign Relations, Sub-Committee on the United Nations Charter. Pacific Settlement of Disputes in the United Nations. Staff Study No. 5. Washington, D.C.: Government Printing Office, 1954.

Activities of Non-diplomatic Representatives of Foreign Principles in the United States. Hearings before the Committee on Foreign Relations, United States Senate, 88th Congress, First Session, Part 9 (May 23, 1963).

Newspaper sources

The New York Times and the *Palestine Post*, later *Jerusalem Post*, provide English-language coverage of the daily actions of the CCP since 1948. Two English-language news review publications are useful for the most recent actions of the CCP: *Middle East Record* (Jerusalem, Israel: Israel Program for Scientific Translations, yearly); and *Mideast Mirror: A Review of Middle East News* (Beirut: The Arab News Agency, yearly). English translations of Arab daily papers such as *Al Ahram* can be obtained through American embassies.

Secondary sources dealing specifically with the CCP

Azcárate, Pablo de. *Mission in Palestine 1948—1953*. Washington, D.C.: Middle East Institute, 1966. Political memoirs by the first principal secretary of the CCP. Frequently very perceptive in both a political and a philosophical sense. Much inside information of interest to serious students of diplomacy. Work uneven in value, however, because of author's limited perspective which results in a number of factual and interpretative errors.

Eytan, Walter. *The First Ten Years*. New York: Simon & Schuster, 1958. A diplomatic history of early Israeli foreign policy by the first Director General of the Israel Foreign Office. Praises Bunche and criticizes the CCP. Emphasizes CCP decision to treat Arabs *en bloc*. Articulates view

189

that failure of peacemaking by the United Nations was due to CCP and Arab policy. No second guesses regarding Israeli policy.

Gabbay, Rony E. *A Political Study of the Arab-Jewish Conflict: The Arab Refugee Problem (A Case Study).* Geneva: Droz, 1959. A massive study, even longer than its title. Reams of descriptive data on most phases of refugee question until mid-1950s. Little analysis of CCP tactics and political relationships. Conclusions not very impressive, and documentation becomes cumbersome at many points. Remains an essential reference source for an early history of the refugee problem.

Hamzeh, Fuad Said. *International Conciliation with Special Reference to the Work of the United Nations Conciliation Commission for Palestine.* The Hague: Drukkerij Pasmans, 1964. A formal-legal approach which in the end comprises a tautology: the CCP should have carried out its mandate by carrying out its mandate. Moralistic and polemical. Many definitions and attempts at analyses are not precise. Little regard for contextual factors. Little regard for anything beyond legal concerns, and even they are not well understood and presented.

Hurewitz, J. C. "The United Nations Conciliation Commission for Palestine: Establishment and Definition of Functions." *International Organization* 7 (November 1953): 482–97. Article does not seek to appraise field work of CCP. Emphasizes change in thinking during 1949 regarding role of CCP—which was reflection of CCP failure in field. CCP first seen as the UN organ for Arab-Israeli conflict. Bunche and others then changed view of CCP role, making UNTSO autonomous. CCP thus given more narrow scope of action.

Johnson, Joseph E. "Arab v. Israeli: A Persistent Challenge." *Middle East Journal* 18, no. 1 (Winter 1964): 1–13. Reflections by the CCP Special Representative on the refugee question during 1961–62. Stresses role of United States in bringing about change in Arab-Israeli conflict. Discloses role of Zionist lobbying in the United States and the United Nations. Gives indication of basic concepts underlying his proposals on the refugee question.

Lenord, Larry. "The United Nations and Palestine." *International Conciliation*, no. 454 (October 1949), pp. 607–786. Early compilation of relevant UN documents on Palestine question. Descriptive data presented on basis of first three progress reports of CCP.

Peretz, Don. *Israel and the Palestine Arabs.* Washington, D.C.: The Middle East Institute, 1956. An objective study, largely narrative rather than analytic. Arab policies and CCP tactics given little attention. Ambiguous use of word "pressure" and ambiguous documentation at points. Very detailed treatment of negotiations regarding blocked accounts. A carefully written reference source, particularly with regard to the influence of Israeli domestic politics on its foreign policy.

190

BIBLIOGRAPHY

Shwadran, Benjamin. "The Palestine Conciliation Commission." *Middle Eastern Affairs* 1, no. 10 (October 1950): 271—85. Good chronology of early CCP action. Frequent assertions without supporting reasoning or documentation. Not entirely objective presentation. Conclusions thin.

Other secondary sources dealing to some degree with the CCP

Articles

Alami, Musa. "The Lesson of Palestine." *Middle East Journal* 3, no. 4 (October 1949): 373—405.
Badeau, John S. "Development and Diplomacy in the Middle East." *Bulletin of Atomic Scientists* 22, no. 5 (May 1966): 5—10.
Childers, Erskine B. "Palestine: The Broken Triangle." *Journal of International Affairs* 19, no. 1 (1965): 87—99.
Clapp, Gordon R. "An Approach to Economic Development in the Middle East." *International Conciliation*, no. 468 (April 1950), pp. 203—17.
Davis, John H. "Arab-Israel Conflict: A Challenge to Leadership." *Arab Journal* 2, no. 3 (Summer 1965): 28—32.
Giniewski, Paul. "La Paix Israeli-Arabe, Est-Elle Possible?" *Politique Etranger* 20 (July 1955): 355—68.
Glick, Edward B. "The Vatican, Latin America and Jerusalem." *International Organization* 11, no. 2 (Spring 1957): 213—19.
Hodes, Aubrey. "Signpost to a Solution." *New Outlook* (March—April 1964), pp. 32—39.
Howard, Harry. "The United States and Israel: Conflict of Interest and Policy." *Issues* 18, no. 4 (Summer 1964): 14—27.
Hurewitz, J. C. "The UN and Disimperialism in the Middle East." *International Organization* 19, no. 3 (Summer 1965): 749—63.
Lehrman, Hal. "The UN Tangle over Jerusalem." *Commentary* 9 (February 1950): 105—14.
London, Isaac. "Evolution of the U.S.S.R.'s Policy in the Middle East." *Middle Eastern Affairs* 7, no. 5 (May 1956): 169—78.
Mezerik, A. G., ed. "Arab—Israel Conflict and the United Nations." *International Review Service* 8, no. 73 (1962).
Mohn, Paul. "Jerusalem and the United Nations." *International Conciliation*, no. 464 (October 1950), pp. 435—71.
Peretz, Don. "The Arab Refugees: A Changing Problem." *Foreign Affairs* 41, no. 3 (April 1963): 558—70.
————. "Israel's New Arab Dilemma." *Middle East Journal* 22, no. 1 (Winter 1968): 45—47.
————. "Problems of Arab Refugee Compensation." *Middle East Journal* 8, no. 4 (Autumn 1954): 403—16.

Stevens, Georgiana G. "Arab Refugees: 1948–1952." *Middle East Journal* 6, no. 3 (Summer 1952): 281–98.

Books

Acheson, Dean. *Present at the Creation.* New York: W. W. Norton, 1969.
———. *Strengthening the Forces of Freedom.* Washington, D.C.: Government Printing Office, 1950.
Afifi, Mohammad El-Hadi. *The Arabs and the United Nations.* London: Longmans, Green, & Co., Ltd., 1964.
Ben Gurion, David. *Israel: Years of Challenge.* New York: Holt, Rinehart & Winston, 1963.
Berger, Earl. *The Covenant and the Sword.* London: Routledge & Kegan Paul, Ltd., 1965.
Bernadotte, Folke. *Instead of Arms.* New York: Bonniers, 1948.
———. *To Jerusalem.* London: Hodder & Stoughton, 1951.
Binder, Leonard. *The Middle East Crisis.* Chicago: University of Chicago Center for Policy Study, 1967.
Campbell, John C. *Defense of the Middle East.* New York: Harper & Bros., 1960.
The Carnegie Endowment. *Egypt and the United Nations.* New York: Manhattan Publishing Co., 1957.
Cremeans, Charles D. *The Arabs and the World.* New York: Frederick A. Praeger, 1963.
Davis, John. *The Evasive Peace.* London: John Murray, 1968.
Dib, G. Moussa. *The Arab Bloc in the United Nations.* Amsterdam: Djambatan, 1956.
Ethridge, Willie Snow. *Going to Jerusalem.* New York: Vanguard Press, 1950.
Feis, Herbert. *The Birth of Israel.* New York: W. W. Norton, 1969.
Glubb, Sir John Bagot. *A Soldier with the Arabs.* London: Hodder & Stoughton, 1959.
Goodwin, Geoffrey. *Britain and the United Nations.* New York: Manhattan Publishing Co., 1957.
Hadawi, Sami. *Palestine: Loss of a Heritage.* San Antonio: Naylor Co., 1963.
Halperin, Samuel. *The Political World of American Zionism.* Detroit: Wayne State University Press, 1961.
Hurewitz, J. C. *Middle East Politics: The Military Dimension.* New York: Frederick A. Praeger, 1969.
———. *The Struggle for Palestine.* New York: W. W. Norton, 1950.
———, ed. *Diplomacy in the Near and Middle East, A Documentary Record: 1914–1956.* New York: D. Van Nostrand Co., 1956.
Khadduri, Majdia. *The Arab-Israeli Impasse.* Washington, D.C.: Robert B. Luce, 1968.

Khalil, Muhammad, ed. *The Arab States and the Arab League.* Vol. 2, Beirut: Khayats, 1962.

Khouri, Fred J. *The Arab-Israeli Dilemma.* Syracuse: Syracuse University Press, 1968.

Kilic, Altamur. *Turkey and the World.* Washington, D.C.: Public Affairs Press, 1959.

Kimche, Jon. *Seven Fallen Pillars.* London: Secker & Warburg, 1953.

————— , and Kimche, David. *A Clash of Destinies.* New York: Frederick A. Praeger, 1960.

Kirk, George. *A Short History of the Middle East.* New York: Frederick A. Praeger, 1961.

Laqueur, Walter Z. *The Road to Jerusalem.* New York: Macmillan Co., 1968.

————— . *The Soviet Union and the Middle East.* London: Routledge & Kegan Paul, 1959.

Lewis, Barnard. *The Middle East and the West.* Bloomington: Indiana University Press, 1964.

Lie, Trygve. *In the Cause of Peace.* New York: Macmillan Co., 1954.

MacDonald, Robert W. *The League of Arab States.* Princeton: Princeton University Press, 1965.

McDonald, James G. *My Mission in Israel: 1948–1951.* London: Victor Gollancz, Ltd., 1951.

Monroe, Elizabeth. *Britain's Moment in the Middle East: 1914–1956.* London: Chatto & Windus, 1963.

Nasser, Gamal Abdel. *The Philosophy of the Revolution.* Buffalo: Economics Books, 1959.

Polk, William R. *The United States and the Arab World.* Cambridge, Mass.: Harvard University Press, 1965.

————— *et al. Backdrop to Tragedy.* Boston: Beacon Press, 1957.

Safran, Nadav. *The United States and Israel.* Cambridge, Mass.: Harvard University Press, 1963.

————— . *From War to War.* New York: Pegasus, 1969.

Sharabi, Hisham. *Palestine and Israel.* New York: Pegasus, 1969.

Stevens, Georgiana G., ed. *The United States and the Middle East.* Englewood Cliffs, N.J.: Prentice-Hall, 1964.

Study Group, the Hebrew University of Jerusalem. *Israel and the United Nations.* New York: Manhattan Publishing Co., 1956.

Truman, Harry S. *Memoirs: 1946–1952.* Vol. 2. New York: New American Library, 1965.

Williams, Ann. *Britain and France in the Middle East and North Africa, 1914–1967.* New York: St. Martins Press, 1968.

Zanabili, Abdelmanim. *Les Etats Arabes et les Nations Unies.* Aurillac, Suisse: Imprimerie du Cantal, 1953.

Zeine, Zeine N. *Arab-Turkish Relations and the Emergence of Arab Nationalism.* Beirut: Khayat's, 1958.

193

Zurayk, Constantine K. *The Meaning of the Disaster.* Translated by R. B. Winder. Beirut: Kashaf Press, 1956.

UN Peacemaking

Articles

Bloomfield, Lincoln P. "Peacekeeping and Peacemaking." *Foreign Affairs* 44, no. 4 (July 1966): 671–82.

Lefever, Ernest W. "The Limits of U.N. Intervention in the Third World." *Review of Politics* 30, no. 1 (January 1968): 3–18.

Mack, Raymond, and Snyder, Richard. "The Analysis of Social Conflict— Toward an Overview and Synthesis." *Journal of Conflict Resolution* 1, no. 2 (June 1957): 212–46.

Martin, P. "Peace-Keeping and the U.N.: The Broader View." *Journal of International Affairs* 40 (April 1954): 191–204.

Mathews, Robert O. "The Suez Canal Dispute: A Case Study in Peaceful Settlement." *International Organization* 21, no. 1 (Winter 1967): 79–101.

Michalak, Stanley J. "Peacekeeping and the United Nations: The Problem of Responsibility." *International Studies Quarterly* 11, no. 4 (December 1967): 301–19.

Perkins, Whitney T. "Sanctions for Political Change—The Indonesian Case." *International Organization* 12, no. 1 (Winter 1958): 26–42.

Tandon, Yashpal. "Consensus and Authority behind United Nations Peace-keeping Operations." *International Organization* 21, no. 2 (Spring 1967): 254–83.

——— . "The Peaceful Settlement of International Disputes." *International Relations* 2, no. 9 (April 1964): 555–87.

UNESCO. "The Technique of International Conference." *International Social Science Bulletin* 5, no. 2 (1953).

——— . "Techniques of Mediation and Conciliation." *International Social Science Bulletin* 10, no. 4 (1958).

Books

Aron, Raymond. *Peace and War: A Theory of International Relations.* Translated by Richard Howard and Annette B. Fox. Garden City, N.Y.: Doubleday & Company, 1966.

Boulding, Kenneth. *Conflict and Defense.* New York: Harper & Bros., 1962.

Brook, David. *Preface to Peace.* Washington, D.C.: Public Affairs Press, 1966.

Bunche, Ralph. *Peace and the United Nations.* Tenth Montague Burton Lecture on International Relations. Leeds: Jowett & Sowry, Ltd., 1952.

Chase, Stuart. *Roads to Agreement.* London: Phoenix House, Ltd., 1952.

Claude, Inis. *Swords into Plowshares: The Problems and Progress of International Organization.* 3d ed. New York: Random House, 1964.

Dunn, Frederick S. *Peaceful Change.* United States Memorandum No. 8. Prepared for the American Coordinating Committee for International Studies, 1937.

Goodrich, Leland, and Simons, Anne. *The United Nations and the Maintenance of International Peace and Security.* Washington, D.C.: The Brookings Institution, 1957.

Gordenker, Leon. *The United Nations and the Peaceful Unification of Korea.* The Hague: Martinus Nijhoff, 1959.

——— . *The UN Secretary-General and the Maintenance of Peace.* New York: Columbia University Press, 1967.

Hankey, Lord. *Diplomacy by Conference.* London: Ernst Benn, Ltd., 1946.

Hinsley, F. H. *Power and the Pursuit of Peace.* Cambridge, Mass.: Cambridge University Press, 1963.

Ikle, Fred Charles. *How Nations Negotiate.* New York: Harper & Row, 1964.

Jackson, Elmore. *Meeting of Minds.* New York: McGraw-Hill Book Co., 1952.

Kahn, Herman. *On Escalation: Metaphors and Scenarios.* New York: Frederick A. Praeger, 1965.

Korbel, Josef. *Danger in Kashmir.* Princeton: Princeton University Press, 1954.

McNeil, Elton. *The Nature of Human Conflict.* Englewood Cliffs, N.J.: Prentice Hall, 1965.

Miller, Linda B. *World Order and Local Disorder: The United Nations and Internal Conflicts.* Princeton: Princeton University Press, 1967.

Rapoport, Anatol. *Fights, Games, and Debates.* Ann Arbor: University of Michigan Press, 1960.

Schelling, Thomas C. *Arms and Influence.* New Haven: Yale University Press, 1966.

——— . *The Strategy of Conflict.* Cambridge, Mass.: Harvard University Press, 1960.

Taylor, Alastair N. *Indonesian Independence and the United Nations.* Ithaca: Cornell University Press, 1960.

Webster, Sir Charles. *The Art and Practice of Diplomacy.* New York: Barnes & Noble, 1962.

Young, Oran R. *The Intermediaries: Third Parties in International Crises.* Princeton: Princeton University Press, 1967.

195

INDEX

INDEX

Abd al-Nasir, Jamal, 107, 125, 130, 138 and *n*
Arab Bloc, 35-36, 40-43, 46-47, 49-52, 56-59, 61, 72, 83, 97-99, 107-9, 110-11, 130, 142-43. *See also* Conciliation Commission for Palestine, and the Arab Bloc
Arab-Israeli War (1948-49), 23-24. *See also* Armistice agreements (1949)
Arab-Israeli War (1956). *See* Suez Crisis
Arab-Israeli War (1967), 33, 106, 123, 145. *See also* United Nations, and 1967 Arab-Israeli conflict
Arab League, 75-77, 92
Arab nationalism, 20-21, 99, 107
Aras, Rustuv, 78*n*, 80*n*
Armistice agreements (1949), 33, 35, 40, 43, 81-82, 90. *See also* Conciliation Commission for Palestine, and the 1949 armistice
Azcárate y Flores, Dr. Pablo de, 38-39, 40*n*

Balfour Declaration (1917), 21-22
Barco, James, 38, 86-87
Beirut conference, 42-43, 45-47; opening of, 45
Ben Gurion, David, 46-47, 77, 127 and *n*
Bernadotte, Count Folke, 24, 26, 27 and *n*
Boundary problems, 50-53, 54-55, 57-58, 78, 145
Britain. *See* United Kingdom

Bunche, Ralph, 27 and *n*, 30, 35-36, 39-40, 42, 44, 63-64. *See also* Rhodes talks

Clapp, Gordon, 61-62
Clapp Mission, 61-62, 68-69, 101
Conciliation, definition of, 13-15
Conciliation Commission for Palestine (CCP), 2, 3, 31-32, 70-71, 72-77, 95, 101-3, 140, 145-46, 166-69; and the Arab Bloc. 41, 64, 74, 83, 97-99, 102, 119-21; and Beirut conference, 35-48; creation of, 21, 26-30; decline of, 56, 75-76, 95-97, 146-47; and frozen assets, 56, 58-59, 104-6, 112-14, 115-22; and the General Assembly, 63-67, 80-81, 82-83, 93-97, 110-12, 146; and Israel, 63-64, 74, 85, 99-101, 111-18; and the Lausanne conference, 48-55, 56-63, 101-2; and the 1949 armistice, 40-41; and the Paris conference (1951), 87-93, 118; and the Refugee Office, 84-86, 91-93; and the Special Representative, 104, 123-26, 129, 140, 143-44; as a three-government organ, 97-103. *See also* United Nations Relief and Works Agency
Conciliation Commission for Palestine (CCP) Secretariat, 38-39; and the United Nations Secretariat, 39-40
Conflict management. *See* Peacekeeping
Conflict resolution, definition of, 12
Congo. *See* United Nations in Congo

199

THE JOHNS HOPKINS UNIVERSITY PRESS

This book was composed in Baskerville text and Bulmer and Baskerville display
type by Port City Press, Inc. It was printed by Universal Lithographers, Inc.
on Perkins and Squier R, 60-lb. paper. The book was bound
by L. H. Jenkins, Inc. in Bancroft Joanna Arrestox cloth.

Library of Congress Cataloging in Publication Data

Forsythe, David P   1941—
  United Nations peacemaking.

  "Published in cooperation with the Middle East
Institute."
  1. United Nations. Conciliation Commission for
Palestine. I. Middle East Institute, Washington, D.C.
II. Title.
JX1977.2.P34F67   341.5′2   71-181557
ISBN 0-8018-1352-2